BANNING PUBLIC LIBRARY
W9-BCC-804

# Made in the USA

**Also by Vaclav Smil**

*China's Energy*
*Energy in the Developing World* (edited with W. Knowland)
*Energy Analysis in Agriculture* (with P. Nachman and T. V. Long II)
*Biomass Energies*
*The Bad Earth*
*Carbon Nitrogen Sulfur*
*Energy Food Environment*
*Energy in China's Modernization*
*General Energetics*
*China's Environmental Crisis*
*Global Ecology*
*Energy in World History*
*Cycles of Life*
*Energies*
*Feeding the World*
*Enriching the Earth*
*The Earth's Biosphere*
*Energy at the Crossroads*
*China's Past, China's Future*
*Creating the 20th Century*
*Transforming the 20th Century*
*Energy: A Beginner's Guide*
*Oil: A Beginner's Guide*
*Energy in Nature and Society*
*Global Catastrophes and Trends*
*Why America Is Not a New Rome*
*Energy Transitions*
*Energy Myths and Realities*
*Prime Movers of Globalization*
*Japan's Dietary Transition and Its Impacts* (with K. Kobayashi)
*Harvesting the Biosphere: What We Have Taken from Nature*

# Made in the USA

## The Rise and Retreat of American Manufacturing

Vaclav Smil

The MIT Press
Cambridge, Massachusetts
London, England

MIT Press books may be purchased at special quantity discounts for business or sales promotional use. For information, please email special_sales@mitpress.mit.edu or write to Special Sales Department, The MIT Press, 55 Hayward Street, Cambridge, MA 02142.

This book was set in Sabon by the MIT Press. Printed and bound in the United States of America.

Library of Congress Cataloging-in-Publication Data

Smil, Vaclav.
Made in the USA : the rise and retreat of American manufacturing / Vaclav Smil.
pages cm
Includes bibliographical references and index.
ISBN 978-0-262-01938-5 (hardcover : alk. paper)
1. Manufacturing industries—United States. 2. Industrial policy—United States. 3. United States—Commerce. I. Title.
HD9725.S57 2013
338.4'7670973—dc23
2012051393

10 9 8 7 6 5 4 3 2 1

# Contents

# Preface

Long experience has taught me that too many people approach books dealing with complex topics with too many preconceptions and hence become easily disappointed if the content does not reflect at least some of them. I am afraid that a book about the rise and retreat of American manufacturing written at the beginning of the second decade of the twenty-first century will be particularly subject to such a reception. Those economists (and policy makers) who do not see (as was famously said) any difference between potato chips and microchips, who favor unrestricted globalization, and who celebrate the loss of US manufacturing jobs as a desirable evolutionary step toward a purely service economy will dislike the book's insistence that manufacturing does matter. Equally, those economists (and policy makers) who abhor every aspect of globalization and argue for increased protectionism will dislike my strong agreement with the calls for greatly expanding US exports of manufactured goods.

If this is not an economic analysis written by an economist promoting a particular view or advocating a specific policy, it is also not a history of America's technical prowess written by a historian trying to conform to a distinct paradigm. I am a scientist with a lifelong devotion to interdisciplinary studies, and I have published many books on complex technical, historical, and economic topics, but when writing this book my goal was quite simple: to tell a story, though one that is well documented and thoroughly referenced. That story is truly epic, multifaceted, and, to me, also endlessly fascinating. There are many reasons why the United States came to hold such an exceptional position in the world, but manufacturing does not usually come first to mind. This book explains why and how manufacturing became such a fundamental force in creating and advancing the United States' economic, strategic, and social might. It traces manufacturing's rapid rise during the last decades of the nineteenth century, its consolidation and modernization during the pre–World War II decades, its role in enabling the world's first mass consumption society after 1945, and its post-1974 challenges and most recent reversals of fortune.

How does the story end? Well, it does not; it keeps unfolding—and even a relatively near-term outcome of this process is beyond our ken. That is why I am content neither to offer general policy recommendations for creating optimal conditions for manufacturing's growth nor to advance strong arguments for specific changes aimed at preventing its decline. Washington, DC, has no shortage of special-interest organizations and think tanks to do that (and some have done so in a thoughtful and comprehensive manner). What I will do—convinced that no advanced modern economy can truly prosper without a strong, diverse, and innovating manufacturing sector whose aim is not only affordable, high-quality output but also to provide jobs for more than a minuscule share of the working population—is review some of the recent calls for change made by those concerned about the future of US manufacturing and explain in some detail some of their principal recommendations.

Fundamentally, this is a story about the country's past achievements and its more recent failings, and, as always in my books, I will not make any forecasts; hence I will not answer the question of whether American manufacturing will experience a true renaissance, as its dwindling proponents hope, or whether it will, in employment terms if not in total output value, become an ever more marginal economic sector (as many economists belonging to the "serving potato chips is as good as making microchips" school equanimously anticipate). All I can say is that I see the odds of America's true manufacturing renaissance and the sector's further retreat to be no better than even.

# Introduction

In 1899 Ransom Olds began to assemble his Oldsmobiles, essentially buggies with an engine under the seat. Two years later he marketed his Curved Dash, America's first serially produced car. Two years after that, Cadillac Automobile Company began selling its vehicles, and in 1903 David D. Buick set up his motor company. In 1908 Oldsmobile, Buick, Cadillac, and 20 other car- and part-making firms came under the umbrella of General Motors, established by William Durant, Buick's general manager. The company kept growing and innovating, and by 1929 it had passed Ford in annual sales. It survived the Great Depression and prospered during World War II, when it was the largest maker not only of military trucks but also of engines, airplanes, tanks, and other armaments and ammunitions.

In 1953 President Eisenhower named Charles E. Wilson, the company's president, the US secretary of defense. When Wilson was asked during his confirmation hearings about any possible conflict of interest, he answered that he foresaw no problems "because for years I thought what was good for the country was good for General Motors and vice versa," a reply that became known as an iconic, but reversed in retelling, claim that "what's good for General Motors is good for the country." By 1962, when its share of the US car market peaked at 50.7%, GM was the world's largest manufacturer, with an apparently assured prosperous future. But that was before OPEC, and before Honda and Toyota began selling cars in the United States.

By 1996, when GM moved its headquarters into the glassy towers of Detroit's Renaissance Center, its share of the US car and light truck market was less than 33% as the company became infamous for poorly designed models built with too many defects. A decade later GM was a hopelessly failing corporation, and when it declared bankruptcy, on June 1, 2009, its US market share of light vehicles was just 19.6%, its share of cars just 16%. The bankruptcy eliminated not only the preposterous Hummer but also a long-running (since 1926) Pontiac brand and Saturn, set up in 1985 as "a different kind of car company" to challenge the Japanese designs. Even after the company's stock was refloated, in November 2010, the government kept a 34% stake. This trajectory, from the world's largest automaker to bankruptcy and bailout, embodies the rise and retreat of American manufacturing—with one big difference. Unlike GM, thousands of America's electronics, textile, shoe, furniture, car parts, or metalworking companies were not too big to fail, and simply disappeared during the past two generations.

But the outcomes are not foreordained, and the GM story also carries an intriguing message of rebound: in 2011, helped by a partial economic recovery, GM sold more than 2.5 million vehicles in the United States and a total of just over nine million worldwide, reclaiming its global primacy (while Toyota, beset by its own quality and delivery problems, slipped to fourth place, behind Renault-Nissan and Volkswagen). And Ford rode out the economic downturn without any government help: in 2008 it had only 14.2% of the US market, compared to its peak of 29.2% in 1961, while in 2011 the sales rebound (2.1 million vehicles sold) raised its share to 16.8%.

But this is no return to the days of American automotive dominance. Deindustrialization has been a nationwide phenomenon, and Detroit has been the epicenter: the view southwest from GM's gleaming towers reveals a stunning cityscape where abandoned houses and lots overgrown with weeds and wild trees vastly outnumber the remaining inhabited houses (see figure 1.1). No wonder: even as recently as 2000 the US auto industry employed 1.3 million workers, but by July 2009 the total had been nearly halved, to 624,000. Post-2000 employment in the entire manufacturing sector followed a similar trend.

After World War II, manufacturing jobs rose steadily, reaching a peak of nearly 19.5 million workers in the summer of 1979. By 1980, in the midst of a recession, the total was still 18.7 million. By the end of 1990 it was 7% lower, at 17.4 million; by the end of 2000 it had hardly changed, at 17.2 million; but a decade later it was just 11.5 million (BLS 2012). Of course, many economists have promised that all those who lost jobs in manufacturing would be absorbed by the endlessly capacious service sector. *But there was no net job creation during the first decade of the twenty-first century.* Rather, there was an overall job loss: in January 2001 the United States had 132.5 million nonfarm jobs, whereas in December 2010 the total was 129.8 million, a 2% drop during a decade when the country's population increased by 9.7%.

The last time similar events took place was during the Great Depression of the 1930s, and as in the 1930s the loss of manufacturing jobs (a total of 5.6 million lost between the end of 2000 and December 2010) was the principal reason for this failure even to maintain the overall employment level. At the same time, between 2001 and 2010 the aggregate US trade deficit (mostly resulting from imports of manufactures) was nearly $4.4 trillion, adding to trillions of dollars in budget deficits ($1.4 trillion in 2010 alone) and making the United States the greatest debtor nation in history. These are the realities that led me to take a critical look at the evolution, achievements, failures, and potentials of US manufacturing.

I take a long-term historical perspective to explain the technical accomplishments and the economic, political, and social implications of the remarkable rise of America's goods-producing industries to global dominance, their post-1970s transformations and retreats, and the likelihood of their survival and expansion. I wrote this book because I wanted to narrate the great, and a truly nation-building, story of US manufacturing—and because I believe that without the preservation and reinvigoration of manufacturing, the United States has little chance to extricate itself from its current economic problems, meet the challenges posed by other large and globally more competitive nations, and remain a dynamic and innovative society for generations to come.

To write about manufacturing is to deal with fascinating stories of quintessential human activities that created modern societies and enable their complex functioning. But this truism is not a widely shared perception in a world long since labeled postindustrial, in economies whose added value is dominated by services and not by making things, and in societies whose attention is swamped by consumption and the exchange of sounds, images, and words belonging to a new, immaterial e-universe.

The fact that all of this depends on an enormous variety of manufactures goes, inexplicably, unacknowledged; even more inexplicably, the entire realm of converting raw material inputs into a myriad of finished goods is seen as a relic from the industrial past that appears passé compared to modern virtual realities.

And then there is the archaic term of the activity itself: what, these days, is really manufactured— made (*faciō*) by hand (*manus*)—in affluent economies? Only a shrinking variety of artisanal products—while the mass of consumer goods has been made by machines for decades as mechanization, robotization, and computerization have replaced even those functions that were thought of not so long ago as safe preserves of human skills. Going a step further, affluent countries have been doing less and less of any kind of manufacturing. As Adam Smith counseled in 1776, "if a foreign country can supply us with a commodity cheaper than we ourselves can make it, better buy it of them."

But would Adam Smith, a rational man, approve of the fact that not a single fork or dining plate, not a single television set or personal computer is made in the United States, and that importing all these goods, and tens of thousands of others, has deprived the country of millions of well-paying jobs? Not likely, especially as he advised to "buy it of them with some part of the produce of our own industry, employed in a way in which we have some advantage" (Smith 1776). But trade statistics make it clear that any of America's comparative advantages fall far short of the aggregate value of those cheaper imported commodities, the situation that has brought, starting in 1976, chronically large trade deficits. Smith thought that "this trade which without force or constraint, is naturally and regularly carried on between two places is always advantageous." Would he still think so given these realities of mass unemployment and chronic deep deficits?

Virtually any mass production of goods now has some connections to foreign trade, much as it has social, political, and environmental consequences on scales ranging from local to global. And although manufacturing now receives hardly any public attention compared to the overwhelming focus on the virtual e-world, it remains the single largest source of technical innovation, and its advances transform every branch of the modern economy. The United States' outsized role in creating, expanding, and improving the world of manufactured goods easily justifies a retrospective appraisal of these achievements. The manufacturing sector's recent weaknesses, failures, and retreats—masked to a large extent by its continued growth in aggregate absolute terms—offer a timely (and sobering) opportunity to dissect some of its problems and challenges.

**Figure 1.1**
Satellite images of Detroit reveal a new urban landscape created by America's deindustrialization. Nearly 90,000 abandoned buildings and vacant lots and a quarter of the city's area are returning to a semiwild state as they are overgrown with weeds, bushes, and trees. Image retrieved from Google Earth.

# 1

# Why Manufacturing Matters

*Claims about the dematerialization of modern economies and about a postindustrial world in which manufacturing does not matter are costly misinterpretations of fundamental realities.*

Not only the wealth; but the independence and security of a Country, appear to be materially connected with the prosperity of manufactures. Every nation, with a view to those great objects, ought to endeavour to possess within itself all the essentials of national supply.
—Alexander Hamilton, *Report on Manufactures,* 1791

Life enriched, and burdened, by an enormous and still increasing variety of manufactured products is a recent phenomenon. All but a few people in preindustrial societies lived with a minimum of simple possessions as only the richest could own good-quality artisanal products, made as unique items or in small series. And even the products made in larger quantities—bricks and earthenware containers, simple metal objects—were not cheap enough to be easily affordable. The poorest peasant families owned, as many of them still do in Asia and Africa, only some cooking pots and perhaps a few utensils, often just a single bed, and, in societies where cereals were the staple food, some containers to store a small amount of grain.

Even during the early decades of Western industrialization the items used or owned by new urban immigrants rarely went beyond a rudimentary stove, a few simple pieces of furniture, and a single change of clothes. There is no better and certainly no more visually captivating testimony to material progress than *Material World: A Global Family Portrait.* In this book, the families of 30 nations, chosen for their representative status in their respective societies, display all of their pitiful (or extensive, as the case may be) belongings arrayed in front of their dwellings (Menzel 1994). Another impressive collection of images portraying the gap between the worlds of misery and excess is a series of photographs that won the third Prix Pictet and was published under the title *Growth* (Barber and Benson 2010). But perhaps the best indicator of what makes up the necessities of life in modern mass-consuming societies comes from Pew Research Center polls that identify the things Americans claim they cannot live without. The list of these necessities grew between 1996 and 2006, with the highest percentage gains for microwave ovens (68% of people could not live without them in 2006, a 36% gain in a decade), home computers, dishwashers, clothes dryers, and home air conditioning units (Taylor, Funk, and Clark 2006). Only the subsequent economic downturn brought a U-turn: by 2009 all of the above-named items were perceived as much less necessary (all suffering double-digit declines) than in 2006 (Morin and Taylor 2009). Even so, two-thirds of respondents could not do without a clothes dryer and 88% could not do without a car.

American history offers an unequaled example of a society defined by the large-scale amassing of goods; getting richer in Europe and Japan has always been a comparatively more subdued affair. America's private and public hoarding of manufactured goods has been going on for about 150 years. In public terms we should not think only of vehicles, buildings, or dams owned by the federal government; we should think also about all of that military hardware, from spy satellites and fighter planes to aircraft carriers, nuclear submarines, and intercontinental ballistic missiles. In its early stages private material acquisition had undoubted quality-of-life benefits (from refrigerators to telephones, from elevators to vaccines), but more recently the purchases—or, more accurately, increased debt obligations—have been marked by excess and a lack of taste, a trend exemplified by living in custom-built faux French mansions and driving Hummers, civilian versions of a military assault vehicle.

The most recent burst of such ostentatious acquisitiveness is taking place in the rapidly modernizing economies of China and India. Although it has been limited to urban elites, its intensity has already made these on average still very poor countries the world's leading markets for ridiculously overpriced luxury goods. There can be no doubt that the notion of a successful modern life has become overly defined by the possession of manufactures: for billions of people those goods remain beyond reach, but not beyond hope of acquisition. The importance of manufacturing thus seems trivially obvious—and yet we hear claims that postindustrial societies have found ways to dematerialize themselves as the magic of software drives the electronic worlds where connection, information, and knowledge become superior to mere objects. Such thinking might charitably be labeled misguided; an unadorned judgment is that it is simply nonsense. Others may concede our material needs but tell us that postindustrial societies do not have to make anything and can simply import all the manufactured products they need.

The advantages of outsourcing and international trade have been extolled by the promoters of globalization for decades, but the arrangements have many inherent problems (Bhagwati and Blinder 2009; Fletcher 2011). There are many instances in which moving some segments of manufacturing abroad makes overall sense, and many more instances in which vigorous foreign trade is desirable and beneficial, but an ideologically based pursuit of unlimited free trade, an excessive dependence on imports, and the systematic outsourcing of entire industries will eventually weaken even the strongest economies. Claims that manufacturing has lost its importance, that we should not be worried about its decline, that the prosperity of modern economies comes from services, and that exporting high-value-added services can secure earnings sufficient for importing all the needed manufactured goods are all wrong. In this chapter I will demonstrate the quintessential position of manufacturing in the economy of any large, prosperous, modern nation.

## Manufactured Societies

Many possessions owned by families in modern affluent countries are necessary in order to live with a modicum of dignity. Beds, plates, cutlery, glasses, simple clothes, shoes, soap, and towels are in this category. In cold climates we cherish well-insulated walls, good doors and windows, and reliable furnaces or stoves; everywhere we would like to have a convenient kitchen and lights after dark. For individual commutes to work, reliable vehicles (or bicycles), trains, and subways and streetcars are essential. Other items of material consumption are clearly dispensable frivolities, a category to which a critical inspection could assign most of the items found in modern North American households.

But by a simple count, perhaps most of the items most families own belong to that huge in-between category that does not imply any opulence but that makes daily life comfortable and enjoyable. Such objects range from small appliances to books, from garden tools to sports equipment, from furniture to gadgets for the reproduction of music. And while most people in traditional societies spent most of their lives within the narrow confines of their villages and towns, mass-scale mobility has been one of the most distinguishing features of modern societies and has required the large-scale construction of transportation infrastructure, prime movers, and conveyances as we travel often enormous distances for business or vacations.

Behind all these material needs is a multitude of specialized manufacturing industries that draw on raw resources from all continents (and from offshore waters), employ hundreds of millions of workers worldwide, and are never finished with their work, as new products are created to replace worn-out or obsolete items. And given the large numbers of consumers that can afford to buy these products (now globally on the order of 1.5 billion for higher levels of expenditures, and another two billion or so at intermediate levels), manufacturing had to cease to be what the term's Latin roots imply—literally, made by hand. That is now an anachronism as far as all but a tiny share of everything available on today's market is concerned: high levels of mechanization and automation and the ubiquitous use of electricity-powered tools and machines became the norm, allowing large quantities to be produced at acceptable costs.

The same is obviously true about food consumed in modern societies. In traditional subsistence societies crops were grown mostly for immediate consumption by peasant families, but in modern societies crops are grown overwhelmingly for distant markets, and because of high rates of meat and dairy intakes, most crops are actually destined for animal feeding and not for direct consumption by humans. This arrangement requires the mass manufacture of such items as synthetic fertilizers, pesticides, and herbicides, needed to sustain high yields; the production of tractors, implements, and combines, for timely and efficient cultivation and harvests; and the availability of trucks and ships to carry foodstuffs to distant markets. Because of these inputs it has been possible to feed seven billion people, provide an excessive food supply for nearly two billion, and reduce the total number of malnourished people to less than one billion worldwide (Smil 2001, 2011).

Other existential necessities include the energy supply for households, industries, and transportation, along with the drilling rigs, pumps, compressors, well casings, pipelines, tankers, refineries and mines, coal-cleaning plants, trucks, trains, and bulk carriers needed to extract, process, and distribute fossil fuels. The final uses of these energies take place in boilers, raising pressurized steam for massive electricity-generating turbines; in furnaces; and in prime movers: gasoline-fueled car engines are now the most numerous converters, large diesel engines powering container ships the most efficient kind, and jet engines used in commercial airplanes the most reliable designs (Smil 2010). The largest category of final uses consists of machines, appliances, and light emitters to convert electricity to thermal, kinetic, and electromagnetic energy.

Or we can simply look at the extremes of our lives, where objects surround us as we are born and as we die: sheets, gloves, stethoscopes, injection needles, drugs, and monitors charting every heartbeat until the final flat line. Truism it may be, but it bears repeating in a society where most minds are divorced from the fundamentals of making things: well-being in the modern world is defined by our dependence on a multitude of products, physical objects that must be made by first transforming raw materials (by smelting, refining, reacting, separating, synthesizing) into a wide variety of intermediate products, ranging from metals to plastics, from lumber to flour, which are turned by further processing and final assembly into marketable items.

This description comes close to the official definition of these productive activities without using that less than ideal term, manufacturing. The US Census Bureau defines manufacturing as a sector that "comprises establishments engaged in the mechanical, physical, or chemical transformation of materials, substances, or components into new products. The assembling of component parts of manufactured products is considered manufacturing, except in cases where the activity is appropriately classified in Sector 23, Construction" (USBC 2010). This official definition embraces both the mechanical and the human component of the activity by describing the manufacturing establishments as

> plants, factories, or mills and characteristically use power-driven machines and materials-handling equipment. However, establishments that transform materials or substances into new products by hand or in the worker's home and those engaged in selling to the general public products made on the same premises from

which they are sold, such as bakeries, candy stores, and custom tailors, may also be included in this sector.

But the awkwardness does end not here, and the most obvious problem is with inclusions and boundaries. Virtually all modern manufacturing entails management, payroll, and accounting, and most of it depends on continuous design improvements, research and development activities, and often just-in-time deliveries of parts and components by a variety of carriers. An international comparison shows that in 2005, services purchased by manufacturers from outside firms were 30% of the value added to manufactured goods in the United States and between 23% and 29% in major EU economies. Another comparison shows that in 2008, service-related occupations in manufacturing accounted for 53% of manufacturing jobs in the United States, between 44% and 50% in Germany, France, and the UK, and 32% in Japan (Levinson 2012). US manufacturers thus employ fewer people in actual production operations than in allied service–type functions.

And while many products of modern engineering still fundamentally look outwardly like their early predecessors, they are now very different hybrid systems of parts and services. Cars are the best example of this transformation: they are still complex mechanical constructs (modern vehicles contain some 30,000 parts), but now all of their functions, from engine operation to the deployment of air bags, are controlled by computers, and the requisite software is more complex than that on board fighter jets or jetliners (Charette 2009). GM put the first electronic control unit (ECU) in an Oldsmobile in 1977, and today even inexpensive cars have 30–50 ECUs, requiring some 10 million lines of code, and the 70–100 ECUs in luxury cars need close to 100 million lines of codes, compared to the 6.5 million lines of code needed to operate the avionics and onboard support systems of the Boeing 787 and the 5.7 million lines of code needed for the US Air Force's F-35 Joint Strike Fighter.

Electronics and software now account for as much as 40% of the cost of premium vehicles, and software development alone claims up to 15% of that cost, or, at $10 per line of code, on the order of $1 billion before a new model even leaves the factory. Cars have been transformed into mechatronic hybrids, assemblies of parts unable to operate without complex software. That is why Tassey (2010) argues that we should think of manufacturing as a value stream rather than a static category—but the operational definitions and data collection procedures used by national governments and international organizations are not designed to reflect these complex realities.

When these associated services are provided by manufacturing establishments, the North American Industry Classification System (NAICS) views them as "captive" and treats them as manufacturing activities. But "when the services are provided by separate establishments, they are classified to the NAICS sector where such services are primary, not in manufacturing" (NAICS 2008). Because many manufacturing companies, large and small, now routinely outsource design and R&D activities, as well as market research or payroll (MacPherson and Vanchan 2010), this has become a significant source of undervaluation. And there is more: defining manufacturing as the transformation of materials into new products hinges on the definition of "new," and hence on an inevitably subjective setting of boundaries.

The NAICS offers a longish list of activities that are considered to be suppliers of new products, starting with bottling and pasteurizing milk and packaging and processing seafood, through apparel jobbing (assigning materials to contract fabricators), printing, and producing ready-mixed concrete, to electroplating, remanufacturing machinery parts, and tire retreading. That logging and agriculture are excluded seems only natural, but the NAICS also leaves out many activities that could logically be seen as obvious kinds of manufacturing, including the beneficiation of ores (assigned to mining), fabrications on construction sites (assigned to construction), bulk breaking and redistribution in smaller lots (assigned to wholesale trade), the custom cutting of metals and customized assembly of computers (assigned to retail trade), and the entire sector of "publishing and the combined activity of publishing and printing" (assigned to information) because "the value of the product to the consumer lies in the information content, not in the format in which it is distributed (i.e., the book or software diskette)" (USBC 2010).

In light of these realities, there is no doubt that the lack of a modern, realistic, and inclusive definition of manufacturing is not only of statistical interest, it is a barrier to judging the sector's true performance and to formulating informed policies (van Opstal 2010). Finally, there are differences between the two ways of measuring the sector's output. Manufacturing production quantifies the value added by an establishment minus its purchases of inputs from outside sources, or the sector's sales minus its purchases of raw and intermediate materials and energy. The measure remains the same regardless of whether some services (such as accounting or design) or even actual manufacturing are done by vendors rather than in-house. In contrast, goods output quantifies all spending on domestically produced goods and all goods exports minus the cost of all manufactured imports.

These measures are not identical, as the latter, goods output, includes the retail cost of imported goods (the sum of subtracted imports refers to the payments for foreign production and delivery, not to the purchase price), as well as the costs of domestic transportation, marketing, and financing of the operations. Steindel (2004) found that in the United States, goods output has been increasing relative to manufacturing production for many years. He explained the puzzling divergence by a rising share of imported goods, increased service inputs to the sale of all goods, and a larger share of post-production service inputs to market consumer as opposed to capital goods.

All of this has important consequences. First, we are stuck with an anachronistic term that not only fails to capture the fact that modern manufacturing has become highly, and almost universally, mechanized but also gives no hint that computers and computer-controlled devices are now used in every stage of manufacturing, from design and prototyping to the actual machining, fabrication, quality testing, and packaging of finished products. Second, while the quantitative evaluation of the sector's weight in an economy has always depended on a somewhat arbitrary delimitation of manufacturing's boundaries, this definitional weakness has grown to become a major complication as modern manufacturing is unthinkable without large, and growing, components of R&D, the processing of high-quality special components, customized assembly, national and global marketing, and post-sale servicing (now commonly online), with major producers often outsourcing or subcontracting many to most of these steps.

These practices also make "country of origin" an increasingly questionable categorization. Chances are that any but the simplest of today's machines or devices have been assembled from components that originated in more than one country and that may in turn contain subcomponents made elsewhere. Besides making any meaningful assignation of country of origin impossible, this reality can also greatly inflate the value of exports if they are, as is standard, assigned to the country whose workers performed the final assembly. Rassweiler's (2009) teardown of Apple's iPhone is a perfect example of these complications.

iPhone's key components—its memory, display, screen, camera, transceiver, and receiver—come from Japan (Toshiba), Germany (Infineon), the United States (Broadcom and Numonyx), and South Korea (Samsung), and the final assembly is done by Hon Hai Precision Industry, a Taiwanese company trading as Foxconn and operating a giant plant in Shenzhen, Guandong province. In 2009, exports of iPhones from China to the United States added about $2 billion to the US trade deficit when the accounting uses the total manufacturing cost. But the assembly in China added less than 4% of the total, which means that the value added in China raised the US trade deficit by less than $75 million and that more than 96% of the $2 billion bill actually represented transfers of components, with more than three-quarters of their value originating in Japan, Germany, South Korea, and the United States.

Before I start retracing the history of American industrial production, I must refute two persistent myths concerning modern manufacturing. The first sees manufacturing as a progressively less important endeavor because technical innovation constantly displaces (in absolute or relative terms) mass, and the quantities of material inputs and manufactured products that are required to perform identical economic functions decline with time. The dematerialization of securities, for example, is now complete: no companies or stockbrokers issue paper forms as everything has become an electronic book entry. And most people are aware of the inverse relationship between computer mass and performance. In 1981 IBM's first personal computer had 16 kb of RAM and a mass of 11.3 kg, or just 0.7 g per byte (IBM 2011). I began to write this book in 2011 on a 4 Gb RAM Dell Studio laptop weighing about 3.6 kg, and hence having the mass of about 0.9 μg per kb of RAM.

This dematerialization reduced the mass per unit of RAM ratio to only about 1.3 × 10–9 of its 1981 value in 30 years! In 1981 the mass of about two million personal computers was on the order of 20,000 t, and their aggregate RAM was on the order of 30 Gb; in 2011 the more than 300 million computers sold worldwide weighed only about 1.2 Mt, or only about 60 times the mass in 1981, while their aggregate RAM was more than 1 Eb ($10^{18}$ bytes), or 30 million times greater. With a 1981 mass/RAM ratio, the computers sold in 2011 would have weighed 840 Gt, nearly two orders of magnitude more than all the metals, plastics, glass, and silicon used worldwide, or more than 200 times as much as all the materials used annually in the United States.

But this example is also extraordinarily exceptional: trends from the e-world—driven by an ever denser packing of transistors on a microprocessor (microchip)—have been a realm unto themselves, and nothing remotely similarly has taken place in other major fields of manufacturing. Impressive improvements have been common in many branches of modern manufacturing, but reductions in the mass per unit of performance ratio by seven orders of magnitude are utterly impossible in other major industries, be it ferrous and color metallurgy, chemical syntheses, furniture building, or food processing. Indeed, in most branches of nonelectronic manufacturing even reductions of an order of magnitude (that is, new designs performing the same functions with only a tenth of the mass of earlier products) are uncommon.

Perhaps the most common example of such a success is the heavy diesel engine. In 1897 the first machine had a mass/power ratio of more than 330 g/W, and in 1910 the first engine installed on an oceangoing ship rated about 120 g/W, while today's most powerful marine diesel engines rate nearly 30 g/W, a reduction of an order of magnitude (Wärtsilä 2012; Smil 2010). On the other hand, there have been many cases of reducing the unit mass of products by 20%–50%, with examples ranging from the mass of aluminum soft drink cans to the mass/power ratio of modern electric locomotives. But all of those substantial relative reductions have not added up to any absolute declines in demand for materials.

Available data show that during the past generation even the affluent economies, which already enjoyed the world's highest rates of per capita consumption, saw further increases in aggregate material inputs, while the world's most populous and rapidly modernizing countries, above all China, India, Indonesia, and Brazil, experienced extraordinarily high rates of demand for virtually every kind of material. As a result, there has been no aggregate global dematerialization as far as any metal, any construction material, any plastic, or any kind of biomass is concerned. The demand for these manufacturing inputs is reaching historical highs because even the most impressive relative reductions have been more than negated by the combination of continuing global population growth and rising per capita demand for virtually all kinds of industrial and consumer goods.

## Manufacturing and Service Economies

The second view I wish to expose is more fundamental and even more dismissive than the first one: it does not posit any diminishment of mass, it simply sees modern manufacturing as a largely (if not an almost entirely) dispensable activity, a matter of a secondary importance that can be taken care of by simply importing whatever is needed from the cheapest foreign sources and paying for the purchases by earnings from high value-added services whose contribution now dominates GDPs of all affluent countries. Or, as one of many recent conclusions favored by economists has it, manufacturing's declining share of GDP is "something to celebrate" (Perry 2012).

Manufacturing seems easy to dismiss in societies that find the postindustrial label, originally introduced by Bell (1973) and Illich (1973), the most fitting description of their realities and aspirations. The notion that manufacturing does not have to be a major concern of effective economic policy or an important part of long-term national aspirations—and the logical extension of this notion, namely, that low-cost foreign suppliers can cover any need in a global economy—has been embraced for two very different reasons: because of an entropic perception of economic development and, more commonly by a majority of economists, because of a mistaken interpretation of an indisputable reality.

The first line of reasoning has to do with the obviously unsustainable nature of economic growth that created and continues to support modern societies (Binswanger 2009). In the long run, the growth imperative of modern economies is incompatible with the second law of thermodynamics, called by Nicholas Georgescu-Roegen (1971) the most economical of all physical laws. From this perspective, accessible material at low entropy is the most critical variable, and minimized entropic degradations should be the foremost goal for any rational society. Or, to rephrase this challenge by referring to several recent books, because materials matter (Geiser 2001), we should stop shoveling fuel for a runaway train of economic growth (Czech 2000), embrace the logic of sufficiency (Princen

2005), confront consumption (Princen, Maniates, and Conca 2002), and make a break with the throwaway culture (Slade 2006) by reasserting self-control (Offer 2006).

And according to the most radical reinterpretation, even a steady-state civilization would not be enough. The only thermodynamically acceptable society would have to be supportable without any fossil fuel input and would have to minimize its material throughput (Georgescu-Roegen 1971). In less radical interpretations these ideas have found expression since the 1980s in calls for sustainable economic growth tinged with varying shades of "green," in arguments for service economies aiming at wealth without resource consumption (Stahel 1997), and in proposals for economic de-growth (Flipo and Schneider 2008) or, in a variant phrasing, for managing prosperous economies without growth (Victor 2008; Jackson 2009). And the time to act may be here, as the denouement of exponentials has already begun (Morgan 2010). Obviously, any material- and energy-intensive mass-scale manufacturing is an anathema to these efforts, and the declining fortunes of modern manufacturing are seen as desirable steps toward a long-term goal of true sustainability.

The second line of reasoning leading to unconcern about manufacturing's declining fortunes, and one that is much more common and widely accepted, sees that trend as an essential component of a highly desirable evolution marked by a steady decline in the sector's contribution to the national economic product—and by the obverse trend of an inexorably rising importance of services. These two trends, one downward, one upward, characterize all modern economies. In Germany the value added by manufacturing stood at about 32% in 1970. It was down to 21% by the year 2000 and to 18.9% by 2010. In Japan the shares for the same years stood at 35%, 22%, and 21.2% (UN 2012).

In the United States, manufacturing's share of GDP declined from 27% in 1950 to less than 23% by 1970 and to 13.3% in the year 2000; after a small rise to 14.1% in 2007 it declined to 12.9% in 2009, then rose a bit to 13.5% in 2010. I should note that all of these comparisons are based on the UN's data using ISIC categories (International Standard Industrial Classification, manufacturing being category D). In contrast, the US domestic accounts, using NAICS codes 31–33, indicate even lower shares: 14.2% in 2000, 11.2% in 2009, 11.7% in 2010, and 12.2% in 2011—and only about 11% when subtracting foreign-made components of US-made products (USBC 2012a). In 2011, government services contributed about 13%, financial services (including insurance and real estate) topped the sectoral ranking at about 20%, and all service sectors (including all trade) accounted for about 77% of the country's GDP.

Manufacturing is not the only economic sector that has been seen as increasingly unimportant when compared to services. Agriculture, fisheries, and forestry add an even smaller share to the total economic product: in 2010 they accounted for about 1% in the United States and Germany, nearly 1.5% in Japan, and—an exceptionally high share—2% in France (UN 2012). A brief reflection suggests that this low share is not an appropriate way to value the sector's importance in any populous affluent country: we need only to imagine the EU economy without French or German farming, or trying to replace all the food in any affluent populous country by imports, or the consequences of losing US farm exports, the world's largest source of traded grains and meat.

In 2011 US agriculture accounted for only 1.2% of the country's GDP, but the absurdity of the claim that this small share makes farming a marginal economic activity is best exposed by comparing the loss of that share with the disappearance of an identical share contributed by financial services. Complete loss of agriculture's 1% is not obviously equivalent to reducing financial services' share by 1%. The first loss would bring large-scale suffering and death not only inside the country but worldwide because there is not enough food on the global market to feed the United States solely by imports, and even Brazil could not make up for the loss of US food exports. The second loss actually took place between 2009 and 2011, when the sector's share of GDP fell by 1.4% even as the economy was slowly recovering from the worst post–World War II recession it has faced. And one could argue that a further decline might be desirable if the loss entailed all those speculative, derivative transactions that have been one of the principal causes of many recent economic hardships.

Analogously, using the declining share of GDP to judge the importance of manufacturing in the US economy is to rely on a wrong metric because the sector offers benefits unmatched by other economic activities (Duesterberg and Preeg 2003; MI 2009). Above all, manufacturing creates many backward-forward linkages that include many traditional jobs (from accounting to job training), as well as entirely new labor opportunities (in e-sales, global representation). As a result, sales of every dollar of manufactured products support $1.40 of additional activity, while the rate for transportation is about $1, and the retail sector and professional and business services generate less than 60 cents for every dollar of final sales (MI 2009).

Because of its own needs for better-educated labor and its multiple linkages to intellectual services, transportation, and wholesale and retail operations, manufacturing also acts as a powerful motivator for supporting and expanding suitable training and education: losing manufacturing means reducing opportunities for skill-oriented education, and as the sector accounts for about two-thirds of R&D, its decline means losing innovation capacities and economic multiplier effects. Moreover, manufacturing is a key enabler of the traded sector's strength, and in a globalized world it is impossible to have a strong national economy without internationally competitive trade (Atkinson et al. 2012). In the US case, the import of manufactured goods is the single largest cause of the country's chronic trade deficit—while perhaps the best way to reduce that drain is, particularly given the country's relatively low trade intensity, through the expansion of manufactured exports.

Making the case for perpetuating a strong manufacturing sector in America's service-dominated economy thus rests mainly on three fundamental realities. First, and most notably, manufacturing has been the principal driver of technical innovation, and technical innovation in turn has been the most important source of economic growth in modern societies. Second, despite extensive offshoring, large labor cuts, and a deep erosion of many formerly thriving sectors (apparel, consumer electronics, leather goods, machine tools, primary steel), US manufacturing remains very large and, in absolute value–added terms, still a growing part of the nation's economy, and a reversal of this long-term trend would make the existing socioeconomic challenges even harder to tackle. Third, a relatively low intensity of manufactured exports has contributed to the country's trade deficits, and a further retreat of the US manufacturing sector would eliminate any realistic hope for their eventual reversal.

The first reality means nothing less than crediting manufacturing as the key generator of America's (and indeed the world's) post-1865 economic growth. This attribution has been revealed by efforts to account for the sources of economic growth that was needed to create the world's first mass consumption society. How has US manufacturing achieved those unprecedented levels of high-volume production and high labor productivity? Classical explanations credited the combined inputs of labor and capital as the key generators of economic growth (Rostow 1990); not until 1956 did Abramovitz show that this combination explained just 10% of the growth of per capita output and no more than 20% of labor productivity growth in the US economy since 1870 (Abramovitz 1956).

Most of the large residual, known as the total factor productivity (TFP), had to be due to technical advances, and Solow (1957) supplied its first startling quantification, concluding that 88% of the doubling of the overall US labor productivity between 1909 and 1949 can be attributed to technical changes in the broadest sense, with the small remainder the result of higher capital intensity. In his Nobel lecture, Solow claimed that "the permanent rate of growth of output per unit of labor input . . . depends entirely on the rate of technological progress in the broadest sense" (Solow 1987). Denison (1985) found that 55% of the US economic growth between 1929 and 1982 was due to advances in knowledge, 16% to labor shifting from farming to industry, and 18% to economies of scale. As the latter two variables are themselves largely a result of technical advances, above all mechanization, which released rural labor to industry, Denison's account implies that innovation was behind at least three-quarters of economic growth during that period.

These early studies of TFP viewed technical change as an exogenous variable, with new ideas coming from the outside, to be eventually adopted and internalized by enterprises. This view ignores many ways of continuous innovation within industrial enterprises and the feedbacks among producers, innovators, and markets. An endogenous explanation of technical change as a process induced by previous actions within an economy began with Arrow's (1962) work and became commonplace a generation later (Romer 1990). But Grossman and Helpman (1991) argued that the decompositions of Solow's residual may be inappropriate for drawing any inferences about the underlying causes of economic growth because the identified factors are not independent variables but are dynamically linked, and they also concluded that the exogenous-endogenous dichotomy is more of an externally imposed division than a description of reality.

And as Solow (2000) pointed out, the claim that the tempo of economic growth is a function of a simple variable that can be manipulated by a policy is hardly persuasive, and is unsupported by historical evidence.

Perhaps most notably, a massive post–World War II increase in US R&D manpower and funding aimed at producing waves of technical innovation has not resulted in a comparable rise in economic growth. De Loo and Soete (1999) offered an explanation for this lack of correlation between higher post–World War II R&D and productivity growth, concluding that those activities concentrated increasingly not on product innovation but on product differentiation, which improves consumer welfare but does little for economic growth.

The latest puzzle regarding the effects of technical innovation on economic growth rates was the apparent failure of the nearly universal adoption of the microprocessor to generate a surge in US manufacturing productivity. David's (1990) explanation of this paradox came in the form of a historical analogy with electricity generation, whose impact on manufacturing productivity became very strong only during the early 1920s, 40 years after the beginning of commercial electricity generation. The low rate of labor productivity growth, averaging less than 1.5% per year between 1973 and 1995, was reversed during the late 1990s, and at 2.5% a year it almost equaled the 1960–1973 rate (Dale et al. 2002).

While there may be no perfect way to disaggregate the relative contributions of individual factors driving economic growth, there can be no doubt that innovation, rather than labor or capital, has been its most important driver. In turn, there is no doubt that technical innovation in modern Western societies has originated overwhelmingly in the manufacturing sector. The sector has been always the principal locus of independent invention and technical improvements. In the closing decades of the nineteenth century manufacturing companies were the first entities to foster systematic research in their factories and laboratories, and from these often surprisingly modest origins grew the modern R&D sector.

Governments have become major sponsors of this effort (through national research institutions, universities, and aid to industries), but its principal locus (particularly after subtracting the government spending on military projects) remains in the industrial/manufacturing sector. In 2007 global R&D expenditures reached about $1.1 trillion, with more than 60% coming from industry: US industry funds about 67% of all R&D, the EU mean is about 55% (but nearly 70% in Germany), and shares in East Asia are above 60% (NSF 2010). Another estimate credits the top 1,400 firms with spending $545 billion on R&D in 2007, with the largest 100 firms accounting for 60% of that total.

And the key role of manufacturing innovation is obviously true even when describing great transformations in nonindustrial sectors, be it modern agriculture, transportation, or communications. Global agriculture could not feed seven billion people without the Haber-Bosch synthesis of ammonia, without inputs of pesticides and herbicides, and without field machinery, including irrigation pumps. Intercontinental travel time could not shrink without gas turbines powering jetliners, and the global shipping of bulk materials and countless manufactured goods would be much less affordable without the diesel engines that propel massive tankers, cargo carriers, and container ships. Communication could not be instantaneous and global, and no modern service sector based on data storage and processing (banking, finance, retail, hotel and travel reservations) could exist in today's convenient form, without microprocessors, whose manufacturing had to be preceded by the invention of integrated circuits a decade earlier, which in turn was preceded by the commercialization of silicon-based transistors.

Perhaps the best way to stress this fundamental causality is not to use such terms as technical advances, invention, or innovation but to choose Mokyr's broader and a more fundamental term, "useful knowledge"—and to say that only when it was applied, "with an aggressiveness and single-mindedness" that was not known before, it "created the modern material world" (Mokyr 2002, 297). Only those who believe that modern societies can prosper without manufacturing need to be reminded that manufacturing has been the dominant mode of translating this useful knowledge not only into all the material riches but also into the convenient services that are the hallmarks of modern societies.

The second point, the formidable size of America's manufacturing, is easily illustrated with readily available national statistics. When the comparison is done in constant (2005 dollars) using official exchange rates, the sector was still the word's leader, with $1.762 trillion in 2010 (compared to China's $1.654 trillion), accounting for about 19% of the global manufacturing output (UN 2012). In current monies (2010 dollars), China moved to the lead in 2010 ($1.922 trillion vs. $1.856 trillion), but the relative difference remains large (more than fourfold), with the US 2010 per capita rate at about $6,000 and the Chinese rate at about $1,400.

The per capita level of manufacturing effort was also higher in the United States than in France ($4,100), Canada ($4,900), and Italy ($5,200), but roughly 20% lower than in Germany ($7,600) and 25% lower than in Japan ($8,500).

Another way to appreciate the magnitude of the US manufacturing sector is to realize that in 2010, the value it added to the country's GDP was higher (when compared in nominal terms) than the total GDP of all but seven of the world's economies, a bit behind Brazil and well ahead of Canada; a ranking based on purchasing power parity makes the value added by US manufacturing larger than all but nine of the world's largest economies, behind France and ahead of Italy. And the sector has been growing: when measured in constant monies it expanded by about 60% between 1990 and 2010, nearly matching the growth of overall GDP, and grew by 23% between 2001 and 2010, compared to a 15% increase for the overall GDP. But these encouraging aggregates have been accompanied by huge job losses and the drastic downsizing or near elimination of entire manufacturing sectors.

Dealing with the third point requires a review of the specifics of the United States' foreign trade balance. This is perhaps the best way to disprove the idea that a further decline in American manufacturing is of little consequence because exports of high-value-added services, particularly those in software, information, communications, and data management, can make up for the necessity of importing higher shares of manufactured products—or the notion than any decline of domestic manufacturing capacities can be easily made up by inexpensive imports. The United States has had constant trade deficits since 1976, rising from $6 billion to nearly $152 billion by 1987, falling to as low as $31 billion in 1991, and then soaring to $759 billion by 2006; the economic downturn reduced the annual total to $375 billion in 2009, but in 2010 the deficit rose again to close to $500 billion (USBC 2011b). As a share of GDP, the US trade balance shifted from +0.7% in 1960 and +0.2% in 1970 to –0.7% in 1980, –1.4% in 1990, –3.9% in 2000, and –5.8% in 2006 before it improved to –3.4% in 2010.

During this entire period the country had a positive and rising balance in service trade and a negative, and until 2006 generally worsening, balance in trading of goods (including food, fuels, and raw materials). Recent exports of manufactured products—defined according to the Standard

International Trade Classification—increased (in nominal terms) by two-thirds between 2002 and 2008 before dropping by nearly 20% in 2009 as a result of the economic downturn, and then almost recovering in 2010. But the imports of manufactures also kept on rising, by about 53% between 2002 and 2008, leading to a large trade deficit in manufactured goods that peaked at $630 billion in 2006 and stood at well over half a trillion ($565 billion) in 2010 before reaching another record level of $635 billion in 2011 (USBC 2012a). Exports of services have helped narrow the country's overall trade deficit, but they are not enough to close the huge manufacturing gap.

Service exports took 11 years to double, from $269 billion in 1999 to $553 billion in 2010, and in 2011 they rose to $606 billion, which means that even when assuming an unchanged level of service imports (nearly $430 billion in 2011), the current positive balance in service trade would have to increase 3.5-fold to eliminate the 2011 trade deficit in manufactured goods. Obviously, any further widening of merchandise trade deficits would have to translate into an even faster rate of service export expansion to prevent any additional overall deterioration. While it is most unlikely that surpluses in the service trade could ever eliminate the large deficit in the goods trade, it is quite realistic to envisage that increased exports of manufactured products could greatly reduce (if not entirely eliminate) the deficit in that category. This possibility exists because the United States has been underperforming as an exporter of manufactured products, a point I stress and quantify in the closing chapter.

To sum up: an enormous and still expanding range of manufactured products remains a key defining attribute of modern societies. While there are many impressive examples of relative (per unit of final product, per a specific performance) dematerialization, neither the rapidly modernizing economies nor the postindustrial economies have experienced any dematerialization either in aggregate or in average per capita terms. Manufacturing's importance cannot be judged merely according to its (still declining) share of value added to a nation's GDP; the sector remains the principal source of technical innovation and hence a key driver of economic growth. The United States is a comparatively weak exporter, and hence a higher level of manufactured exports could perhaps be the most rewarding way of, if not fully regaining America's positive trade balance, then it least substantially reducing the country's now chronic trade deficits.

No. 766,768. PATENTED AUG. 2, 1904.

M. J. OWENS.

GLASS SHAPING MACHINE.

APPLICATION FILED APR. 13, 1903.

NO MODEL. 10 SHEETS—SHEET 1.

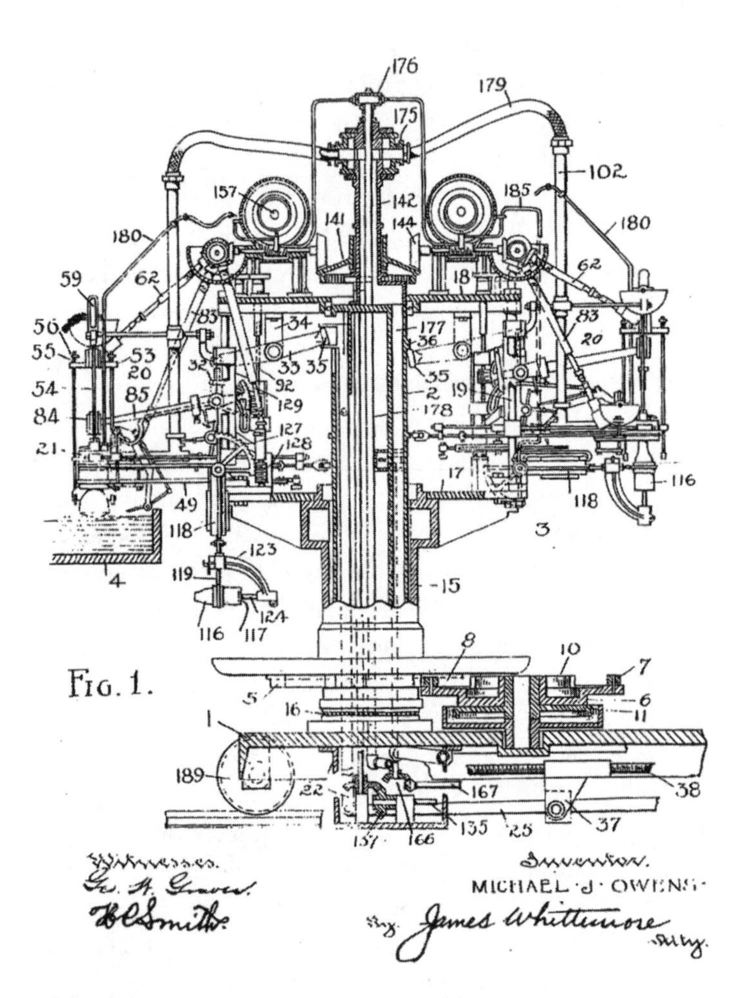


**Figure 2.1**
In 1904 M. J. Owens finally received US patent 766,768 for his glass-shaping machine. This remarkable automaton symbolizes the transition of American manufacturing from manual artisanal work to fully mechanized mass production. Patent drawing available at http://www.sha.org/bottle/pdffiles/Owens1904patent.pdf.

# 2

# The Ascent, 1865–1940

*During the three generations following the Civil War United States transformed itself from a traditional rural economy into the world's leading, and exceptionally innovative, manufacturer.*

I am an American. I was born and reared in Hartford, in the State of Connecticut . . . So I am a Yankee of the Yankees—and practical; yes, and nearly barren of sentiment . . . I went over to the great arms factory and learned my real trade; learned all there was to it; learned to make everything: guns, revolvers, cannon, boilers, engines, all sorts of labor-saving machinery. Why, I could make anything a body wanted—anything in the world, it didn't make any difference what; and if there wasn't any quick new-fangled way to make a thing, I could invent one—and do it as easy as rolling off a log.

—Mark Twain, *A Connecticut Yankee in King Arthur's Court,* 1889

When the thirteen colonies proclaimed their independence from British rule in 1776, their constitution, adopted 11 years later, was a remarkably modern document spelling out the aspirations of a new nation. And, contrary to a common view that the new state had a weak industrial foundation, the newly united states were a relatively strong economic power (McAllister 1989). Like its European contemporaries, it was a traditional society where most of the citizens—close to 80%—engaged in small-scale subsistence farming (with larger-scale agricultural production limited to southern plantations); and with a low level of urbanization, in average per capita terms the early postcolonial Americans enjoyed close to the highest income levels of the contemporary world.

And while at the end of the eighteenth century Britain, their former colonial power, had a much stronger industrial base, the new state had not only a great deal of artisanal household manufacture but also substantial shipbuilding capacities, and its pig iron output accounted for about 15% of the world's total. More important, the country's natural endowment was second to none, and once the industrialization process began in earnest, following the Civil War (1861–1865), its progress rapidly surpassed all European achievements. Reconstructions of historical accounts show that the US gross economic product topped the UK's total during the late 1860s (or, at the latest, in the early 1870s) and that the United States has been the world's leading economy ever since (Maddison 2007).

Given Britain's large and diversified manufacturing sector, it took the United States a bit longer to move to the top spot: in 1870 the UK's share of global manufacturing output was still nearly one-third, compared to less than one-quarter for the United States, but the order was reversed sometime during the late 1880s (in 1890 at the latest), and just before World War I the US share stood at about 36%, compared to less than 15% for the UK. After becoming number one, the United States retained its manufacturing primacy for the next 120 years. In 2010 it was widely reported that the United States had been surpassed by China, but that was true only when the sector's contribution to GDP was measured in current dollars: the totals were $1.923 trillion for China and $1.856 trillion for the United States, but in constant 2005 dollars the United States was still ahead, at $1.763 trillion, compared to $1.665 trillion for China (UN 2012).

Those of us who see economic development through its fundamental physical lens would hasten to point out that none of this would have happened without an enormous increase in overall energy consumption. This increase was accompanied by an epochal transition as biomass fuels (wood and charcoal) and animate energies (human and animal muscles) were displaced by fossil fuels (coal, oil, and natural gas), mechanical prime movers (waterwheels, steam turbines, internal combustion engines), and electricity (in manufacturing used above all to power electric motors, and also for lighting and ventilation). Between 1865 and 1900 the annual primary energy use multiplied nearly 12-fold and average per capita use nearly tripled. But because coal was burned (in boilers and stoves) with higher efficiency than wood in stoves and fireplaces, and because electric light bulbs were much more efficient energy converters than candles or oil lamps, the per capita supply of useful energy (heat, motion, light) at least quintupled.

These higher conversion efficiencies also explain why the energy intensity of the US economy (energy per unit of GDP, measured in constant dollars) declined by about 25% during the last three decades of the nineteenth century. This trend briefly reversed after 1900, when the electrification of industries and households and growing car ownership accelerated the demand for fossil fuels. American statistics allow us to pinpoint the year when the country's huge fuelwood consumption was surpassed by the combustion of fossil fuels (Schurr and Netschert 1960). Coal supplied only 5% of the US primary energy output by the early 1840s, rising to 10% a decade later. By the early 1870s it accounted for a third of the total, and by 1885 it had reached one-half. By that time crude oil, whose extraction began in 1859 in Pennsylvania, supplied about 2% of all energy; 1884 was the first year when America's output of two fossil fuels (natural gas use was negligible) contained more energy than wood. This tipping point was followed by a rapid decline in wood's importance to about 20% of the total by 1900.

But energy alone, no matter how abundant, could not propel the United States to its economic dominance. Rather, the country's enormous post-1865 leap was primarily driven by technical advances. These developments made the United States not only the largest mass producer of goods but also the leader in commercializing new inventions, setting up entirely new industries, introducing new ways of production, and raising labor productivity. More than a century later the country, and the world, still continue to benefit from many of those epoch-making advances. And in terms of labor productivity, American manufacturing did not have to play catch-up with the British performance.

As Broadberry (1994) has demonstrated, that productivity was higher in the United States even in the early decades of the nineteenth century, and by 1860 the United States had a more than twofold advantage; subsequent industrialization made little difference, with relative US/UK labor productivity ratios during the three decades between 1870 and 1900 showing no particular trend as they fluctuated between about 180 and a bit over 200. Sectoral close-ups based on census figures for the years 1907 (UK) and 1909 (US) show particularly large differences in the auto industry (more than fourfold), in metallurgical industries, and in the production of building materials and paper. These large differences persisted throughout the twentieth century; during the 1920s and 1930s American labor productivity was about 2.5 times the British rate (Broadberry 1998).

In surveying the ascent of American manufacturing during the past 150 years I will follow a simple pattern. For each period I first present the key macroeconomic indicators (GDP in absolute and per capita terms, its growth rates, and its sectoral origins) and basic data for the manufacturing sector (total value added, decadal growth rates, changing productivity, exports and imports), and then focus on accomplishments in a few key areas whose progress defined or dominated a particular period. For the pre-1900 decades the special focus will be on innovations in the production of steel, the quintessential material of the nineteenth-century industrialization and still the dominant metal of modern civilization; on the origins and expansion of an entirely new industry to generate, distribute, and use electricity, an industry that was created during the last two decades of the nineteenth century; and on pioneering developments in the invention and commercial design and manufacturing of new machines, devices, and tools for the information and communication sectors, whose even more spectacular advances came during the twentieth century.

In the second part of the chapter I survey what I call the period of consolidation, the first four decades of the twentieth century, before the country's entry into World War I. The special focus will be first on electrification of industries and households. Because of electricity's wide availability and the large range of its final uses, this was perhaps the single most important technical advance in the history of modern civilization as it transformed not only manufacturing and household management but everything else, from medicine (where electricity is used in refrigeration for vaccines and in a multitude of diagnostic devices) to flight (where electricity powers radio, radar, and, most recently, GPS).

The focus then turns to two fundamental American innovations that arose early in the twentieth century and came to define modern manufacturing worldwide: on the one hand, the organization for mass production, a development that was pioneered by Henry Ford's making of affordable automobiles, and on the other hand, the detailed attention to individual operations designed to optimize a specific process and to reach the highest practical efficiency, a quest pioneered by Frederick Winslow Taylor. I close the chapter with a counterintuitive survey of technical and productive advances of American manufacturing during the decade of the Great Depression. That decade of hardship and losses was also a time of remarkable technical advances and admirable gains in productivity.

## Creating the Modern World, 1865–1899

During the first half of the nineteenth century the United States remained an overwhelmingly agrarian economy: in 1860 the urban population (in settlements larger than 2,500 people) was still only 16% of the total. Wood was by far the most important energizer of America's households and industries, and most antebellum manufacturing establishments were

**Figure 2.2**
One of the last large coal-fired electricity-generating plants using steam engines, Edison's New York station was completed in 1902. A few years later all new plants used steam turbogenerators. This engraving appeared on the cover of *Scientific American,* September 6, 1902.

small, artisanal workshops that relied solely on human labor. These workshops accounted for roughly a third of the overall economic output, producing essential items for households, transportation, and industry of the steam age. In 1860 only about 15% of all manufacturers were using steam power, while about 24% relied on water power, but after the war the use of steam power became positively correlated with the size of manufacturing establishments, and by 1880 just over 50% of workers were employed by factories and workshops that relied on steam engines (Atack, Bateman, and Margo 2008).

Another important factor in the early expansion of industrial production was a gradual adoption of what came to be known as the American system of manufacturing (Hounshell 1984). Its key principle, going back to the Venetian shipbuilding of the early modern era, was first deployed in the mass production of manufactured items by the British navy during the Napoleonic wars to produce standardized, interchangeable parts by semi-skilled labor using special purpose-built milling machines in conjunction with jigs (templates) to guide the machining (Coad 2005). The practice was slow to spread both in the UK and the United States, where it was first embraced by the Department of War in its armories in Springfield, Massachusetts, and Harpers Ferry, West Virginia, and by their contractors to make rifles, muskets, and pistols (hence the common term, armory practice).

The practice diffused slowly as the first sewing machines, bicycles, or automobiles were produced in an artisanal way, by skilled machinists and mechanics. But it was eventually adopted by all major industries, from sewing machine manufacture to automakers (Ford's famous contribution will be described later) and from grain harvesting to watchmaking (the last with an annual output of more than 100 million pieces by 1920), and it was fueled by mass immigration, the westward settlement of the country, which required extensive material support, and rising disposable income. One of the greatest visual testimonies to how this manufacturing succeeded is the more than 600 pages of the annual merchandise catalogs of the two great rivals, Montgomery Ward and Sears, Roebuck, which displayed thousands of items making up the universe of American manufacturing by the end of the nineteenth century: I cite the two editions that are readily available in modern facsimiles (Montgomery Ward & Company 2008 [1895]; Sears, Roebuck & Company 2007 [1897]).

The productivity gains afforded by the combination of steam-driven mechanization, the use of interchangeable, standardized parts, and the rise of larger manufacturing establishments are impressively illustrated by examples published by the US Department of Labor. In an artisanal workshop, two men needed 188 man-hours to produce a plow, whereas in a largely mechanized factory 52 specialized workers required only 3.75 man-hours per plow. A seamstress working alone needed 10 hours for the 25 different tasks that went into making a men's shirt, whereas mechanized production, employing specialized workers to perform 39 specific tasks, turned out a shirt in just 80 minutes.

Mechanization, specialization, and commercialization were also the key factors driving gains in agricultural labor productivity, particularly in field work, as American manufacturers introduced new steel plows, harvesters, threshing machines, and grain combines. At least two-thirds of the century's total farming productivity increase came after 1860, and virtually all improvements in livestock output took place after 1865 (Weiss 1993). American agriculture was thus able to boost its output with no, or minimum, price increases and could supply the expanding and industrializing cities with plenty of food and with its surplus labor.

The three postwar decades were an era of exceptionally abundant and truly epochal inventions and innovations; I have argued elsewhere that its advances created the twentieth century (Smil 2005). Although the inventors, scientists, and engineers who came up with these ideas and the entrepreneurs who transformed them into entirely new products and industries came from many European countries (particularly the UK, France, Germany, and Russia), the largest aggregate contribution came from the United States. The full force of these innovations was not felt until the first decades of the twentieth century, but the post-1865 technical advances had an indisputable impact on the era's total factor productivity (TFP). America's TFP was low during the Civil War decade, but after that the data, with estimates available since 1869 and annual series since 1889 (Kendrick 1961), show TFP growth in manufacturing at 0.86% during the 1870s, 1.94% during the 1880s, and 1.12% during the century's last decade, levels higher than the average during the last three decades of the twentieth century and a clear evidence of the era's knowledge-based progress (Field 2009).

This post-1865 emergence of the modern American economy can be characterized in many other ways. Economists would extol the era's rapid growth of GDP in both absolute and per capita terms, the latter rise being all the more remarkable because of the intervening large-scale immigration.

During the 1870s the GDP grew by 71% and the per capita gain was 35%, both being record decadal increments. The analogous rates for the 1880s were only slightly lower, 66% and 33%. A major slowdown during the 1890s (with the GDP up by only 32%) was due to the economic downturn that began in 1893 (when the real GDP fell by 6%) and lasted until 1897. By that time US manufacturing had surpassed the British output to make the United States the global leader, and cheaper American products began their rapid penetration of foreign markets (Wright 1990). There is no doubt that the post-1865 American manufacturing was biased toward adopting labor-saving technical advances as it transformed itself into a capital- and energy-intensive enterprise, producing large batches of goods (Chandler 1977; Cain and Paterson 1981).

Observers concerned with industrial organization would stress the rise of modern business enterprises (MBEs). These were characterized by a large labor force and deepening capitalization—between 1850 and 1890 the capital/labor ratio nearly tripled, with most of the gain made during the 1880s (James 1983)—and their unprecedented mass outputs were able to supply nationwide markets (and exports). MBEs were also distinguished by a growing concentration of manufacturing and the increasing importance of organization, information, and communication in guiding their expansion and innovation. The concentration of production (led by the iron and steel, meatpacking, flour milling, and distilling industries) proceeded so rapidly that its level hardly changed during the twentieth century. By 1900 a third of income from manufacturing came from industries where the largest four enterprises accounted for more than half of all sales. Seventy years later that share was 29% (Nutter and Einhorn 1969).

Political economists and social commentators would point out the growth of enormous monopolies, the challenges faced by labor unions, and the manifold problems that accompanied rapid industrialization, urbanization, and environmental degradation. They would also highlight the stark contrast between the ostentatious consumption by the era's leading industrialists and bankers, on the one hand, and the poverty of immigrants and the hardships of westward-moving settlers on the other. The first reality, satirized in *The Gilded Age*, by Mark Twain and Charles

Dudley Warner, gave the era its common name in American history. In the book's preface the authors wrote facetiously about

> a State where there is no fever of speculation, no inflamed desire for sudden wealth, where the poor are all simple-minded and contented, and the rich are all honest and generous, where society is in a condition of primitive purity and politics is the occupation of only the capable and the patriotic. (Twain and Warner 1873, 1)

Yet another remarkable attribute of the period is the role of individuals in the modernization process: those were the decades of heroic invention and often admirably speedy innovation as engineers and entrepreneurs (often the same individuals) created a new world. No list could leave out Alexander Graham Bell, Thomas Alva Edison, George Westinghouse, and Nikola Tesla, but it should also feature many others, including George Eastman (cameras and film), Charles Hall (aluminum from bauxite), Ottmar Mergenthaler (linotype), and William Stanley (electricity transformers). Those were also the decades of enormous fortunes amassed (through monopolies, low wages, and harsh working conditions) for Andrew Carnegie and Henry C. Frick in iron and steel (Ingham 1978), Andrew W. Mellon and J. Pierpont Morgan in banking (Knox 1900), John D. Rockefeller and Henry H. Rogers in crude oil production and refining (Tarbell 1904), and Leland Stanford and Cornelius Vanderbilt in railroads (Jensen 1975).

**American Steel**

America's manufacturing leap was helped by many outside impulses: by the need to connect the far-flung regions of a new nation, to accommodate massive post-1865 immigration, to expand the cities in which most of these newcomers had found industrial jobs, to build new factories, and to furnish westward-moving settlers with homesteading goods. Steel was the common material denominator in meeting these needs, an indispensable means to America's economic primacy: steel for rails and locomotives, for ships and bridges, for industrial and agricultural machinery, and for household objects; as well, structural steel was critical to skyscrapers, a new kind of building that first appeared in American cities during the 1880s.

Steel in its simplest form is an alloy of iron and less than 1% of carbon, and its many varieties contain additions of other metals, most commonly chromium, nickel, and vanadium. It has a much higher tensile strength and impact resistance than iron. These attributes are needed for rails, strong construction beams, the reinforcing rods or sheets used in making durable objects, and machines. The alloy is an ancient material whose laborious artisanal production restricted it for millennia to such high-price applications as special tools, weapons, or cutlery (Bell 1884). Once larger and more efficient blast furnaces began to smelt cheap iron, the requirements for high-tensile, high impact resistance metal needed for rails or beams were met by a limited production of wrought iron. Large-scale steelmaking became possible thanks to the independent inventions of Henry Bessemer in the UK (in 1856) and, a year later, of William Kelly in the United States in 1857 (Hogan 1971).

Although the US courts upheld Kelly's domestic rights, the process has always been known as Bessemer's steelmaking. Its essence is the decarburizing of molten pig iron in large tilting converters by delivering blasts of cold air for 15–30 minutes to remove such impurities as carbon, silicon, sulfur, and phosphorus. The first Bessemer steel was made in the United States in a Kelly converter in 1861. By 1870 the process accounted for 55% of the total steel output, its share peaking in 1890 at 86% (Temin 1964). Afterward it was fairly rapidly displaced by open-hearth steelmaking. Open-hearth (Siemens-Martin) furnaces, patented and first deployed in Europe during the 1860s, removed the impurities from steel by slow boiling of charged pig iron and regenerating the escaping heat in brick chambers. In the United States such furnaces produced less than 10% of all steel in 1880, but nearly a third by 1900 (King 1948).

The diffusion of the Bessemer process and the conversion to open-hearth steelmaking opened the way for enormous increases in US steel production and shifted technical leadership in ferrous metallurgy from Britain to America (Hogan 1971; Warren 1973; Misa 1995). Right after the Civil War, the United States produced less than 20,000 t of steel, or just a bit more than half a kilogram per capita. By 1870 the total approached 70,000 t, and in 1880 it rose to 1.25 Mt, an 18-fold expansion in a decade. Even so, the rising demand for steel could not be satisfied by domestic production, and substantial imports continued during the 1870s, peaking in 1880, when the United States bought abroad (mainly in the UK) more than 1 Mt of rails, bars, and plates.

After 1890, when domestic steel output rose to 4.28 Mt, imports rapidly subsided, and by 1900 the annual production had topped 10 Mt, prorating to nearly 135 kg per capita. US producers first surpassed British metallurgists in the capacities and productivities of their furnaces, converters, and plants, then topped the aggregate British production. America became the world's largest steel producer in 1887, the largest extractor of iron ores in 1889, and the largest producer of pig iron in 1890. After the Civil War just over 1% of the US pig iron output was converted to steel, but by 1890 the share was nearly 50%, and by 1900 it had risen to 75% (Hogan 1971; DiFrancesco et al. 2010). By the end of the nineteenth century the United States was producing a third of the world's steel, far ahead of both Germany (with about 20%) and the UK (with about 15%). The iron and steel mills of Pennsylvania (centered on Pittsburgh), Ohio (Cleveland), Indiana (Gary), and Illinois (Chicago) became America's largest, and increasingly highly capitalized, industrial enterprises.

In 1869 the average capitalization of US steelworks and rolling mills was less than $160,000, but by 1899, only 30 years later, that mean had risen to nearly $470,000 (Temin 1964). By that time, US steel had finally become competitive with British production. As Allen (1979) showed, during the 1860s British mills were producing pig iron and iron bars and rails for about half the price of American products, and this price advantage had changed little by the late 1880s, when American iron bars were still nearly twice as expensive and steel rails cost nearly 60% more. The situation reversed rather rapidly during the 1890s, however, and comparisons for the early years of the twentieth century show that labor productivity was almost 80% higher in the United States than in the UK. Falling steel prices were also a key reason for the rather sudden emergence of competitive engineering goods and a jump in US exports: the US exports of such goods to the UK more than doubled in 1896 and then nearly tripled in just three years before settling down to a new plateau (Floud 1974).

During the last three decades of the nineteenth century steel became, for the first time in history, both increasingly inexpensive and readily available for use in a large number of applications previously satisfied by wrought iron, wood, or stone. In his history of American steel, Misa (1995) divided the pre–World War I decades into three periods, named after their characteristic steel uses: rails, 1865–1885; cities, 1880–1890; and armor, 1885–1915. For the two decades between 1865 and 1885 steel was synonymous with rails as the cheaper and more durable metal replaced wrought iron rails (whose US production peaked in 1872). While iron rails had to be replaced every 6–12 months, steel rails lasted for more than 10 years. In 1880 iron rails made up about 70% of all track; by 1900 their share was less than 8%. In 1840 the total length of the US railroads was about 4,500 km; before the end of the 1840s it had surpassed the British total, and by 1860 it was 11 times as much (49,000 km). The first transcontinental railroad was completed in 1869.

But the greatest construction spurt, which saw nearly 133,000 km of new track laid, came during the 1880s, when the total length of track in use grew by more than 70%, to nearly 320,000 km, including tracks for two new transcontinental links completed in 1883 (the Northern Pacific line, from Chicago to Seattle, and the Southern Pacific line, from New Orleans to Los Angeles). An additional almost 95,000 km of track was added during the 1890s (including the Great Northern Railroad, from St. Paul to Seattle). This expansion called for more steel than indicated by the overall length of track in use because steel rails gradually got heavier. In 1880 their average weight was about 30 kg/m (60 lb/yd), but starting in the late 1880s rails weighing 43–45 kg/m were used, and during the 1890s the maximum weight of steel rails reached 50 kg/m (Hogan 1971). Steel thus accelerated the westward projection of the American state, while railroad expansion created large new markets for steel used to make locomotives, freight cars, bridges, and telegraph wires.

As the railroad expansion began to slow down, the US steel industry began to diversify into producing new industrial and agricultural machinery and structural components. Sectors with a fast-rising demand for steel ranged from personal and military firearms (the most popular revolvers of the period were three models of the Colt 0.45, introduced in 1873, 1878, and 1898) to the wire and barbed wire required to fence the West. Galvanized steel was used in 1874 for the first popular design of barbed wire, by Joseph Glidden, and soon the market offered hundreds of variants (McCallum and Frances 1965). Major consumers of steel also included cable, nail, and cutlery production and the machine tool industry; toolmakers were producing an increasing variety of designs for metal fabrication, woodworking, and cloth weaving and for the leather, paper, and food industries.

In agriculture, steel became widely used first for John Lane's moldboard plowshares and sulky plows (allowing a farmer to sit while plowing and adjusting the depth of cut by levers) during the 1870s. More steel went into multi-share plows drawn by teams of heavy horses or by steam power, into mechanical reapers and grain threshers, and, during the 1890s, into the first horse-drawn wheat combines. After 1877, when Lloyd's Register of Shipping classified steel as an insurable material, the metal rapidly displaced wood and iron. Steel ships also became the principal carriers of iron ore on the Great Lakes, and during the 1880s more steel began to go into heavy armor for the US Navy's ships.

Steel as tinplate also found a large market in food canning, and many entirely new markets for steel arose with the post-1860 emergence of America's rapidly growing (and the world's largest) oil industry, which needed drilling rigs, well casings, welded pipes, vessels, and distillation columns for refineries and the containers used to transport and store the fuel. The most commonly used nineteenth-century US container, a steel barrel with the volume of 42 US gallons (nearly 160 liters), was chosen by the US Bureau of the Census in 1872 as the standard measure of oil output and trade. Anachronistically (as crude oil now moves in pipelines and tankers and is stored in large tanks), the oil industry still clings to the unit.

During the 1880s a new and unprecedented demand emerged for steel as a structural material in the first skyscrapers, built in Chicago and New York. The race began with William Le Baron Jenney's ten-story steel-skeleton building—with steel used for beams and girders and iron and steel for columns—in Chicago in 1885 (Turak 1986). Soon after there came another essential steel-consuming invention that allowed buildings to go higher: the first American electric elevator was installed in Baltimore in 1887, and Otis, the company that still dominates the market, put in its first New York elevators in 1889 (Otis Elevator Company 1953), making it much easier (prior to that, elevators were powered by steam engines) to build new cities of steel. A year later came Manhattan's first 20-story-tall World Building, and in 1897 Henry Grey invented a way to roll H beams in a single piece directly from an ingot. H beams then replaced the riveted I beams in the much taller skyscrapers built during the twentieth century.

The new automobile industry was restricted to small artisanal production until after 1900 (and early carriage-like car bodies used mostly wood and canvas rather than steel) and thus had only a limited demand for the metal. But before the century's end more steel was used for weapons (field guns, since 1861 Gatling guns, since 1884 Hiram Maxim's self-powered machine guns), and the metal was also an indispensable component of another completely new industry that began to generate and transmit electricity during the 1890s. The rise of this industry is remarkable because it had to be created almost entirely de novo.

**The Edisonian Electric System**

It was not even a case of putting the cart before the horse—there was no horse to begin with. When Joseph Wilson Swan (recognized in the UK as the rightful inventor of durable incandescent light bulbs) and Thomas Alva Edison (far from the first American to work on incandescent light, but the first one to succeed with the first commercially viable design) solved the challenge of electric lighting during the late 1870s, there was no system in place that would generate electricity and transmit it to houses and factories. Dynamos, improved and commercialized during the 1870s (mainly thanks to Werner Siemens and Zénobe-Théophile Gramme), could supply continuous current (mostly to power arc lights in public urban spaces), but individual consumers of electricity in general, and households in particular, could not install their own steam engines and connect them to dynamos to power their lights. The only other option for households or workshops, expensive and inconvenient, would be to rely on groups of batteries.

Edison anticipated the need for an entirely new system of generation, transmission, and supply, and also realized that it would have to be competitive with the well-established, well-financed, and highly profitable gas-lighting industry (Josephson 1959). Consequently, months before he could demonstrate his first practical light bulbs he began to design larger dynamos and evaluate the likely operating costs in order to compare them with the price of illumination by gas (Friedel and Israel 1986). The speed with which the first working prototypes were translated into commercial realities is easily appreciated by listing the sequence of major milestones in developing the new industry.

The world's first electric system—using about 100 bulbs to light the buildings of Edison's Menlo Park laboratory in New Jersey (one of the world's first true R&D establishments), nearby streets, and the local railway station—was revealed by Edison on December 31, 1879. The first outside installation of electric lights was done for the steamship *Columbia* just three month later, and by then work had begun on the first short underground electricity distribution network in Menlo Park. The first streetlights were lit in November 1880. Meanwhile, Edison had also designed a record-size dynamo capable of powering hundreds of lamps of the first urban system, planned to start deliveries in Manhattan in May 1881.

That proved to be an overly optimistic target as the new entity that was to undertake the project, Edison Electric Illuminating Company, was set up in December 1880 and the final project contract was signed only on March 23, 1881. Boilers and steam engines could be ordered from established suppliers, but all other components of the electrical system, ranging from sockets and switches to insulated underground wires and meters, had to be designed, tested, and serially produced from scratch because the leading American maker of gas-lighting fixtures refused to make any parts; moreover, Edison's major stockholders were reluctant to provide further funding.

That is why during 1881 Edison proceeded with installations of small systems serving only a workshop or a group of offices. In March 1881 Edison was granted a critical patent for a more economical electricity distribution system that cut the cost of copper to only 16% of the originally estimated value and made the installation of more than 24 km of underground cables much more affordable. A larger dynamo was readied at the same time (Beauchamp 1997). Edison had to scale down his original plant to light up the entire district between Canal Street and Wall Street in lower Manhattan and ended up with an area of about 2.5 km$^2$ between Wall Street and the East River, whose high density of financial and publishing offices guaranteed a ready market. The station itself was housed in two adjacent buildings in Pearl Street, and the first light was switched on experimentally in J. P. Morgan's office on September 4, 1882. Four months later the station powered 5,000 light bulbs, whose electricity consumption was measured, starting in early 1883, by an electrolytic meter, yet another Edisonian invention.

Subsequent progress was rapid as improved versions of the Pearl Station system diffused around the United States: their count surpassed 1,300 in 1891, when they powered some three million lights. Friedel and Israel (1986, 227) concluded that the completeness of Edison's system "was more the product of opportunities afforded by technical accomplishments and financial resources than the outcome of a purposeful systems approach," but there can be no doubt that his contributions were those of an exceptional holistic conceptualizer. Edison clearly identified the most important technical hurdles, overcame them by intensive research and testing effort, and transformed those innovations into commercially viable innovations (Hughes 1983).

When I was writing *Creating the 20th Century* (Smil 2005), I read scores of appraisals of Edison's work, but the one I liked most, and the one that is most apposite as far the topic of this book is concerned, was offered in 1908 by Emil Rathenau, Germany's leading industrialist and the founder of the Allgemeine Elektrizitäts Gesellschaft, on the occasion of Edison's 70th birthday. In his speech Rathenau recalled how impressed he was with Edison's thoroughness, evident in the objects displayed at the Electrical Exhibition in Paris in 1881, a veritable homage to America's nineteenth century manufacturing at its best:

> The Edison system of lighting was as beautifully conceived down to the very details, and as thoroughly worked out as if it had been tested for decades in various towns. Neither sockets, switches, fuses, lamp-holders, nor any of the other accessories necessary to complete the installation were wanting; and the generating of the current, the regulation, the wiring with distribution boxes, house connections, meters, etc., all showed signs of astonishing skill and incomparable genius. (Quoted in Dyer and Martin 1929, 127)

As is common with early stages of all major inventions, Edison's system was also very inefficient, it was not easy to scale up, and at the time of its introduction there was no way to convert electricity to mechanical power on scales suitable for household and industrial uses. As originally conceived, Edison's system could not be an economical means of supplying electricity to millions of households and tens of thousands of workshops and factories. Remarkably, all of its shortcomings were addressed before the end of the 1880s by the fundamental inventions of the steam turbine, more efficient lights, transformers, and electric induction motors, and by the century's end these challenges were also largely resolved in commercial practice. What remained for the first decades of the twentieth century was to diffuse these new techniques and make electricity the dominant energizer of American manufacturing.

Edison had to use steam engines, the largest commercially available prime movers, in all of his plants built during the 1880s. After more than a century of improvements the largest (compound-type) steam engines had capacities in excess of 1 MW (Dickinson 1939), but their typical efficiency in prolonged operations was only about 15%, and despite a steady decline in the mass/power ratio they remained heavy and bulky; further, the speed they could impart to the attached dynamos was limited because a relatively slow piston motion (Ewing 1911). The poor performance of the pioneering installations (Edison's early plants had an overall efficiency of less than 3%) was solved by replacing steam engines and dynamos with turbogenerators, steam turbines that rotated on the same shaft as alternators.

Charles Algernon Parsons filed his British steam turbine patent in April 1884, and the first small (75 kW) commercial turbogenerator was installed in Newcastle-on-Tyne in 1890 (Parsons 1936). Scaling up had proceeded so rapidly that by 1899, Parsons's company was building the first 1 MW units for a large German station. The US manufacturing of steam turbines began only after George Westinghouse acquired the US patent rights in 1895, but it progressed rapidly, with a 1.5 MW unit shipped in 1900 to the Hartford Electric Light Company (MacLaren 1943; Bannister and Silvestri 1989). By that time it had become obvious that the days of large steam engines in power plants were numbered, and steam turbogenerators became the largest, and in many ways the most important, prime movers of the twentieth century, with American manufacturers—particularly Westinghouse and GE—leading their performance and capacity improvements.

Edison was such a proponent of direct current (DC) transmission that, starting in 1887, he actually waged a short-lived (about three years') but intensive campaign of demonizing alternating current (AC). He reversed himself abruptly in 1890. David (1991) has explained Edison's behavior as a deliberate business strategy: by vehemently opposing AC he tried to prop up the value of his entirely DC-based system before all of his remaining stake in the electric business was bought by the newly formed Edison General Electric Company in 1899, in whose work he stopped participating a year later.

The victory of AC would have been impossible without another innovation that had to be improved and commercialized. Transformers were needed because the best way to generate and use electricity is at low voltages, while the best way to transmit it across long distances with minimal losses is with high voltages. Transformers can economically and efficiently change the voltages of vast flows of electricity. Their development began in the early 1880s both in Europe and in the United States, and by 1886 it was an American design, by a Westinghouse engineer, William Stanley, that emerged as the prototype of all future transformers (Stanley 1912). In 1895 Westinghouse and General Electric connected the new Niagara Falls station (generating at 5 kV) to Buffalo with an 11 kV line. That sealed the dominance of AC, and by 1900 the largest devices could transform inputs of 50 kV (Passer 1953; Hunter and Bryant 1991).

But nothing made as great a difference to the expanding market for electricity as the large-scale introduction of AC electric motors (Bailey 1911; Dunsheath 1962; Pohl and Müller 1984). Their DC predecessors began to diffuse during the 1870s. These early versions ranged from small, battery-powered units for driving Edison's stencil-making electric pen, used to duplicate documents, to fairly powerful machines for small exhibition locomotives (electrified from the third rail). By 1885 Frank Sprague, Edison's former employee, had developed the first relatively powerful DC motors (the largest capacities of 15 hp, or about 11 kW). A year later 250 of them were bought by manufacturing enterprises, mainly printers, and by 1899 several thousand of them had an aggregate capacity of more than 10 MW (DuBoff 1979).

But most DC motors of the 1880s were small (up to a few hundred watts) and unreliable devices (Hunter and Bryant 1991), and a superior design became available only thanks to the invention of the induction AC motor by a Serbian engineer, Nikola Tesla. After emigrating to the United States Tesla worked first for Edison before setting up his own company in 1887 and applying for two scores of patents for a new polyphase AC motor (Ratzlaff and Anderson 1979; Cheney 1981; Seifer 1996). Westinghouse Electric bought the key patents of Tesla's efficient and reliable design in July 1888 and the next year marketed a small electric fan, the first mass-produced household products powered by AC electricity. AC machines had a lower mass/power ratio (smaller and lighter for the same power rating) than DC motors and were also simpler and hence easier to construct, and cheaper and very durable. In the same year Mikhail Osipovich Dolivo-Dobrowolsky introduced the first three-phase induction motor in Germany (Tesla's original design was for a two-phase AC motor) that delivered a more even power output.

Electric motors made slow inroads in some industries during the 1890s, but their wider adoption in households (starting with vacuum cleaners

ayment Receipt

rro Bay Library (OM)
5-772-6394
w.slolibrary.org
iday, November 20, 2015 3:13:31 PM

776
the, Mark E.

rd Type: Visa
rd Number: XXXXXXXXXXXX3985
ansaction ID: 71231
th No.:
ount: $7.00

tle : MADE IN THE USA
em barcode : 32063012969788
terial type : ILL
ason : ILL Fee
arge : $7.00

tal charges : $7.00
id : $7.00
------------------------------------
count balance: $0.00

ank You!

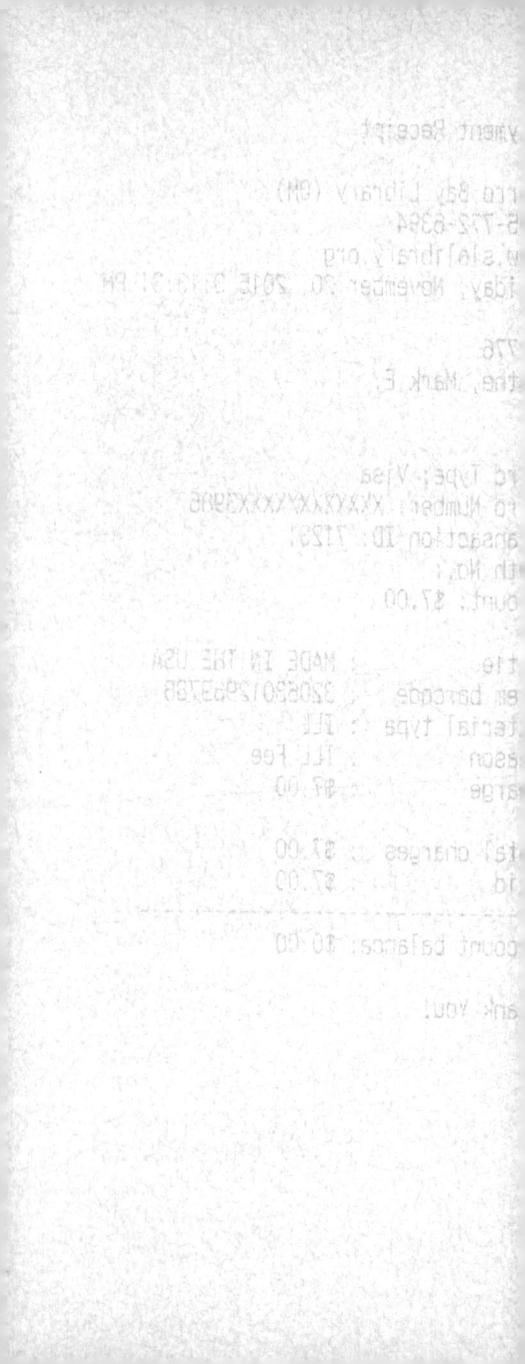


and refrigerators) and manufacturing (to power stationary and portable machinery) had to wait until the early decades of the twentieth century, when the combination of growing generation capacities of central power stations and expanding transmission ensured a reliable electricity supply. As a result, in 1889 only 4% of all primary energy in manufacturing was supplied by purchased electricity (Jerome 1934), and illumination of public and private spaces remained the leading application of the growing electricity supply. More light bulbs could be accommodated by drawing on the same power, thanks to the improving performance of incandescing filaments. While Edison's first cardboard fiber lights converted only 0.2% of electric energy to light, improved designs reached an efficiency of 0.5%, and by 1906 the first tungsten filaments had raised the performance to about 2%.

**Manufacturing for the Information Age**

The modern information era—a time of inexpensive availability of textual, aural, and pictorial information distributed by wired connections and wireless broadcasts—has been characterized by a steadily expanding array of devices and options. For today's teenagers, 24/7 TV news channels, mobile phones, and the Internet have always been part of their lives, and photographs, records, and movie houses seem to be prehistoric relics. People born during or before the 1970s remember the diffusion of personal computers in the 1980s, the arrival of the first Internet browsers in the mid-1990s, and the first Wi-Fi laptops. For their parents, the information age was defined by newspapers, long-playing records, the switch from black-and-white to color TV, and monopoly-owned telephone networks. And for their grandparents, the markers of the information age were a good radio receiver and a bulky TV set.

But the modern information age began long before any of these events, during the second half of the nineteenth century, and its advent was heralded by both well-known events (Alexander Graham Bell's famous first phone call to Thomas Watson was on March 13, 1876; the first brief silent movies were shown in 1894 and 1895) and developments that only historians of technical advances would recall (such as the early work on wireless transmission by David Hughes and Oliver Joseph Lodge). These innovations changed everything from printing words (linotype) and illustrations (halftones instead of laborious engravings) to making long-distance communication instantaneous and personal (telephones), from capturing images and news of faraway places (photographs and moving pictures) to listening to recorded music and preserving memories (phonographs, records, cameras)—and they also included a fundamentally different way of producing cheap paper. The basic concepts underlying these inventions were realized and the prototypes were translated into practical devices with impressive speed.

My brief survey starts with a revolutionary change in making paper, the dominant material for preserving and conveying information during the pre-electronic era. Traditional papermaking depended on a limited supply of cotton, linen, flax, and hemp fibers recovered from rags. The mechanical pulping of wood, adopted on a larger scale in Europe by the 1870s and producing an inferior, rapidly deteriorating paper containing lignin and resins, is now widely used to make material for packaging and some newsprint. The first two methods of producing virtually pure cellulose fibers from wood were American inventions: the alkaline process, first used in 1863, was soon largely displaced by a sulfite process (wood chips were boiled with bisulfites of calcium or magnesium) that was patented first by Benjamin Chew Tilghman in 1867 and subsequently improved by European engineers.

The impact of these innovations was rapid. In 1850 the annual US production of rag paper averaged less than 5 kg per capita, but by 1900 (after its total had doubled during the 1890s) it had surpassed 30 kg per capita, for a population more than three times the size of the 1850 population. This increased paper supply led to the emergence of an entirely new paper-based manufacturing. Erasable writing slates, those ancient tools of literacy, were replaced by school notebooks: in 1895, Montgomery Ward's 160-page School Spelling Tablet cost just three cents. The catalog from which it could be ordered was another beneficiary of inexpensive paper: its first issue, in 1872, was a single page, but by 1895 it had more than 600 pages (Montgomery Ward & Company 2008 [1895]).

Newspapers and journals began to add pages and started special editions; and new titles, including illustrated magazines, sold cheaply. Classic works became available in mass market editions, as did practical guides to arts and crafts, agricultural management, or small manufacturing. Paper manufacture became important in nonliterary arenas as well. Margaret Knight, a Maine-born inventor, designed the first sturdy paper bag with a flat bottom and also the first machine to make such bags, in 1867. With better machine design, introduced by Luther Childs Crowell in 1872 and further improved by Charles Stilwell in 1883, brown paper bags became one of the cheapest and most commonly used manufactured items before the ubiquitous use of plastics.

Printers now had cheap paper, but still faced the high cost of laborious manual typesetting. The first practical solution of mechanical typesetting came with Ottmar Mergenthaler's linotype, whose construction occupied 15 years of his life after he emigrated to the United States from Germany. The composing machine had to perform automated composing, justifying, casting, and distributing of the type with speed and accuracy, achieving maximum tolerances of 0.01 mm, in order to print clearly every character. And even before that took place it was necessary to manufacture precise yet inexpensive matrices that could withstand thousands of hours of repeated use, a task that called for specialized machines. Mergenthaler's first working prototype was ready in the summer of 1886, and by 1892 the Model 1 had become a large-scale commercial success. Three years later more than 1,000 linotypes were at work, and later, more complex designs dominated the industry until the 1950s. By the time the last linotype was shipped, in 1971, Mergenthaler's company and its successors had produced nearly 90,000 machines. If Gutenberg's movable type marked the first revolution in the history of printing, Mergenthaler's machine marked the second one.

The typewriter is yet another example of a device with a high degree of mechanical complexity. It was a thoroughly American invention that began with an 1868 patent by Christopher Sholes, Carlos Glidden, and Samuel Soule. They sold their rights to a couple of entrepreneurs, who contracted with E. Remington & Sons, well-known manufacturers of guns and sewing machines, to design and produce a commercial model (Zellers 1948). Remington's 1874 typewriter design looked like a sewing machine, having a treadle for paper advancement, and produced an invisible text as the bars hit the ribbon against the platten's underside. In 1878 Byron Brooks patented the typing of capitals and small letters with the same key, three year later James Hammond introduced a revolving cylinder, and visible designs became dominant by the late 1890s (Typewriter Topics 1924).

For millennia, image reproduction was an artisanal process performed one sheet at a time. Mechanical presses made this process faster, but, as in the case of typesetting, the original image still had to be laboriously cut or engraved. Early photography, during the first half of the nineteenth century, did not change this: taking pictures was limited by the size of the equipment, long exposure times, and the laborious processing of negatives. Moreover, there were no inexpensive ways to copy these images in mass printed matter, and the illustrated journals had to rely on engravers to convert photographic images to reproducible engravings.

Sensitive dry plates reduced exposure times, but only roll film and simple cameras made it possible to take true snapshots of events and people with ease, and only an ingenious method of breaking up continuous photograph surfaces into printable dots allowed them to be reproduced in publications. American inventors and manufacturers were the leaders in commercializing both of these innovations. George Eastman first patented a process for coating glass plates and then substituted for the glass a triple-layer negative film made of paper, soluble gelatin, and gelatin emulsion, and designed a simple camera that was sold for the first time during the latter half of 1888.

Soon the improved versions of this camera became cheaper than the original model, which sold for $25 (by 1895, the cost of the newer models ranged from $3.50 to $13.50). The stripping film was replaced by transparent rolls, which were first used in October 1889 in the Number 1 Kodak camera, whose numerous improved versions (using more sensitive films) were kept in production for the next hundred year; the last version of the popular Kodak Instamatic was produced in 1988 (Coe 1988.). What made the company even more famous than its inexpensive cameras was its superior slide films. Kodachrome was the choice of professional photographers for decades, the last roll being developed in 2010.

Halftone printing, made possible by breaking up a continuous image into a printable pattern of dots, was pioneered by Frederic Eugene Ives, who produced his first halftones during the late 1870s. By 1885 he had perfected the technique by overlaying pictures with finely etched screens; photographing those sets resulted in a dotted, and hence printable, image pattern (Ives 1928). This procedure reduced the cost of newspaper illustrations to less than a tenth of the previous expense (Mott 1957), and because printing halftones was cheaper than typesetting the equivalent amount of printed space, publications embraced the new technique enthusiastically, and have relied on it ever since. During the 1880s Ives also prepared the first primary color separations, using blue, red, and green filters; made their halftones; and used perfectly aligned three-ink printing to make color reproductions.

Although Edison claimed he would do for the eye what his phonograph did for the ear, his Kinetograph (a camera) and Kinetoscope (a viewer) were developed mostly by his assistants and relied on the previous work of Étienne-Jules Marey in France (whom Edison met in Paris in 1889). Real motion pictures evolved from putting together a number of specific technical advances made during the late 1880s and the early 1890s, mostly by French engineers; in December 1895, Louis Lumière showed the first short clips in Paris. In movies (as in the automobile industry), the Americans had a secondary role in the initial commercialization, but their entrepreneurship soon more than made up for it by developing the world's largest movie industry, which required new designs of cameras, films, and lights and of editing and projection equipment.

Finally, a few paragraphs on the development of devices to communicate and convey information by voice. Early research on electric telephony (going back to the 1830s) did not lead to any practical devices. Matters advanced during the mid-1870s thanks to the research done on multiplex telegraphic transmission by Elisha Gray and Alexander Graham Bell. This contest ended with Bell filing his patent application on February 14, 1876, just two hours ahead of Gray's filing of a conceptually nearly identical caveat (Evenson 2000). Gray did not challenge Bell's primacy, and Bell revealed his awkward design to the public in 1876 at Philadelphia's Centennial Exposition. This prompted Edison to act. Edison's subsequent invention of a variable resistance carbon receiver, a diaphragm modulated by electric current, opened the way to the first practical commercial telephones (Josephson 1959). Better diaphragm designs followed, culminating in Anthony White's solid-back transmitter in 1892, whose improved versions then served for eight decades before they were replaced by electronic versions.

As in the case of any device dependent on infrastructure (in this case, local and long-distance lines and telephone exchanges), telephone ownership progressed slowly. In 1878, one year after the Bell Telephone Company was set up, the United States had 10,000 telephones. A decade later the total surpassed 150,000, and by 1900 the number had risen to 1.35 million, or one phone for every 56 Americans (Garcke 1911).

Transcontinental calls became more common only after World War I, as did automatic telephone exchanges. But long-distance calling remained expensive, and in 1900 even local bills amounted to as much as a third of the mean urban monthly wage. The cheaper telegraph remained the most common means of rapid long-distance contact.

Sound recordings began with Edison's phonograph in 1878, but the inventor's hope that it would eventually be bought by every American family was a great miscalculation. Edison kept on tinkering with his design into the second decade of the twentieth century, when it became obvious that the gramophone offered a superior recording alternative. In 1888, after four years of research, Emile Berliner, a German immigrant who had settled in Washington, developed a sound recording system using a lateral stylus on a hard surface (Berliner 1888). The first 1,000 gramophones were sold in 1894 with hardened rubber as the early material for the records. The rubber was soon replaced by shellac, and that material was used for the next 50 years, when it was displaced by vinyl. An even less expensive and incomparably farther-reaching way of recording and transmitting sound began its development during the 1890s. Wireless broadcasting was based on the fundamental discoveries of Heinrich Rudolf Herz, Nikola Tesla, David Hughes, and Edouard Branly, and the first practical steps were taken before World War I, but the manufacturing of affordable radio receivers and the commercial transmission of radio waves had to wait until after 1918.

As this brief survey shows, by the late 1880s, the United States had become the world's leader in manufacturing. While the country did not dominate all fields of new technical advances and did not pioneer all manufacturing sectors—automobiles and steam turbines are probably the two most important examples where the United States did not have an early lead—the overall primacy was indisputable. This position was the result of high labor productivity, thanks to an exceptionally high consumption of energy in manufacturing; superior output figures; and an unprecedented concatenation of technical and organizational advances as new inventions were rapidly translated into commercial products.

Nobody captured this reality better than that most astute observer of the contemporary American scene, Mark Twain. Immodest as it may seem, Mark Twain's description of his Yankee stranger at King Arthur's court cited in this chapter's epigraph is an accurate portrait of the country's technical prowess during the last decade of the nineteenth century: a Yankee could truly "make anything a body wanted," and if there was no quick and easy way to do so he "could invent one—and do it as easy as rolling off a log" (Twain 1889, 20). The first decades of the new century saw the further strengthening of this manufacturing dominance.

## The Decades of Consolidation, 1900–1940

At first glance, the eventful decades from the start of the twentieth century to the start of World War II have little in common. The first decade of the twentieth century resembled the 1880s in its rapid economic growth: GDP was up by 56%, and in per capita terms the gain was 29%, compared to 66% and 33% respectively during the 1880s. In technical terms the decade showed much continuity with the previous 20 years, which had been

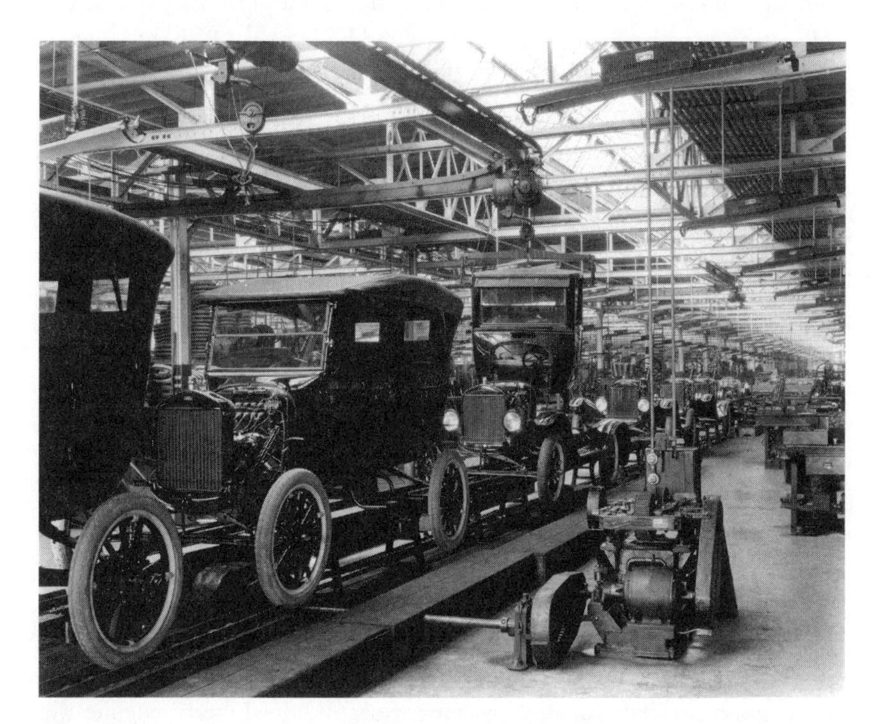

**Figure 2.3**
The assembly line of the Ford Model T, shown here in 1924, was the paragon of modern industrial mass production. Image available at http://motorcitymusclecars.files.wordpress.com/2011/02/modeltassembly_1924.jpg.

dominated by the appearances and rapid adoptions of new inventions. The most notable American inventions in the first decade of the twentieth century included such diverse accomplishments as the first powered flight, accomplished by the Wright brothers in 1904, and the first conic rotary drill, patented by Howard Hughes in 1909. While America's pioneering role in flight and in the development of commercial aviation is widely appreciated, even historians of technical innovation rarely extol the much less glamorous concurrent innovations in oil exploration and production.

And yet, a century later, those fundamental achievements continue to provide effective foundations for the hydrocarbon industry. Rotary drilling rigs (unlike their percussion predecessors, which pulverized rock by the repeated raising and dropping of a heavy metal bit) have a heavy rotating circular table (driven initially by a steam engine, later by diesels) with drill pipes inserted in its middle. They came into widespread use only after the rotary cone drill was invented by Howard Robard Hughes, who began manufacturing it in 1909 in partnership with Walter B. Sharp (Brantly 1971). Improved designs, including the first diamond drill, introduced in 1919, and the first three-cone bit, in 1934, increased the average penetration rate, and the entire process of drilling and well completion was further helped by Erle P. Halliburton's cement jet mixer, introduced in 1919 (Allaud and Martin 1976). Improved versions of these fundamental inventions are still with us.

The second decade saw all Western economies affected by World War I. Although World War I was not such a great divide for the United States as it was for Europe, US economic growth declined substantially, with the real GDP expanding by less than 17% during the decade and by a mere 1% in per capita terms, the slowest growth since the second decade of the nineteenth century. The country entered the world conflict only in 1917 and had to boost its manufacturing capacity to produce record numbers of old and new weapons, the latter category including tanks, trucks, and airplanes. Although this manufacturing mobilization was modest when compared with the effort required to win World War II, it advanced the art of mass production. Perhaps most notably, the Liberty engine, the war's most important aeroengine, was designed in May 1917 in less than a week by Jesse G. Vincent of Packard Motors and E. J. Hall of Hall-Scott Motor Car. Its prototype was ready in less than six weeks, and the engine's serial production had reached more than 20,000 units when the wartime run ended in early 1919 (Schipper 1919).

But the first two decades of the twentieth century differed radically from the last two decades of the nineteenth century in one key aspect: they saw a sharp increase in the energy intensity of the US economy, a trend explained by the diffusion of coal-fired electricity generation and by the first wave of mass car ownership, which required large increases in the supply of gasoline. Between 1900 and 1920 the energy intensity of the US economy rose by about 22% when all fuels are included, and by about 45% when the calculation is done only for coal and hydrocarbons. The peak intensity was reached during the years 1915–1920 in a brief, fluctuating plateau, and after one more upward blip in 1923, the measure commenced what would be a continuous secular decline, falling to more than 25% below its 1920 rate by 1940.

The third decade's often cited sobriquet, the roaring twenties, applied not only to some of the era's boisterous urban lifestyles but also to its economic achievements: inflation-adjusted GDP grew by about 45% between 1920 and 1929, and by nearly 30% in per capita terms. The electrification of manufacturing was approaching its completion, and increasing numbers of urban residents came to enjoy a distinctly higher quality of life than at any other time during the country's history. This situation was abruptly reversed with the onset of the Great Depression, the most pronounced and longest-lasting economic downturn in modern history. One of its key consequences, the rise of a much more interventionist government, can be still felt eight decades later.

Key figures illustrate the precipitous nature and the unprecedented extent of the economic retreat. In 1929 the country's nonfarm unemployment rate was fairly low, at 5.3%; the very next year it had nearly tripled, to 14.2%; in 1931 it surpassed 25%, and it peaked in 1933 at nearly 38% (the total unemployment rate that year, farm plus nonfarm, reached 24.9%). The rate declined gradually to 21.3% by 1937, but the following year it rose again, to nearly 28%, and by 1940 it was still above 21%; only the war brought full employment. In absolute terms this meant that the nonfarm labor force shrank rapidly from about 35.7 million in 1929 to less than 28 million by 1932 and that the 1929 total employment figure was not surpassed until 1939, when the count reached 36.03 million. The workforce decline in manufacturing was much steeper, from 10.7

million to 7 million (35% down) between 1929 and 1932, and again, it took a decade to get permanently back above the 1929 total.

The plunge in manufacturing was worsened by the passage of the infamous Smoot-Hawley Tariff Act of 1930, which brought reciprocal retaliation by America's trading partners and cut foreign trade by more than half (Irwin 2011). During its lowest point, in 1933, the country's economic product was more than 25% below the previous (1929) peak. That drop was entirely erased by 1936, and in 1937 the growth rate reached 5%, but in 1938 there came another 3.5% decline. Although the GDP ended the decade almost 25% above its depressed 1930 level, only another world war put the country on a path of renewed economic expansion.

The first four decades of the twentieth century saw the consolidation of those extraordinary technical advances that had taken place during the last four decades of the nineteenth century. The most important development embodying this process of technical and managerial consolidation was the electrification of industrial production. US manufacturing had also begun to benefit from innovations aimed at raising the volume of its output and improving the quality of its finished product. These developments had profound effects on US manufacturing and the American way of life, and have proved to be durable transformations of universal importance. Electric motors remain the dominant prime movers in every sector of manufacturing, and the mass production of complex but affordable consumer goods, guided by a quest for optimization and subject to strict quality control, remains the universal model in global manufacturing.

The economic setbacks of the 1930s overshadowed a range of gradual advances that, in retrospect, appear to be unmistakable harbingers of a new consumer society. Despite plenty of individual hardship, it was only during the 1930s that large numbers of Americans got the taste of an incipient affluence that would include the common ownership of cars, radios, and electrical appliances. This was possible because US industries became the leading innovators in mass manufacturing, and also pioneered the modern airline industry. In terms of manufacturing advances and technical progress, the decade was a success.

### Electrification of Industries and Households

The productivity of societies is circumscribed by their dominant prime movers, energy converters capable of producing kinetic energy in a variety of forms suitable for human needs (Smil 2010). Animate prime movers—human and animal muscles—remained dominant even after ancient and medieval societies introduced the first mechanical prime movers, wind sails, waterwheels, and windmills. The steam engine, the first inanimate prime mover powered by the combustion of fossil fuels, functioned as a key enabler of nineteenth-century industrialization. Electric motors convert electricity into mechanical energy but they are not strictly speaking prime movers, as that electricity is generated by converting fossil fuels, falling water, or wind (and since the 1950s also by heat from nuclear fission) by such *prima facie* prime movers as steam turbogenerators, water, and wind turbines.

But, in a broader sense, electric motors have been the dominant prime movers of modern manufacturing, an outstanding example of those pervasive general-purpose techniques that are the true engines of growth in modern economies (Bresnahan and Trajtenberg 1995) and whose impact goes far beyond providing a convenient supply of power at lower cost than their predecessors. The large-scale introduction of electric motors in industry also allowed a more rational and more efficient design of entire factories. It multiplied their productive capacities, improved working conditions and safety, and created entirely new products and markets. This epochal transition from steam to electric power in US manufacturing has been well documented and perceptively analyzed by DuBoff (1979), Devine (1983), Schurr (1984), Woolf (1984), Schurr and colleagues (1990), Hunter and Bryant (1991), and Goldfarb (2005).

The first installations of electric motors in industrial plants mimicked the use of steam power (Devine 1983). The prime mover was different but the rest of the arrangement remained the same: motors (instead of steam engines or waterwheels) were connected by pulleys and belts to long, slender iron or steel line shafts that were suspended from ceilings and spanned entire factory floors; their rotation was transmitted to shorter, parallel-mounted countershafts connected by belts to individual machines. The multiple disadvantages of this arrangement are obvious. Efficiency was inherently poor because of large friction losses and because the entire assembly had to rotate even if only a single machine was operating; conversely, the entire process had to stop if only a single belt slipped or ripped or a single countershaft broke. An accident anywhere along the distribution line shut down an entire work floor.

Maintenance needs were high owing to the periodic tightening of slack belts and their continuous oiling, which also became a source of dirt and dangerous slicks on walls and floors. The entire system was dangerous. Because the belts for the transmission between floors passed through ceiling holes, they facilitated fire dispersal, and the complex arrangements of rotating shafts, pulleys, countershafts, and belts created a noisy and perilous environment prone to accidents. And although multiple pulleys allowed speed and power changes, such adjustments could not be controlled accurately. The shift to a less cumbersome, more efficient, and more flexible electric group drive began in 1892 in GE's plant in Schenectady, and more companies in upstate New York chose this arrangement after 1895 once they could use inexpensive hydroelectricity from the Niagara Falls power plant. In this arrangement motors powered relatively short shafts that served a small group of machines in different parts of a factory.

The falling prices of centrally generated electricity convinced managers that a unit drive, with a suitably sized motor powering individual machines, was the best choice, and this arrangement, which began to spread after 1900, has persisted ever since. Its many advantages include the complete elimination of any friction losses in power transmission; the precise control of power delivery, allowing more accurate machine operation; the possibility of using machines in ways that either optimize the processing sequence or maximize the use of available space; and the liberation of ceilings from dangerous congestions of moving iron, steel, and leather, which made it possible to install translucent or well-lit ceilings, adequate ventilation, and, in enterprises working with heavy loads, overhead traveling cranes. The electric motors themselves had no competition in terms of efficiency, ruggedness, and reliability. They could be put to a variety of uses, from delicate micromachining tasks to lifting large weights, and were low in cost: mass-produced motors are inexpensive, particularly given their longevity.

Moreover, motors could also be used to power mobile—portable or wheeled—tools. Only a few other inventions have had such a transforming impact on industrial production, with all of the noted improvements translating into substantial productivity gains. A truly large-scale diffusion of industrial electric motors could take place only once the electricity supply became generally assured and prices declined to affordable levels. In 1900 the average efficiency of converting coal to electricity was less than 4%. By 1925 it was approaching 15%, and a decade later it surpassed 20% (Schurr and Netschert 1960). The efficiency and cost of electricity generation improved with larger units: the maximum rating of steam turbogenerators rose steadily from 1 MW in 1900 to 200 MW in the early 1930s before its growth stopped for two decades. These capacity increases enabled the central plants to serve larger service areas and called for longer transmission lines and higher voltages; the maximum US voltages rose to 230 kV by 1923 and, except for the 287.5 kV link between Hoover Dam and Los Angeles, which was completed in 1936, they stayed at that level until 1954.

Electricity output rose nearly tenfold between 1900 and 1920, then more than doubled during the 1920s. This was reflected in business enterprises' rising reliance on externally produced electricity. In 1899 only 4% of industrial prime movers were powered by purchased electricity; the share surpassed 20% a decade later and 50% after the end of World War I, reaching 75% by 1929 (Jerome 1934). And whereas in 1899, slightly more than one-fifth of all electric motors made in the United States went to industries, by 1910 that share had risen to nearly half, and by the late 1920s most new motors were destined for industrial use. As a result, during the 30 years before the beginning of the Great Depression, the total capacity of mechanical drive power installed in US manufacturing more than quadrupled, from about 7.3 GW to 32.2 GW, but the capacity of electric motors grew more than 70-fold, from just 350 MW to 25.2 GW (DuBoff 1979).

In 1899 less than 5% of the total capacity of industrial prime movers was in electric motors. By 1917 the total capacity of electric motors had surpassed that of industrial steam engines, and by 1929 the substitution was virtually complete as the share of electric power rose to more than 82%, peaking a decade later at nearly 90%. Penetration rates varied by industry: the printing industry—newspapers and magazines—was the earliest adopter, preceding other industries by about two decades; by 1909 nearly 80% of its power capacity was in electric motors. Other early conversions took place in the textile industry, metal fabrication, and instrument manufacturing, while late adopters included the food and beverage industries and papermaking (Goldfarb 2005).

The key to appreciating electrification's impact is to realize its substantial multiplier effects. Replacing a large coal-fired steam engine powering complex shaft and belt assemblies with a number of electric motors powering individual machines did a great deal more than bring large direct savings on an enterprise's energy bill or improve its labor and capital productivity. Modern manufacturing simply became unthinkable without electric motors, and soon afterward the same could be said about everyday household chores as electricity took over cooking, heating, cooling, cleaning, and washing and as it began to power radios and, just before World War II, the first TV sets.

The diffusion of residential electricity connections took off only during the second decade of the century. In 1908 only 8% of all US households had access to electricity, with the share rising to nearly 35% by 1920, 68% by 1930, and 79% by 1940. This diffusion of residential service was accompanied by substantial declines in average prices, from about 16 cents per kilowatt-hour (kWh) in 1902 to about 7.5 cents per kWh by 1920, 6 cents per kWh in 1930, and less than 4 cents per kWh in 1940 (USBC 1975). Incandescent lighting retained the largest share of household electricity use until the 1930s. Its efficiency was greatly improved with the introduction of tungsten filaments by GE in 1910, resulting in an efficiency of up to 1.5%, and by coiling the filament and filling the bulbs with a mixture of nitrogen argon, introduced by Irving Langmuir in 1913, which produced an efficiency of 1.8%. The first fluorescent lights appeared during the 1930s; their efficiency surpassed 5%.

Various electricity-powered household converters, such as irons, fans, cookers, hot plates, and water heaters, became available during the 1890s, but, much like cars, they were expensive and owned by few; purchases of household gadgets and appliances powered by electricity became common only after 1920.

A converter that eventually helped change the distribution of America's population first appeared at the very beginning of the twentieth century. Willis Haviland Carrier sold his first air conditioning unit in 1902, but the use of these devices remained limited to industrial settings and, starting in the 1920s, theaters and department stores. The mass adoption of window units came only during the 1950s, and beginning in the 1960s the availability of central AC units began to make the Sun Belt more appealing. Major appliances were introduced only after 1900. The first bulky and heavy vacuum cleaners were sold in 1905, to be followed quickly by William Hoover's upright, in 1907, and the Electrolux canister, in 1921; the first washing machines appeared in 1907, and the first practical refrigerators in 1913.

But without exception, large-scale diffusion came only during the 1920s: by 1929 annual sales amounted to 890,000 refrigerators, 760,000 washing machines, and 225,000 electric ranges (USBC 1975). Early refrigerators were heavy and expensive, but their greatest drawback was the absence of an inexpensive and safe—nontoxic, nonflammable—refrigerant: none of the gases commonly used (ammonia, isobutane, methyl chloride, sulfur dioxide) fit that bill (Nagengast 2000). The era of a truly mass ownership of household iceboxes began only after Thomas Midgley introduced the use of inert and nonflammable chlorofluorocarbons (CFCs) as inexpensive refrigerants. It took half a century more to realize that their large-scale use had the dangerous effect of gradually destroying the stratospheric ozone (Smil 2006). By 1935 GM's Frigidaire and other brands sold eight million units with CFCs, and by 1940 annual sales approached two million units as every second US household owned a refrigerator, a level of ownership that Europeans reached only during the 1960s.

All fundamental technical challenges of radio broadcasting were solved before World War I (Smil 2006), and radio sales rose from about 100,000 sets in 1923 to almost five million units by 1929 and nearly 10 million by 1939. A new manufacturing sector created thanks to broad access to affordable electricity was that of making diagnostic, medical, and dental devices. Half a century after the launch of the Edisonian electric system, America's electricity-centered manufacturing—making the machines and components for the generation, transmission, and distribution of electricity and converters for industrial, institutional, and household use—evolved to become one of the country's largest industries. Carmaking was another industry that originated during the 1880s and whose large-scale expansion took place only after 1900, but by 1930 it had added more value than any other sector, becoming the quintessentially American kind of manufacturing, whose achievements and problems continued to have an enormous global influence for decades to come.

**Modern Industrial Production: Mass and Efficiency**

The electrification of factories raised their productivity, and rising disposable incomes presented manufacturing enterprises with opportunities for selling more expensive products, but US manufacturers had to solve three major, conjoined challenges to take advantage of these new realities. These challenges were to make their products at affordable prices and on unprecedented scales while maintaining acceptable quality. With relatively simple goods made of just one basic material, this called "only" for inventing an ingenious way of fully mechanized production. The evolution of a fully automatic glass bottle-making machine shows why the quotation marks are justified.

Until the closing decades of the nineteenth century all mass-produced glassware was made by blowing molten glass into molds and finishing the product with hand tools. Semiautomatic machines to make bottles or jars began to appear during the 1860s, but it took Michael Joseph Owens more than 40 years before he succeeded in making the first fully automatic design in 1903 (ASME 1983). His first commercial model, ready in 1905, could make more than 17,000 bottles a day, compared to the fewer than 3,000 turned out by a workshop employing six men and boys; seven years later a much improved version of Owens's initial design raised the daily total to 72,000 bottles. The resulting advantages of low cost and appealing and hygienic packaging were obvious, but an even more important consequence of that kind of fully mechanized manufacturing was the elimination of the centuries-old practice of employing young boys in glassworks to perform tasks ranging from stoking furnaces to moving blown and cooled products.

But the mass manufacturing of complex products called for different solutions, and optimizing individual tasks was the answer that emerged at the beginning of the twentieth century. These developments were not without their precedents. The stepwise division of labor had been used from the 1830s in butchering hogs in Cincinnati, and half a century later, in Chicago's infamous Union stockyards, the process was perfected to handle 14 million animals a year (Wade 1987). But dismembering a dead animal is a labor sequence not in the same class as assembling a car, and dissecting a manufacturing process down to individual hand movements is different from advocating rational approaches to production. Those more effective steps took place thanks to the failed experiences of an early car manufacturer and the unlikely consequences of developing a superior cutting steel.

The automobile was a thoroughly European invention. Its origins during the 1880s were indisputably German—Karl Benz, Wilhelm Maybach, and Gottlieb Daimler were the leading inventors—with French engineers adding a great deal of subsequent refinements and improvements (Flink 1988; Smil 2006). Throughout the 1890s American carmaking was a surprisingly restricted, unfocused affair that produced expensive machines only rich customers could afford, and at the beginning of the twentieth century France was the country with the largest annual output of automobiles. Within a decade all that became nothing but a short footnote to carmaking history, thanks to the innovations introduced by Henry Ford.

Ford began his car-building career in 1896, when he was the chief engineer of the Edison Illuminating Company in Detroit, by building a small quadricycle (Ford 1922). He left his first job in the auto industry in 1902 after four years as the chief engineer and manager of Detroit Automobile Company when it was rebranded as Cadillac, and a year later set up the Ford Motor Company (FMC) with monies provided by the city's large coal dealer, Alexander Malcolmson, and began to make his alphabetically designated models (Brinkley 2003). In 1907 Ford's Model K was selling for $2,800 (FMC 1908), an equivalent of about $67,000 in 2010 dollars.

Ford's Model N, introduced in 1906, was the company's first relatively inexpensive automobile. Its production reached about 7,000 units by 1908. The Model T, launched on October 1, 1908, became the huge success it did because, from the start, the company got many things right. As E. B. White (1936) put it, "it was the miracle God had wrought. And it was patently the sort of thing that could happen only once." Ford's goal was to build a car "for the great multitude" that would use the best materials yet the simplest designs so it could be sold at a price low enough that anybody on a salary could own one. This down-market move required a very basic vehicle—the early models did not even have a battery, and their headlamps had to be lit by carbide gas—but quality was not compromised as the chassis was built of vanadium steel and, despite its precarious appearance, the machine had a phenomenal durability; millions of Model Ts remained on the road during the Great Depression years of the 1930s.

But the machine became no less famous for the way it was made: perhaps no other manufactured item is so iconically associated with a new way of production. The system deployed to make Model Ts did away with the artisanal manufacturing that had dominated all kinds of industrial production throughout the nineteenth century and was the norm in early automobile workshops and small plants. Neither of its two basic arrangements, either small groups of workers completing entire vehicles at fixed stations using parts brought or carted from stores or specialized workers walking among the stations to perform their singular task, was efficient, and both were logistical nightmares, resulting in a very low labor productivity. Even in Ford's best operation a worker could not complete more than 13 cars a year.

Ford did not pioneer either the use of standardized components, a practice common in some manufacturing sectors since the 1880s, or the moving assembly line, which was first used for chassis production in 1911 not at the FMC but at the Everitt-Metzger-Flanders Company by two of Ford's former managers, W. E. Flanders and Max Wollering (Lewchuk 1989). Their cable tow-line boosted the output to 100 chassis a day. Ford's rope-drawn line followed in 1913, and between October and December it cut the chassis assembly time from more than 12 hours to less than three, and a year later to just 93 minutes, when the plant was producing a thousand Model Ts a day (Flink 1988). The conversion of the final assembly to a moving line took more than 14 months, and other operations throughout the plant, including metal casting, the mechanical conveyance of cast pieces to factory floor, and the machining and testing of critical car parts, were speeded up by the simultaneous multiplication of tasks (Bond 1914).

The entire operation consisted of using identical, ready-to-install components, with no individual adjustment requiring specialized labor. The performance of repetitive simple tasks required some dexterity but no particularly demanding skill—an arrangement permitting payment of a uniform wage—to mass-produce identical (or nearly so) vehicles, which maximized the economies of scale. All of this was done at a speed fast enough to shatter all previous productivity records but that still allowed maintaining a fairly good quality. The essence of the operation was caught by a contemporary observer:

> the work has been analyzed to the minutest detail with a view to economizing time. Men are given tasks that are very simple in themselves, and, by dint of repetition day in and day out, acquire a knack that may cut the time of the operation in two. A man may become a specialist in so insignificant an operation, for instance, as putting in a certain bolt in the assembling of the machine. (Bond 1914, 8)

This approach required a clear chain of command and absolute control of the workforce in the plant, but right from the start, Ford also managed information from dealers that allowed him to match production to sales and to lower inventory costs. Economies of scale were converted into Ford's rising dominance of America's car market and falling prices for the product. The annual output rose from nearly 18,000 cars during the first year of Model T production, 1908–1909, to nearly 203,000 cars in 1913, surpassing by more than five times the production of Willys-Overland, in second place, and by a stunning 70 times the output of the largest British carmaker (Lewchuk 1987).

Peak production was reached in 1923, with just over two million vehicles. In 1908–1909 the Model T accounted for about 15% of the US car output, but by 1914 its share had nearly tripled, to 44%, and in 1917 it peaked at 48%, with all vehicles produced between 1915 and 1925 boasting the same color, a standard black varnish. The labor required to make a car declined from more than 400 hours in 1909 to less than 150 hours by 1915 and to just 50 hours by 1926 (Wilson and McKinlay 2010). The first models sold for $850–$875, but by 1914 the price was down to $440, and the post–World War I prices were as low as $265. When the production of Model Ts ended in 1927, the company's official tally stood at 14,689,520 vehicles (Houston 1927).

Much has been written about the human cost of assembly-line manufacturing, particularly during its early unregulated phase, when the work was done in conditions unacceptable according to today's numerous workplace regulations. There is no doubt that it was exhausting, stressful, exploitative, often dangerous, and in some ways even dehumanizing, resulting in high labor turnover. But standardized manufacturing processes made it possible for large numbers of unskilled, often illiterate or semiliterate workers, including many new immigrants, to earn a decent wage, and when in 1914 their pay was more than doubled, to $5 per hour, and their workday was cut from nine to eight hours, there were no better-paid workers anywhere (Lewis 1986). Not surprisingly, the *Economist* in its survey of major twentieth-century achievements called this development "the most dramatic event in the history of wages."

A century later some fairly definite judgments are possible (Wilson and McKinlay 2010). Basic bureaucratic control was a key precondition of Ford's success. Thereafter the introduction of the assembly line gave the company more than a decade of unsurpassed profitability. The practice had spread rapidly to other carmakers, and during the 1920s the strategy of building a single, and barely changing, model gave way to annual model alterations. The wholesale systemic changes Ford introduced, such as keeping all labor in-house rather than using outside contractors, promoting better component design, and using new materials, were at least as important for Ford's success as the assembly line, and the entire system was not as rigid and dependent on unskilled repetitive labor as has been commonly assumed. And whatever its merits and problems, Fordism has cast a very long shadow. As Wood (1993, 535) has demonstrated, at the labor process level even the much admired Japanese model of carmaking, often see as the antithesis of deskilled work, "rests on the fundamental bedrock of Fordism—work study, assembly lines, and mass production and marketing."

Ford's innovation went far beyond a moving assembly line. His key aim was an unprecedented vertical integration, and already by 1915 the company was producing all the major components used in its cars. In 1917 Ford began to build what would become a decade later the world's largest integrated manufacturing complex. Dearborn's River Rouge plant covered 800 ha and, at its peak, employed more than 100,000 workers. It shipped a finished automobile every 49 seconds. The plant consumed raw materials—iron ore, limestone, coal, silicon, soybeans—most of them transported by Ford's ships and trains, and produced a complete array of intermediate inputs, including coke, pig iron, rolled steel, plate glass, plastics, and final items for car assembly.

Scientific management in manufacturing began with a quest for better steel tools. Frederick Winslow Taylor, best known in this field, was from a rich Philadelphia Quaker family, but his interests led him to progress from apprentice patternmaker to engineer and finally senior manager at the Bethlehem Steel Corporation, where in 1898 he decided to find out why even the best-tempered cutting tools kept failing. In extensive systematic experiments conducted with J. Maunsel White, a metallurgist, Taylor discovered that the heat treatment of tools doubled or even tripled the previous metal-cutting speed. These high-speed steels were used in high-performance grinding machines designed by Charles Norton and James Heald in 1903 and 1905. Without these machines it would have been impossible to mass-produce the parts needed for Ford's Model T, and in subsequent decades improved versions of high-speed steels and precision grinding machines (most notably those of the Cincinnati Milling Machine Company and the Heald Machine Company during the 1930s) were indispensable to all large-scale runs of car and airplane designs (Rolt 1963). But long before this great accomplishment Taylor began to study what he perceived to be an enormous waste of a key economic resource, the inefficient use of labor. He was particularly interested in what he called the "systematic soldiering" of workers, or deliberate performance far below the labor's potential.

In the fall of 1880, while working at the Midvale Steel Company, Taylor began a series of experiments designed to quantify all key variables involved in steel cutting. These experiments continued for 26 years and consumed more than 360 t of iron and steel, and their estimated cost was at least $150,000. Their complex results were summarized in 12 formulas and then reduced, after 15 years of work, to a simple set of slide-rule calculations so that the optimum conditions for executing a particular cutting job could be set by a good mechanic in less than 30 seconds. After three decades of effort Taylor summarized his efficiency management findings in *The Principles of Scientific Management* (Taylor 1911).

The book opens by contrasting concerns over the exploitation of natural resources, at that time a fashionable topic, thanks to Theodore Roosevelt's interest in conservation, with society's ignorance of wasted labor:

> We can see and feel the waste of material things. Awkward, inefficient, or ill-directed movements of men, however, leave nothing visible or tangible behind them. . . . And for this reason, even though our daily loss from this source is greater than from our waste of material things, the one has stirred us deeply, while the other has moved us but little.

This, he argued, had to change, as optimized labor productivity would lower prices and benefit everybody. Except, his detractors would say, the workers themselves, whose higher earnings came from excessively stressful work as they tried to complete their tasks in preassigned times (Kanigel 1997).

As is often the case with the critics, too many did not read Taylor carefully (or at all). He stressed that his method should not set excessive quotas: if the "man is overtired by his work, then the task has been wrongly set and this is as far as possible from the object of scientific management." He maintained that the combined knowledge of managers falls "far short of the combined knowledge and dexterity of workmen under them," and hence he argued against any antagonistic attitudes of management and workers in favor of "the intimate cooperation of the management with the workmen." He saw scientific management of labor as the combination of several key elements:

> Science, not rule of thumb. Harmony, not discord. Cooperation, not individualism. Maximum output, in place of restricted output. The development of each man to his greatest efficiency and prosperity.

There is no accident that these maxims seem much like those followed by Japan's seemingly invincible car, camera, and electronics companies of the 1970s and 1980s when their managers strove to eliminate all unproductive labor activities as well as excessive workloads, to do away with an uneven pace of work, to make workers partner in production by encouraging them to make suggestions that would improve productivity, and to avoid labor-management confrontations to the greatest extent possible (Smil 2006). Taylor's precepts were far from welcome when he first tried to put them into practice: after three years of promoting them at Bethlehem Steel, he was fired in 1901. But once his great opus came out a decade later his ideas spread widely, first in the United States and, especially after World War II, abroad. Today, a century after their systematic formulation, Taylor's principles of scientific management guide global manufacturing.

**Manufacturing during the Great Depression**

Manufacturing was hit hard by the greatest economic downturn of the twentieth century, and even by 1940 many sectors, including the tire, tractor, and carpet industries, had not returned to the record sales of the late 1920s (USBC 1975). On the other hand, the electrification of American industries and households had suffered no setbacks. In 1940 total electricity generation, as well electricity use in manufacturing, was up by more than 50% compared to 1929, and while the annual sales of large industrial motors were lower in 1939 than in 1929 (not surprisingly, as the electrification of manufacturing was basically completed by the early 1930s), during the same time the production of small electric motors, those with capacities of less than 750 W, had more than doubled, the sales of electrical ranges had grown by 50%, the sales of radios had nearly doubled, and sales of refrigerators had risen more than threefold (USBC 1975).

These advances were just one element, if a key one, that made possible the decade's most remarkable achievement: the record growth in total factor productivity. In no other decade of the twentieth (or late nineteenth) century did the annual growth in TFP in the US private nonfarm economy even come close. Between 1929 and 1941 the rate was 2.31%, compared to 2.02% during the 1920s and 1.9% during 1948–1973. Growth in output per hour was higher during the 25 years of post–World War II expansion (2.88% vs. 2.35%), even as growth in output per unit of capital input was barely positive during that period (0.18%), while during the 1930s it averaged nearly 2.5%, far ahead of the second-best record of 1.32% for the years 1941–1948 (Field 2006).

Analogical comparisons restricted to manufacturing show that substantially higher growth rates were recorded only during the 1920s, a finding best explained by the gains from industrial electrification and the reconfiguring of factories that took place during that decade. Although the growth in TFP in manufacturing was nearly halved during the 1930s compared to the 1920s it was still higher (as was the output per hour and output per unit of capital inputs) than the rates reached during the long post–World War II economic expansion that ended in 1973. In sectoral terms the most impressive growth rates of TFP in manufacturing during the 1930s were in machinery production, electrical equipment, and paper products. As a result, a large share of the immediate post–WW II productivity was already in place before the attack on Pearl Harbor (Field 2003).

As a result, US manufacturing retained, and in some sectors expanded, its global productivity primacy, and the United States of the 1930s was far ahead of Germany, the leading economic power in Europe, as well as ahead of Japan, Asia's technically most advanced economy. Woltjer (2010) shows that during the years 1935–1936 the average output of an American manufacturing worker was twice as high as in Germany; that the United States had a clear edge even in industries whose modern development was led by German scientists and engineers (in chemicals, dyestuffs, and drugs, German productivity was 14% below the US level; in fertilizers, disinfectants, and glues it was 22% lower); and that the largest differences in output per worker were nearly threefold (in the paint and varnish industry, as well as in the food, drink, and tobacco industries), with the difference reaching nearly sevenfold in crude oil refining, an obvious American strong point. Yuan, Fukao, and Wu (2010) have shown that in 1935, Japan's labor productivity in manufacturing was only 24% of the US level (and China's was a mere 7%).

Many factors combined to bring about that extraordinary American performance. The 1930s were the first decade that industrial production in general, and manufacturing in particular, entered almost fully electrified and hence able to benefit from more efficient reconfigurations of factory floor layouts, higher operating flexibilities, and an improved working environment. The spreading use of new materials—stainless steels, wood treatments, quick-drying lacquers, plastics—made many products more durable or faster to make, while a more common reliance on instrumentation brought both capital and labor savings. Important advances were also made in the energy sector, above all in crude oil refining and thermal electricity generation. In 1936 Sun Oil was the first refiner to use Eugène Houdry's catalytic cracking process to derive a higher share of high-octane gasoline.

Houdry's process was made even more efficient when Warren K. Lewis and Edwin R. Gililand invented the fluid bed catalytic cracking process in 1939, an innovation that was adopted so fast that by 1942 it was producing 90% of the United States' aviation fuel. The efficiency of thermal electricity generation rose with the rising use of oil and natural gas and the installation of more efficient and larger boilers and turbogenerators, resulting in falling rates charged to large industrial users: between 1929 and 1940, fuel used per kWh was reduced by 20% and prices fell by 25% (USBC 1975). No less important, the capacity for scientific and engineering R&D was strengthened greatly during the 1930s. Between 1927 and 1933 the total number of scientists and engineers working in US manufacturing rose by 74%, but between 1933 and 1940 it nearly tripled, to almost 28,000; that rate, averaging 13.3% per year, was unmatched even during wartime, when the mean annual expansion of R&D employees in manufacturing slowed to 8.4% per year (Field 2008).

As a result, the 1930s saw significant technical progress in so many sectors of manufacturing that the remainder of this section could simply be allotted to a list of such advances. Instead, I will focus on those advances that laid the foundations for the large post–World War II expansion in certain manufacturing sectors. In the field of materials, the most consequential class of innovations was the new plastics. In the mechanical realm important advances included the maturation of the car industry, the introduction of the first long-range passenger airplanes, and the adoption of diesel engines for trucks and locomotives. The most notable advances in manufacturing for the information and entertainment sectors took the form of movies with sound and color, color photographic film, and apparatus for the first TV broadcasts.

The history of plastics began during the nineteenth century. Starting in 1910, Leo H. Baekeland's Bakelite became the first commercially successful product in electric insulators and telephones. The 1930s were the decade of perhaps the most important plastic breakthroughs, and American research chemists and engineers, together with their counterparts in Germany (polysterene by IG Farben in 1930) and England (polyethylene by ICI in 1933), were among the leading creators of these new materials (Smil 2006). Most of these advances in plastics came from DuPont's basic research on polymerization, launched in 1927, and from the rapid commercialization of an entire cluster of new discoveries.

By far the most important new materials were neoprene, first synthesized by Wallace H. Carothers and his team in 1930, and polymer 66, synthesized by the same team in 1936, which became one of the world's best-known synthetic materials when the company chose to call it nylon (Hermes 1996). Nylon toothbrushes, the first retail items to incorporate the product, were introduced in 1938; stockings followed the next year. DuPont's last great contribution of the 1930s was a slippery plastic resistant to high and low temperature and to acids, polytetrafluoroethylene, better known as Teflon. Two other notable American contributions of the 1920s and 1930s included vinyl, formulated by Waldo L. Semon at BF Goodrich in 1926, and polyvinylidene chloride, or Saran Wrap, developed by Ralph Wiley at Dow Chemical Corporation in 1933.

The maturation of the car industry was evident in a nearly complete shift to fully enclosed vehicles with more streamlined metal bodies and the introduction of features that became widely adopted only after World War II: the first front-wheel drive (on a Cord in 1930), the first power brakes, and the first air conditioning (in a Packard in 1938). Further optimization of assembly lines raised labor productivity, which was up by 19% during the 1930s, and the latest versions of Ford's assembly plants opened for production in 1931 in Dagenham, Essex, England, and a year later in Nizhny Novgorod, the Soviet Union, while the River Rouge plant continued to receive many young foreign engineers who wanted to study the famous operation. Among them were an Italian who came for a short visit in 1939, and a Japanese who came for a longer stay in 1937. After World War II these two men rose to the leadership of two leading car companies, Giovanni Agnelli as the CEO of Fiat and Kiichiro Toyoda as the president of Toyota Motor Company.

American companies also emerged as the undisputed global leaders in aircraft manufacturing. Although commercial aviation began as early as 1919, it was only after the adoption of the fully enclosed aluminum fuselage that the industry could contemplate profitable service carrying more than a handful of passengers over longer distances. Reciprocating engines caused considerable vibration and noise, flight in the mid-troposphere subjected the planes to much turbulence, the absence of radar made flying risky, and air travel was still expensive and relatively slow, but for the first time, a modicum of comfort was achieved on regularly scheduled flights to distant destinations.

In June 1936 American Airlines began scheduled flights using the McDonnell Douglas model DC-3, named the Dakota, which eventually became the most successful propeller-driven aircraft in history, appreciated for its sturdiness and reliability (Davies, Thompson, and Veronica 1995). The plane was originally configured as a sleeper with 14 berths for transcontinental service but was soon converted to 21 seats. Just over 16,000 DC-3s were eventually built in the United States and abroad, and in 2010, when the plane celebrated the 75th anniversary of its first flight, there were some Dakotas flying in cargo service. In 1939 the Boeing 314, better known as the trans-Pacific Clipper, began scheduled service to Asia with Pan American Airways. The massive hydroplane included a stateroom, a dining room, and seats convertible into bunks (Bauer 2000).

On the rails, GM joined the unfolding diesel revolution in a fairly spectacular manner. By 1933 the company had a powerful—600 hp, 447 kW—experimental two-stroke engine ready, and in May 1934 it powered the *Pioneer Zephyr*, the world's first stainless streamlined train, on its record-breaking run from Denver to Chicago, averaging 124 km/h and cutting the previous travel time almost in half (Ellis 1977; GM 2011). Six year later there were 90 similarly streamlined diesel-powered trains in service. But GM was slower in developing diesel-powered trucks; it set up its diesel division only in 1938, five years after Kenworth Motor Truck Company began its US production.

Innovations in communication and information were marked by the first full-length Technicolor movie, which was made in Hollywood in 1935. In the same year Kodak began selling the first color transparency film. Radio manufacturing was already a mature industry, but a welcome innovation came in 1933, when Edwin Armstrong discovered the way to eliminate AM's annoying static interference by developing wide-band frequency modulation (FM); the first FM broadcasts began in New Jersey in 1937. The development of American TV broadcasting was complicated by a lengthy patent dispute between Philo T. Farnsworth and Vladimir K. Zworykin. Both of them began developing TV systems in the early 1920s, and although the US Patent Office eventually, in 1935, decided in Farnsworth's favor, RCA's engineers based the first commercial system on Zworykin's design and began broadcasting in 1939. (A brief BBC service had begun in 1932, with higher-resolution programs available in 1936.) World War II interrupted the widespread adoption of many technologies, and opportunities for a new mass-manufacturing sector opened up only after 1945.

**Figure 3.1**
Vice President Richard Nixon makes a point to the Soviet premier Nikita Khrushchev during the famous "kitchen debate" at the American National Exhibition, Sokolniki Park, Moscow, July 24, 1959. The debate can be viewed at http://www.youtube.com/watch?v=3G5I9h6CFaM&noredirect=1.

# 3

# Dominance, 1941–1973

*Without an unprecedented manufacturing surge the United States could not win the first global war, and a steadily expanding manufacturing was also a key to the country's domination of the post–World War II world.*

After twenty years, many Americans want a new house or a new kitchen. Their kitchen is obsolete by that time. . . . The American system is designed to take advantage of new inventions and new techniques.

—Richard Nixon, "Kitchen debate" with Russian premier Nikita S. Khrushchev, Moscow, July 1959

In 1940 the United States was the world's leading industrial power and the largest producer of goods in virtually every manufacturing sector. US manufacturing was also the world's most productive by any measure, in most sectors being twice as good as its nearest competitors, and the most diversified, partly the result of unsurpassed access to affordable energy in general and to inexpensive electricity in particular. The Great Depression cut the US manufacturing output and reduced the country's labor force by millions. By 1940, when the US economy had almost completely recovered, a new crisis loomed: Japanese and German aggression was to change two regional conflicts into a global war.

Japan's road to war began in 1931 with the invasion of Manchuria, followed in 1937 by an attack on China proper. Germany embarked on its aggressive path with Hitler's rise to power in 1933 and the rearmament policy of 1935. In 1936 came the reoccupation of the Rhineland, and in 1938 the annexation of Austria and the Sudetenland. The attack on Poland and war with Britain and France began in September 1939. The United States stayed neutral through 1940 and did not change this position even after Hitler's armies attacked the USSR in June 1941 and approached Moscow in a matter of months. But the country was not entirely neutral: some initial steps toward expanding the manufacturing of military hardware were taken in 1940 and then stepped up as a result of the Lend-Lease Act, passed on March 11, 1941, which sought to send massive shipments of war supplies to Britain and China and, starting in October 1941, to the USSR as well (Kimball 1969).

Even so, when Japan attacked Pearl Harbor on December 7, 1941, the United States was unprepared to fight a global war: only 5% of all military spending during 1940–1945 took place before the attack (Field 2008). At that point the United States saw it had no choice but to mobilize its enormous latent productive capacities, and its response was unprecedented, rapid, and generally highly effective. Wartime mobilization was helped by the fact that during the preceding decade, the federal government had increased its involvement in economic and social matters, largely in response to the devastation of the Great Depression, and was more ready to exercise a dominant role than it might have been during the late 1920s. The remarkable accomplishments of this brief period have been detailed in many surveys and specific accounts (Nelson 1946; Janeway 1951; Milward 1979; Adams 1994; Jeffries 1996; Harrison 1998; Tassava 2008; Herman 2012).

In this chapter I look at the manufacturing highlights of those years, starting with the rapid expansion of the country's industrial output, which required first an unprecedented construction effort and progressed to the mass production of war material, dominated by ammunition, bombs, vehicles, tanks, airplanes, and ships. I also describe a number of pioneering contributions in engineering, scientific research, and industrial design that eventually led to entirely new industries, whose post-1950 expansion resulted in new webs of global transport and trade. None of these was to prove more important than the new field of commercial computing.

On the other hand, the inevitable disruptions and inefficiencies associated with a rapid mobilization for war and a similarly rapid postwar reconversion to a civilian economy meant that between 1941 and 1948, growth in manufacturing productivity was actually much lower than during the 1930s. Moreover—and contrary to the common belief about war's unique capacity for accelerating technical progress—the production of every major consumer item in the first decade of the postwar mass consumption was based on foundations put in place during the 1930s.

Although the wartime developments may not have been as consequential in direct economic terms as has been commonly assumed, mobilization for war gave rise to new technical, managerial, and social modalities that helped change the country's economic and social structure, and the new expectations and aspirations were eventually reflected in new political realities.

During the quarter century of postwar economic expansion between 1948 and 1973, America's manufacturing progress made it possible to create, for better or for worse, the world's first true mass consumption society, to reach new peaks of industrial production, and to start diffusing the powers of electronic computing. These accomplishments were made easier by abundant and inexpensive supplies of natural resources, the absence of any foreign economic competition that could seriously weaken US primacy, and, as has become clear in retrospect, a relative strategic stability of the bipolar superpower contest during the decades of the Cold War. All of these realities changed, often abruptly and fundamentally, during the last quarter of the twentieth century. As a result, the 25 years between 1948 and 1973 remain a remarkable singularity. The United States will never again be in such an advantageous and enviable economic and strategic position as it was during those years.

## World War II and Its Immediate Aftermath, 1941–1947

Basic macroeconomic statistics convey the unprecedented extent of economic mobilization and manufacturing expansion that was required to win the war against two leading powers on their respective continents and—an often neglected component of the wartime effort—to aid the country's allies. In 1940, total federal spending was $9.47 billion, less than 9.5% of that year's GDP, and defense spending reached $1.66 billion, a mere 1.64% of GDP and 17.5% of federal spending. Over the next three years federal spending rose, respectively, by about 37%, 132%, and 111%, reaching as much as 47% of GDP, while defense spending shot up by 269% in 1941 and 260% in 1942. Over the next three years its rate of increase was rapidly reduced, declining to just 3.5% in 1945, when the absolute direct war outlays peaked at $64.5 billion (in 1940 dollars), or nearly 90% of all federal spending and 37% of the country's GDP (USBC 1975; Milward 1979; Tassava 2008).

**Figure 3.2**
Rosie the Riveter became the symbol of America's wartime labor mobilization in manufacturing. Color image available at http://upload.wikimedia.org/wikipedia/commons/1/12/We_Can_Do_It!.jpg.

With defense spending so low in 1940, it was not surprising that non-war output still accounted for more than 80% of all industrial production in 1941. During the next four years war production dominated, reaching as much as two-thirds of the total in 1943 and 1944. This massive war-time expansion of industrial output was overwhelmingly a result of the rising production of durable manufactures. Steel, aluminum, and rubber were its material foundations: compared to 1939, the steel and rubber output roughly doubled by 1944, and aluminum smelting nearly quin-tupled. During the same period the shipbuilding output expanded more than 17-fold, munitions about 20-fold, and aircraft production 28-fold (Milward 1979).

The war's costs were unprecedented, both in human and in economic terms. Nearly 16.4 million men and women served between 1941 and 1945, the total translating into a participation ratio of 12.2%, higher than the 11.1% during the US Civil War. World War II also surpassed the Civil War in combat deaths, 292,131 compared to 184,594, and wounded combatants, 670,846 versus 412,175 (Leland and Oboroceanu 2010). The total cost of the conflict was put at nearly $300 billion in current dollars, equivalent to about $3.75 trillion in 2010 dollars. In per capita terms this works out to about 15 times the cost of the Civil War, nine times the cost of the Korean War, and eight times the cost of World War I. The overall real costs—adding in the long-term costs of health and social consequences and of environmental degradation—were obviously even higher.

For individuals and families working in wartime manufacturing, the most obvious economic benefit was a much higher disposable income, whose rise was particularly striking when compared to the losses of the preceding decade. Between 1929 and 1933 average disposable income fell by 47%, and the 1929 rate was surpassed (very slightly) only in 1941, but between 1941 and 1945 the mean income rose by 54% (and in 1947 it was up by another 10%). For the society as a whole there was an even greater impact as a result of postwar measures that would not had happened without the participation of millions in the conflict. The most important of these measures was the GI Bill of Rights (the Servicemen's Readjustment Act of 1944), which paid for veterans' education and training (by the time of its expiry in 1957, 7.8 million veterans had participated) and also provided loan guaranties for nearly 2.5 million new homes (US Department of Veterans Affairs 2011).

Although the rapid expansion of wartime manufacturing has been the subject of many studies,, historians have paid much less attention to the reconversion of industries to civilian production (Ballard 1983). The task was formidable. Demobilization released about 9.8 million men, an equivalent of about 17% of civilian employment in 1947. As well, defense spending was cut by nearly 50% in 1946 and by 70% in 1947, when it reached just 5.5% of GDP. The unemployment rate rose only slightly, from 1.9% in 1945 to 3.9% in 1946 and 1947 (and it was only a bit higher in manufacturing), or no higher than it was in 1929 before the Great Depression—a great relief to the millions scarred by the experiences of the 1930s. But the return to a peacetime economy was not effortless. Alexander (1994) showed that extraordinary planning went into the reconversion. This need was envisioned even before the beginning of hostilities. The US Chamber of Commerce and the National Association of Manufacturers published their reports and guidelines already in 1943. In 1944 the Defense Plant Corporation began canvassing its lessees for their interest in buying equipment or real estate, and in the same year new procedures for the quick settlement of canceled contracts were put in place (by the end of 1945, cancellations totaled $64 billion).

Even so, a substantial share of wartime manufacturing facilities was lost to any productive use. About a third of these capacities, dedicated to ammunitions and naval vessels, had no possible civilian uses (surplus Liberty ships and T-2 tankers created a glut of commercial vessels), and much of the remaining factory equipment and stores of raw material and parts were scrapped or sold for recycling. Not surprisingly those sectors that saw the greatest wartime expansion (magnesium, rubber, iron and steel) suffered the greatest pullbacks. One shift that helped keep the unemployment rate down was the large-scale withdrawal of women, as well as very young and older workers, from the workplace. About 2.2 million women left, many involuntarily, and by 1947 about 30% of all women worked, compared to 35% in 1944, but the overall share of female labor declined only marginally, from 29.3% in 1944 to 27.4% in 1947.

Greater female participation in manufacturing was just one of several important legacies of World War II. Equally lasting was a collaboration involving the federal government, private businesses, and organized labor. Their unavoidable wartime cooperation and symbiosis—government put up the monies, private companies delivered the goods and secured labor stability by paying good wages—continued in many ways for decades after the war. As Reich (2011), put it,

> During the three decades from 1947 to 1977, the nation implemented what might be called a basic bargain with American workers. Employers paid them enough to buy what they produced. Mass production and mass consumption proved perfect complements . . . productivity also grew quickly. . . . So did median incomes. . . . As the economy grew, the national debt shrank as a percentage of it. . . . Government paid for all of this with tax revenue from an expanding middle class with rising incomes.

This manufacturing and taxation strategy was undoubtedly a major factor in maintaining decades of high rates of economic growth during the immediate postwar years, but also in sustaining the growth of what Dwight D. Eisenhower later called the military-industrial complex (Eisenhower 1961; Hooks 1991). Another important consequence has been an unprecedented involvement of state-financed basic and applied scientific and engineering research in the development of new techniques in general and weapons in particular. The Manhattan Project, which saw the development of the first nuclear bombs, was by far the grandest wartime demonstration of this new symbiosis. State financing of activities considered critical to defense has continued ever since and has become an integral part of the military-industrial complex.

**Mobilizing for War**

Accounts of World War II manufacturing almost invariably note the impressive increases in total production, the huge influx of new workers into war-related manufacturing, and the social changes brought about by war's dislocations, but, curiously, what had to happen before the first series of tanks or fighter plans left new factories has received much less attention. This mobilization for wartime production required detailed planning, intensified extraction of mineral resources, extensive conversion of civilian manufacturing to wartime needs, and the adaptation of old facilities and large-scale construction efforts to build huge new factories able to turn out war machines at unprecedented scales.

The requisite governmental bureaucracy to fund, manage, or oversee this effort had to be put in place (Catton 1948). This effort was led by the War Production Board, which was formed in January 1942 (its chairman, Donald Nelson, tried to balance military and civilian needs), and, from May 1943, the Office of War Mobilization, which had the final power to resolve myriads of inevitable conflicts among military services and between them and civilian demand. The Defense Plant Corporation directed government funds to build government-owned but privately operated factories, and by 1945 it had disbursed $7 billion for new aircraft and shipyard factories. The construction of the Pentagon, which began in September 1941 and finished in January 1943, was the most obvious physical expression of this new bureaucratic expansion. This bureaucracy had to fund first the construction of new barracks and associated structures for millions of new troops, and new plants and associated housing for their workers (Albrecht 1995).

The first phase of America's war manufacturing was thus to make more building machinery and more construction materials, and to build the world's largest manufacturing spaces. The Dodge engine plant in Chicago (which made Wright engines for B-29 bombers), designed by Albert Kahn's company, became the largest building in the world, with the roofed area larger than 30 city blocks. Some of the giant aircraft-manufacturing plants, including those in Marietta, Georgia (which made B-29 bombers and is now a Lockheed Martin plant), Wichita, Kansas, and Tulsa, Oklahoma, are still making airplanes. On the other end of the size spectrum was the Quonset hut, a lightweight semicylindrical structure of corrugated steel, developed at the Quonset Point Naval Station in 1941; by 1945 more than 150,000 units had been produced and shipped around the United States and to Europe and Asia to serve as temporary housing, offices, isolation wards, and bakeries (Naval Historical Center 2011).

Large shipyards and aircraft factories made a particularly large demand on housing for their workers; the largest one, the Sun Shipping and Dry Dock Company in Chester, Pennsylvania, employed more than 35,000 people. These demands were met by designing both simple but decent family homes and poorly insulated, mass-produced plywood box houses. In terms of layout the housing ranged from unimaginative, regimented rows of look-alike homes to thoughtfully designed neighborhoods; unfortunately, both of these later served as models for sprawling suburbs. The wartime construction efforts also included erecting entire new towns or vastly expanding existing settlements associated with the Manhattan Project, such as Oak Ridge in Tennessee, Los Alamos in New Mexico, and Hanford in Washington.

Accelerated resource extraction is best illustrated by comparing the annual output totals of three fossil fuels and three metallic ores in 1940 with their respective wartime outputs just three or four years later. These multiples were 1.34 for coal, 1.27 for crude oil, 1.4 for natural gas, 1.43 for iron ore, 1.58 for copper ores, and 14.2 for bauxite, while the extraction of magnesium, whose lightness made it an excellent choice for the aircraft industry as well as for ammunition, increased 30-fold between 1940 and 1943 (USBC 1975). And with electricity being the key energizer of all manufacturing activities, it is not surprising that its overall generation rose by 55% in just four years and its consumption in manufacturing increased by nearly 75%, by 1944 accounting for just over half of nationwide electricity use.

The huge wartime influx of labor into factories in large cities generated two powerful wartime trends whose transformative consequences turned out to have lasting effects: migration to new centers of manufacturing, including the cities-bound migration and employment of southern blacks in northern and western US urban areas, and the increased participation of women in the labor force (Anderson 1981). Census figures show that between 1940 and 1950, America's urban population increased by about 22 million people, compared to an increase of just 5.5 million during the 1930s. The westward shift was particularly strong: between 1940 and 1945 California's population gained nearly 36%, Washington's gained more than 35%, and Oregon's increased by nearly 20% (Nash 1985).

The large-scale black migration from the South to the West was an entirely new phenomenon. In 1943, during the peak migration year, 700,000 African Americans left the South, and of these, 120,000 arrived in Los Angeles. This migration not only transformed the population structure of many western cities, particularly in the states of Washington, Oregon, California, Arizona, and Nevada, it also greatly contributed to the rise of the civil rights movement a generation later. The feminization of the labor force was not that rapid in relative terms. Because between 1940 and 1944 as many women as men joined the labor force (about five million of each sex), women's share of the total labor force rose just over 25% in 1940 to just over 29% by 1944, compared to just 20% in 1920 (USBC 1975). But the composition of this new influx signaled a major shift.

In 1910 about 51% of all single women were in the civilian labor force, a share that was actually slightly above the 1940 rate of 48%, and in absolute terms there were nearly as many single women employed in 1920 as in 1940 (6.43 million vs. 6.71 million). As a result, the war-driven influx of single women into the labor force amounted to an absolute gain of only about 800,000 singles (achieving peak employment in 1944 of 7.5 million) and a relative shift from 48% to nearly 59% of all women in that category. In contrast, the participation of married women registered a gain of nearly 3.5 million between 1940 and 1944, from 5.04 million to 8.43 million. While in 1900 fewer than 6 out of every 100 married women worked outside their home, that rate rose to just under 12% by 1920 and to almost 17% by 1940—but it surpassed 25% by 1944, when nearly 36% of all divorced and widowed women were also employed (USBC 1975). This shift had a lasting impact. The labor participation rate of married women dropped briefly after the war, to just over 21% in 1947, but by 1951 it was again above 25%. A decade later it was just over a third, and by 1969 it had surpassed 40%.

Many wartime jobs held by women were in service positions outside the manufacturing sector, as well as in secretarial and other service jobs directly supporting wartime production, but the bulk of them were on factory or shipyard floors, an indispensable contribution that was captured by the portrait of Rosie the Riveter (Gluck 1987). Ironically, the woman whose photograph served as the base for an iconic "We Can Do It!" poster of 1942—Geraldine Doyle, her head wrapped in a polka-dotted bandana, and sporting a muscular-looking right biceps—quit her metal-pressing job after just two weeks, worried that she, a cellist, could injure her hands; she died in December 2010 at age 86 (Chuck 2010). The consequences of the wartime feminization of manufacturing ranged from changes in parenting and greater disposable income to opportunities for extramarital infidelity, and from long-overdue gains in women's equality to a higher frequency of divorce and the travail of broken families. There is no doubt that these experiences had many long-term social and economic impacts during the postwar years.

Wartime production was critically dependent on the large-scale conversion of peacetime manufacturing facilities. In 1939, US military spending was only about $2 billion per year, and even if all the productive capacities of existing defense contractors could be tapped, they were grossly inadequate to meet the escalating demand. Most of the nation's production for war, which during the two years of peak output accounted for as much as 80% of all industrial output, was thus done by nondefense industries. Some manufacturers, fearing postwar losses to their competitors, resisted any conversion, while others, particularly in allied industries, underwent a rapid transformation, such as shifting from making car engines to producing aeroengines.

But a remarkably large share of war production came from makers who had never previously built such products. A good example is Henry J. Kaiser's decision to organize the California Shipbuilding Corporation.

Before the war Kaiser was a leading industrial builder—his contracts during the 1930s included both the Hoover Dam on the Colorado River and the Grand Coulee Dam on the Columbia River—but he had no experience in shipbuilding. The large-scale and rapid wartime construction of mass-produced, welded Liberty ships (one vessel in a Richmond shipyard was completed in less than five days) made him the country's leading shipbuilder (Lane 2001). Kaiser's expansion is a perfect illustration of the pronounced wartime trend toward a rising concentration of manufacturing: in 1940 the country's top 100 companies produced 30% of all goods; by 1943 their share had more than doubled, to 70%.

Between 1941 and 1944 the annual production of military ships rose 25 times, with most of this increase accounted for by landing craft, whose output rose more than 36 times. In terms of complex procurement, organization, and coordinated manufacturing, the two most remarkable gains came in producing destroyers, from 16 in 1941 to 128 in 1943, and aircraft carriers, from a single one in 1941 to 15 in 1943 (Connery 1951; Lane 2001). Similarly impressive production increases were made at opposite ends of the armaments spectrum, by the manufacturers of personal small arms and the makers of high-performance airplanes.

The full-size M1 Garand rifle was chosen as the US Army's weapon in 1936, but before the war the government-owned Springfield Armory made fewer than 50,000 units. In 1945 it shipped 3.5 million rifles, and more than 500,000 were also made by the Winchester Repeating Arms Company. Deliveries of the lighter and easier to use M1 carbine, designed by Winchester, began in mid-1942, and it became America's most produced small arm, with more than 6.5 million units (and a low of price of just $45) shipped during the war. Such large volume required many manufacturers, led by GM and even including IBM and Underwood Typewriter Company, to substantially increase output. The munitions industry matched that pace: during 1944 its volume, measured in dollars per man, was nearly 70% above the British level and 2.6 times the output in the USSR or Germany (Harrison 1988).

Aircraft production was the largest manufacturing sector of the wartime economy; it employed two million workers and accounted for nearly a quarter of all wartime expenditures (Army Air Forces 1945). Photographs of activities in the giant American aircraft factories of World War II make it clear that these were the true prototypes of modern large-scale, high-tech manufacturing (Yenne 2006). During the last quarter of 1940 only 514 planes were delivered to the Army Air Forces. In 1941 the total rose to 8,723, in 1942 it tripled to 26,448, then it nearly doubled to 45,889, and the peak year of 1944 saw 51,547 new planes, nearly 15,000 in the first quarter of that year (Holley 1964). America's total wartime production was 295,959 airplanes (two-thirds combat, one-third support planes), of which the US Army and Navy received more than 230,000, with the rest going mainly to the UK and the USSR. For comparison, Britain's wartime production was 117,479 aircraft, Germany's was 111,787, and Japan's was 68,057.

But the best appreciation of the intensity of America's wartime mobilization may be had by comparing the domestic resources devoted to the war effort. Harrison's (1988) data show the US level peaking at 54% of national income in 1944, higher than the British peak of 47% in 1943 and much lower than the maximum German rate of 60% in the same year; only the Soviet peak was considerably higher, at 66% in 1942. But more has to be considered. For Germany it was, by choice, a total war, and for the USSR, out of necessity, once attacked, it was a fight for the union's very survival. Both these countries drew on other resources, Germany plundering the entire occupied Europe, the USSR receiving US aid. In contrast, the United States was a substantial net exporter of military matériel and food. And, given the size of its economy, its mobilization for war amounted to by far the highest absolute sum among all belligerent nations. Its share of 54% of national income in 1944 came to about $800 billion (in 1990 prices), compared to peak annual outlays of about $250 billion in Germany, $180 billion in the USSR, and $170 billion in the UK (Harrison 1998).

But an overall verdict on wartime manufacturing must look beyond the obvious facts that winning the war required unprecedented levels of government outlays and that the new industrial capacities that employed millions of new workers were built to turn out primarily destructive products that would have no, or only a limited, place in a peacetime economy. That mission was a complete success. But a critical look reveals that World War II actually had a depressing effect on the country's productivity growth and, with a few notable exceptions, was not a remarkable engine of innovation.

America's admirable achievements during the war were primarily mobilizational and organizational, relying on the combination of huge government investment, military oversight, and the deployment of just about every employable worker (in 1944 the unemployment rate was just 1.2%). The mass influx of inexperienced and untrained labor into the workforce led to inevitable inefficiency and waste, as did the race for the fastest possible opening of new factories and attempts to ambitious production quotas. Some wartime products had exceptionally high rates of defects, perhaps the most notorious case being the early series of Liberty ships, which had numerous hull and deck fractures and in some cases even broke in half without warning owing to the combination of deficient welding and low-quality steel (Elphick 2001).

**Old and New Weapons**

There were only three classes of military manufactures in which the total wartime US output did not surpass the production of all other belligerents: tanks and self-propelled guns, artillery, and mortars. In those weapon categories the USSR came out ahead: it made nearly 20% more tanks and twice as many artillery pieces and mortars. But the United States produced nearly 80% more machine guns, twice as many military aircraft, and 14 times as many trucks as did the USSR, and it was also ahead in total munitions. The Soviets built only 25 destroyers and two cruisers, a small fraction of the number of naval ships launched by the United States—349 destroyers, 40 cruisers, and 22 aircraft carriers (Harrison 1998).

These enormous wartime manufacturing achievements are not diminished when they are set in an appropriate historical perspective. The diffusion of mass-production techniques and the electrification of manufacturing during the first three decades of the twentieth century, along with the high rates of productivity gains during the 1920s and record ones during the 1930s, the latter also combined with numerous technical innovations, laid the base for the innovations of wartime and the early postwar years. Consequently, it is reasonable to conclude that the productivity gains and technical advances of the first postwar decade had less to do with wartime developments than with the methods, materials, and machines that had been introduced before the war, and that World War II was not such a mighty accelerator of manufacturing productivity and innovation as has been often claimed.

The two overriding concerns of wartime manufacturing were speed and scale, goals inimical to optimizing cost and efficiency. Moreover, the enormous influx of inexperienced labor—between 1941 and 1943 the makers of transportation equipment hired 2.6 million new workers, the total number hired in the iron and steel industry was more than 800,000, and in all manufacturing sectors it was nearly 4.5 million (Field 2008)—meant that some of the gains in average hourly productivity rate disappeared. Kendrick's (1961) calculations show the compound annual growth of hourly output was 2.35% between 1929 and 1941 but only 1.71% between 1941 and 1948.

There were also frequent shortages of inventories, but perhaps the most intractable problems arose from trying to convert aircraft construction from its traditional workbench production methods to mass-scale assembly lines. Both Ford and GM offered to run such lines, but replicating the success of mass car production was not easy, both because airplanes were much more complicated machines (some containing hundreds of thousands of parts) and because assembly lines in car factories could not accommodate the frequent design changes that are common in military aircraft production. The two most costly examples of these problems involved long-range bombers, the B-24, also known as the Liberator, and the B-29, the Stratofortress.

In May 1940 Henry Ford promised that his company could "swing into the production of a thousand airplanes of standard design a day," and by November 1941 his government-financed Willow Run Bomber Plant in Ypsilanti, Michigan—an enormous facility, featuring a mile-long building and employing 40,000 workers—had begun manufacturing B-24 bombers, but by mid-1943 its maximum output was not quite 14 airplanes a day (Ferguson 2005). And even after the plant output rose, the quality of the finished airplanes was so poor—earning them the facetious nickname, "Will It Run?"—that it became a subject of congressional investigation, and many planes were sent directly to special modification centers before they could be accepted by the US Army Air Forces (Herman 2012). The same was true of many B-29 bombers completed in late 1943 and early 1944 (Willis 2007).

In contrast, cooperation between GM and the Grumman Aircraft Engineering Company of Bethpage avoided any rigid copying of assembly-line practices and achieved high productivity and cost efficiency in making such famous planes as the F4F Wildcat and the F6F Hellcat (Thruelsen 1976). But GM had its own major failure when it attempted to produce a heavy fighter plane, the XP-75, using many already existing components, a move that would obviously have sped up mass production. Many problems uncovered during the prototype testing required substantial redesigns, and by the time a better version was ready, in September 1944, there was no need for yet another type of combat aircraft, and the contract was terminated after only six planes were completed (Holley 1987).

There were notable wartime advances in manufacturing—above all in electronics, and the rapid development of nuclear weapons that would not have taken place in the war's absence—but the lead times that were required for formulating specifications, for the design and approval process, and for prototyping and testing of any weapon before it entered mass production made it unavoidable that the ships, trucks, airplanes, and small arms used during World War II relied almost completely on prewar designs and prewar manufacturing methods. As a result, most of the iconic machines that helped win the war, including the Liberty class ships, GM trucks, and the three most famous wartime planes, were not the products of war; they were products *for* war and had all been conceived before the war started, with many key components in serial production during the 1930s.

When large numbers of cargo ships had to be built rapidly it was decided not to power them by much more efficient diesel engines—whose adoption in shipping had begun before 1910 and whose dominance in newly built ships of all kinds was clear by the late 1930s—but by steam engines. At that time that was a truly archaic mode of naval propulsion, but all Liberty (EC2) ships ran on three-cylinder steam engines, each requiring two oil-fired boilers (Bunker 1972; Elphick 2001). By 1945, US and foreign shipyards had built 2,751 of these relatively small (10,500 dwt), slow (less than 20 km/h), fracture-prone ships (US Maritime Commission 2011). They consisted of 250,000 prefabricated parts, with the main 250 t sections welded rather than riveted for faster production. The ships served as principal cargo and troop carriers. After the war they were sold cheaply to shipping companies, and some continued in service for another two decades.

Similarly, the imperative of speedy manufacturing of reliable designs based on extended manufacturing experience led to the selection of gasoline engines rather than diesels to power America's dominant wartime truck. GM's Diesel Division was set up just a few years before the war, in

1938, and when the company had to produce large numbers of trucks for the US Army it turned to what it knew best. Its CCKW350 truck (Jimmy) was powered by a 92 hp, 4.4 L gasoline engine whose pedigree went back to the 1929 Chevrolet inline 6 and whose production began in 1941. GM eventually made nearly 530,000 CCK trucks powered by the 270 (Meyer 2011).

Producing military vehicles, be they trucks or the war's most famous US vehicle, the Jeep, produced by Willys-Overland and Ford (640,000 vehicles were made by 1945), was technically the easiest part of America's massive production of war machines. By 1940 the United States was by far the world's largest maker of light- and heavy-duty gasoline-fueled automotive engines, passenger cars, and trucks, and at least half a dozen car and truck companies had a great deal of experience with integrated mass production and the ability to retool and convert rather rapidly to new product lines. Between 1941 and 1943 the US car industry completely converted to wartime manufacturing. Factories making automotive engines could be also converted to the production of aeroengines, but these transformations turned out to be more difficult.

The most commonly used transporter was the Douglas C-47 Skytrain and its many modifications, including the C-53 Skytrooper, the C-49, and the R-4D, all being variants (with larger wing tanks, cargo doors, cargo boom hoists, and strengthened floors) of the DC-3, introduced in 1936 and the most successful piston aircraft in history. During the war more than 10,000 military DC-3s were built in Long Beach and Santa Monica, California, and in Oklahoma. The P-51 Mustang, America's iconic World War II single-seat fighter, was commissioned in March 1940 by the Royal Air Force from North American Aviation. Its first test flight took place less than six months after the order was placed, and from December 1943 it was powered by the Rolls-Royce Merlin engine (Ethell 1981; O'Leary 2010). This V-12 engine, generally considered Britain's best piston aeroengine, was first tested in 1933 and went into production in 1936, when it was used to power the first Spitfires (Air Ministry 1940). Between 1941 and 1945 the Army Air Forces took delivery of nearly 15,000 Mustangs.

And the development of America's most formidable long-distance strategic bomber of World War II, the Boeing B-29 Stratofortress, began in 1938. A design conforming to the army's specification was completed in May 1940, and the first orders for the plane were placed in May 1941

(LeMay and Yenne 1988; Vander Meulen 1995; Willis 2007). Unlike with the military versions of DC-2 or the mass production of the P-51, making the B-29 (in Washington, Kansas, Georgia, and Nebraska) turned out to be an exceptional challenge for thousands of subcontractors, who faced frequent design changes and constant modifications of planes already under construction. Boeing built nearly 4,000 B-29s during the war, all going to the 20th Air Force in the Pacific, most of them to attack Japan. A formation of nearly 300 of them firebombed Tokyo on March 9–10, 1945, and two of them carried the first nuclear bombs five months later.

As far as the most advanced airborne prime mover was concerned, the United States benefited from the transfer of know-how and actual prototypes of British jet engines, but by the time these machines were ready for combat service the war was essentially over. The first working model of the British jet engine, Frank Whittle's W.1, powered an experimental Gloster E.28/39 aircraft on May 15, 1941 (Golley and Whittle 1967). In 1941 a dismantled version of the W.1 was sent to GE's engine factory in Lynn, Massachusetts, where its subsequent modifications proceeded so rapidly that the first American turbine-powered airplanes, the XP-59A Airacomet, flew for the first time on October 2, 1942, five months before the British Meteor (Smil 2010).

But neither US nor British jets made any difference to the outcome of World War II. Airacomet's low thrust made it inferior to America's best gasoline-fueled propeller-driven planes, the Republic P-47D (the Thunderbolt, the largest and the heaviest single-engine fighter of the war) and North American Aviation's P-51D Mustang (maximum speed 580 km/h); and unlike Gloster Meteor, the first British jet fighter that began combat missions against Germany in July 1944, the Airacomet never saw any wartime service. But after the war it did not take long before new designs of US jet engines completed their conquest of military fighter and bomber designs, and by the mid-1960s they had also entirely displaced piston aircraft on all long-distance routes.

No survey of wartime production can omit the making of the world's first fission bombs, a scientific, engineering, and manufacturing achievement that had no equal. The Manhattan Engineer District, the official name of the Manhattan Project, set up in the summer of 1942, cost about $2 billion, eventually employed more than 100,000 people, and faced enormous scientific and engineering challenges that had to be resolved, along with unprecedented engineering and organizational tasks (Compton 1956; Groves 1962; Rhodes 1986; Manhattan Project Heritage Preservation Association 2012). Enrico Fermi directed the effort that culminated in the first sustained chain reaction on December 2, 1942, while Robert Oppenheimer became the scientific director of the actual effort to build the bombs in Los Alamos.

Construction of the uranium bomb required the separation of uranium 235, a fissile isotope that makes up only 0.72% of the metal's natural mass. Massive facilities for uranium isotope separation had to be designed and built in Oak Ridge, Tennessee, a task that needed enormous amount of energy, as well as (to avoid using scarce copper) more than 13,000 t of silver borrowed from the US Treasury to make the giant solenoids used for separating uranium isotopes in calutrons, modified cyclotrons designed by Ernest O. Lawrence (Reed 2011). Besides the uranium bomb, the scientists of the Manhattan Project also designed a weapon using plutonium 239 that was produced by the irradiation of uranium 238 in graphite-moderated reactors in Hanford, Washington. By the early summer of 1945 Oak Ridge had produced enough $^{235}U$, roughly 50 kg, to make the 12.5 kt bomb that destroyed Hiroshima at 8:15 a.m. on August 6, 1945, while the Hanford operations yielded 6 kg of $^{239}Pu$ for the 22 kt bomb dropped on Nagasaki three days later.

When the two atomic bombs ended the war in the Pacific, the United States reached the apogee of its global power, thanks to a combination of the enormous achievements of the previous four years and the concurrent economic destruction or weakening of all other major economies. No other country in history was ever as powerful as the United States was on September 2, 1945, the day General Douglas MacArthur presided over the ceremony on the deck of the USS *Missouri,* anchored in Tokyo Bay, at which Japan's foreign minister Mamoru Shigemitsu signed the instrument of surrender (Shigemitsu 1958; MacArthur 1964). Victorious in wars against Germany and Japan, the United States had the world's most modern mechanized armed forces with global-reach capabilities and, after forcing Japan's surrender by bombing Hiroshima and Nagasaki, it was the world's sole nuclear power.

Its economic weight was even more impressive. While Europe, most of the European part of the USSR, and Japan had their industrial capacities either destroyed or severely damaged, the wartime US GDP (all values in constant dollars) peaked in 1944 at nearly 75% above the 1940 level and pulled back only marginally (by just over 1%) in 1945. In 1938 the combined GDP of the other five largest belligerents—the USSR, Germany, the UK, Japan, and France—was nearly 70% higher than the US total, but in 1945 the US total was 20% higher. During the first half of 1945 the US output of goods and services accounted for more than 40% of the worldwide economic product, and even for the entire year, with recovery under way in Europe and in the USSR, the share was, according to Maddison (2007), 35%, compared to just 15% a decade earlier. And with so many European and Japanese factories in ruins, America's manufacturing capacity had an even higher share of the global total, briefly (in May 1945) in excess of 40%.

The US economy also became the largest source of foreign aid, thanks to the Economic Recovery Program, better known as the Marshall Plan. In Europe, 16 countries received $13 billion (all values in this paragraph are in 2005 dollars) between 1947 and 1952, with Germany alone absorbing about $9.3 billion, and the total US assistance to Germany reached $29.3 billion (60% of it as grants) between 1946 and 1952. During the same period Japan got $15.2 billion, more than three-quarters of it as grants, including food shipments that prevented postwar starvation, raw materials, oil, and manufactured inputs. Only a small part of the amount lent was ever repaid (Serafino, Tarnoff, and Nanto 2006).

This unprecedented dominance of the United States was to be short-lived. In relative terms, it began to erode almost immediately with the economic reconstruction in Europe, Russia, and Asia. In 1945 the US GDP was only 1.1% below its 1944 peak, but it fell by 11% in 1946 and by 1% in 1947 before it began to recover. What followed was, to use Rostow's (1960) often cited phrase, "the era of high mass consumption," a quarter century of virtually uninterrupted economic growth, rising disposable incomes, unprecedented material prosperity, and high personal mobility. But before surveying that period I must describe the wartime genesis of electronic computing, an innovation that would play a vital role in the postwar decades of prosperity.

## The Beginnings of the Computer Era

For centuries, the term computer denoted a person performing tedious calculations, in Europe since the late seventeenth century with the help of a slide rule. During the 1880s computers got their first powerful mechanical helper when William Seward Burroughs and his American Arithmometer Company introduced practical adding and printing machines. Two decades later Burroughs Adding Machine Company was selling thousands of units every year, and by the mid-1920s the cumulative sales of its bulky and heavy calculators reached one million (Cortada 1993). Leading US companies involved in complex design, particularly aircraft makers, employed roomfuls of these human calculator–aided computers until the1950s.

The most advanced modern mechanical calculator was a differential analyzer machine (calculus by wheels and discs) built by Harold Locke Hazen and Vannevar Bush between 1928 and 1931 (Bush and Hazen 1931). This mechanical analog computer solved differential equations by integration and was used during World War II to calculate missile trajectories. The first electromechanical calculating machines relied on relays to represent binary digits. Georg Stibitz built the first American prototype at Bell Laboratories in 1936, Konrad Zuse worked on his machine in Germany between 1936 and 1941, and Howard Aiken completed his massive (5 t and 760,000 parts) Harvard Mark I in 1944 (Cohen 1999).

The electronic age began in 1906, when Lee de Forest added a grid electrode to John Fleming's diode (a sensitive detector of Hertzian waves) and when his triode (he called it the Audion) became the first highly sensitive practical amplifier. For the next nearly 50 years, until the great diffusion of television after World War II, "electronics" was synonymous with radio, and both radio and early television relied on vacuum tubes (tetrodes and pentodes, containing four and five electrodes, were added to triodes), bulky components whose electrodes were encased in glass and had a relatively high failure rate.

Modern computers—fully electronic machines using binary-based operations to execute stored programs according to external instructions—emerged during the 1940s owing to a combination of gradual advances that made it possible to build the first prototypes and set a trajectory toward the manufacture of the first commercial machines in the early 1950s. The theoretical foundations of electronic computing were put in place during the 1930s. The first attempts to build electromechanical and electronic computing devices also began during the late 1930s, and the first prototypes emerged during the early 1940s. There were at least three independent beginnings. In Germany, Konrad Zuse worked between 1936 and 1945 in total isolation, and in May 1941 succeeded in building the first Turing-complete electromechanical computer, the Zuse Z3, which was destroyed two years later in the bombing. In 1946 Zuse also designed the first high-level programming language, *Plankalkül*. As his efforts remained unknown until after World War II, they had no influence on the events that eventually led to the first practical computers in the United States and Britain.

The world's first electronic computer remained unknown for an even longer period of time. The existence of the British Colossus, built in 1943 by Tommy Flowers at the Post Office Research Laboratories in London, was kept secret until 1974. Ten machines eventually worked at the Bletchley Research Establishment, deployed not as general-purpose computers but as dedicated code breakers; their most famous accomplishment was the breaking of the German code generated by the supposedly inviolable Enigma (Lorenz SZ42) cipher machines (Sale 2000). In North America, the first electronic computer was dismantled shortly after it was completed. John Atanasoff of Iowa State College conceived a device combining digital arithmetic and vacuum tubes in 1937 and, with the help of his graduate student Clifford Berry, built its first prototype in 1939 and a better version capable of solving simultaneous linear equations in 1942, but did not patent his design before he abandoned the project to do wartime research for the US Navy (Burks and Burks 1988).

The efforts of the three pioneers, Zuse, Atanasoff, and Flowers, thus did not lead directly to commercial computing. But in 1941, John Mauchly of the University of Pennsylvania visited Atanasoff in Iowa and familiarized himself with the latter's work. Then, between June 1943 and November 1945, Mauchly joined with John Presper Eckert to build the electronic numerical integrator and computer, or ENIAC, a machine intended to do ballistics calculations for the US Army. (The contract was with the Army Ordnance Department; with extensions, it cost about $487,000.) The ENIAC was programmed manually by interconnecting wires (later by switches) and was the most massive electronic device ever built, containing nearly 17,500 vacuum tubes and weighing 27 t, with the main console 24 m long and requiring 150 kW of electric power (Weik 1961; Burks and Burks 1981; Rojas and Hashagen 2000).

The ENIAC was unveiled publicly on February 14, 1946, and has been generally considered the first working programmable electronic digital computer—although nearly three decades later a US district court recognized the Atanasoff-Berry design as the first electronic computer and voided the ENIAC patent (US 3,120,606), held by that time by Sperry Rand, the successors of Remington Rand, the company that absorbed Eckert and Mauchly's enterprise in 1950 (Burks 2002). In 1946 the ENIAC was used not only for calculating ballistics trajectories but also by the Los Alamos Laboratory for its computations during the design of the hydrogen bomb. After some improvements, the ENIAC was moved from Philadelphia to the army's Aberdeen proving grounds in Maryland, where it operated between 1947 and 1955.

In 1944 Mauchly and Eckert conceived, to use Cerruzi's (2003, 22) wording, "something like a stored program principle," but the key distinguishing features of modern computers were clearly formulated a year later by John von Neumann (1945) in a consulting report for the US Army Ordnance Department and the Moore School of Electrical Engineering at the University of Pennsylvania. Von Neumann's report is an admirably clear and relentlessly logical document spelling out the main subdivisions of the system, principles governing the arithmetical operations, their requisite circuits, and the need for considerable memory. Since that time computers have changed immensely, but they retain the basic von Neumann architecture as they store both the program and the data in their memory.

By 1946 both the theoretical and the practical foundations for the further development of electronic computers were in place. A standard chronological narrative of computer evolution would add the beginnings of yet another fundamental step toward modern computing, the American invention of the transistor, a miniature solid-state semiconductor device, an equivalent of a vacuum tube that can amplify and switch electronic signals. On December 16, 1947, two Bell Labs researchers, Walter Brattain and John Bardeen, succeeded in amplifying power and voltage after applying electrical contacts to a germanium crystal, thereby, as is commonly claimed, inventing the transistor (Bardeen and Brattain 1950). There are three major problems with this standard story.

First, theirs was a point-contact transistor, not what William Shockley, the research group's leader, was hoping to get, and by 1951 he had come up with his junction field-effect transistor, the type that would eventually transform modern computing (Shockley 1951). Second, it was made of expensive germanium, not of inexpensive silicon, whose use in electronics dates to 1906, when Greenleaf W. Pickard patented the silicon point-contact diode, in popular parlance the cat's whisker used to receive radio signals. During the subsequent decades the notion of amplification with mineral crystal devices was surprisingly common, and some engineers, including Russell Ohl and O. V. Loseev, actually built simple crystal amplifiers (Shockley was aware of Ohl's work).

Third, in the early 1920s Julius Edgar Lilienfeld developed the concept of a field-effect transistor and filed a patent application first in Canada in 1925 and a year later in the United States (Lilienfeld 1930). The application clearly describes a method and a device for controlling and amplifying the flow of current between the two terminals of a conducting solid without any evacuated space and incandescent filaments. As even the Bell System Memorial site concedes, "it's perfectly clear that Bell Labs didn't invent the transistor, they re-invented it," while failing to acknowledge the large amount of pioneering research and design done since the very first decade of the twentieth century (Bell System Memorial 2011).

In any case, a crude point-contact device built by Brattain and Bardeen in 1947 was not the right kind of transistor to transform electronic computing and could not be rapidly converted into a commercial transistor. In 1948 Gordon K. Teal and J. B. Little succeeded in growing germanium crystals, and in 1951 Teal and Ernest Buehler opened the door to an inexpensive commercial silicon-based transistor by making larger silicon crystals and mastering improved methods for crystal pulling and silicon doping. Even after Bell Labs offered to license the field-effect patent in 1951, another three years elapsed before the first commercial semiconducting amplifying device made of grown-junction silicon was marketed by Texas Instruments in 1954. Gordon Teal demonstrated the achievement by submerging a germanium transistor amplifier of a record player in hot oil. The music died as the device failed; then he switched to a silicon-based amplifier and the music played on (Texas Instruments 2011).

In retrospect, it is hard to believe there was no immediate postwar rush to turn the prototypes of electronic computers into commercial machines. After Eckert and Mauchly left the University of Pennsylvania in 1946 they set up the Eckert-Mauchly Computer Corporation, but before they achieved any commercial breakthrough the company was bought in 1950 by Remington Rand, and the first commercial UNIVAC (universal automatic computer) was sold to the US Census Bureau in 1951. But once computer use took off, during the late 1950s and early 1960s, American electronics companies such as Fairchild Semiconductor, Texas Instruments, and IBM were the most accomplished developers of both hardware and software and the leading creators in this new sector of modern manufacturing.

## A Quarter Century of Superiority, 1948–1973

The quarter century of America's global economic dominance was a singularity whose replication is impossible: it resulted from a combination of American strength as the country emerged victorious from World War II and the relative weaknesses of its competitors, both allies and enemies. The recovery of the war-damaged economies of Europe and Asia took the better part of the first postwar decade. The UK surpassed its wartime GDP peak only in 1953 in absolute terms and a year later in per capita

**Figure 3.3**
Intel's first microprocessor, the Intel 4004, was released in 1971. Color image available at http://www.4004.com.

mean. Japan surpassed its prewar record GDP, reached in 1939, also in 1953, but the per capita rate only in 1957. Subsequent economic growth in Western Europe and Japan was helped above all by the extension of Pax Americana, by cheap crude oil, whose abundant supply led to a rapid displacement of the more costly (and more polluting) coal, and by transfers of technical know-how from the United States.

The first benefit was guaranteed by NATO in Europe (NATO had been in existence since 1949, with Germany joining in 1954) and by the US-Japanese security treaty signed in San Francisco in September 1951, which allowed America's allies to reduce their defense expenditures. Low crude oil prices were the result of the combination of continuing US self-sufficiency and a rapidly rising extraction from Middle Eastern oil fields discovered since the late 1930s (Smil 2008). And America's technical and managerial advances spread through the large-scale acquisition of patents and licenses, as well as through the growth of multinational companies.

The postwar economic pullback in the United States bottomed out during the third quarter of 1947; that year's GDP was about 14% below the 1944 peak, but the next year it grew by 4.2% and, with the exception of three small dips, growing only by 0.5% in 1949, 0.6% in 1954, and 0.9% in 1958, it stayed positive for the next 25 years. By 1950 the US GDP was still marginally below its 1944 wartime peak, but after growing by an average of just over 4% per year during the 1950s the US economy was more than 40% larger in 1960. The average growth rate was even higher during the 1960s, nearly 4.5%, when the overall size of the economy expanded by 50%. As a result, in 1970 the United States accounted for no less than 30% of the world's economic activity, a highly disproportional share for a country with (at the time) less than 6% of the world's population.

This strong postwar growth brought appreciable per capita gains despite the concurrently high birth rates: nearly 80 million births took place in the United States during the baby boom generation of 1945–1964 as the total population grew by 37%, but in 1970 the average per capita GDP was slightly more than 50% above the 1950 rate (USBC 1975). Throughout most of this period manufacturing remained the most important contributor to the US economic expansion: it produced 26% of GDP in 1948, 27% in 1950, and 28% in 1955. By 1960 its share was 25.4%, and it changed little to 1965 (25.7%), but by 1970 it had declined to less than 23% and by 1973 to just below 22% (USBC 1975). In absolute terms the total value added by manufacturing rose more than fourfold, from about $70 billion to $300 billion between 1948 and 1973. In constant dollars the increase was roughly 2.3-fold.

There were some short-term fluctuations, but the total number of people employed in manufacturing was growing slowly, from 14.7 million in 1948 to 17.2 million in 1965 and 19.1 million in 1973, when manufacturing still employed more people than any other economic sector. But the surging size of the US government (federal, state, and local) made it a close second-largest employer, with 17.3 million jobs in 1973, compared to just 7.9 million in 1948. While the entire manufacturing labor force in 1973 was 30% larger than a quarter century before, and the production labor force had increased by about 20%, new annual capital expenditures in manufacturing had more than quadrupled, as had the value added per production worker-hour. Average hourly earnings, after growing by about 7% a year, were more than three times the 1948 mean (in current dollars), while the average number of work hours had remained unchanged at about 40 per week (USBC 1975).

As already noted, the 1930s were the decade of the highest productivity gains in American economy (averaging more than 2% per year), and the 1920s saw the highest total factor productivity (TFP) gains in manufacturing (Field 2006). Between 1941 and 1949 TFP growth in the private nonfarm economy slowed down considerably, to about 1.3% per year, and as a consequence of massive capital deepening, the TFP in manufacturing had actually declined at an annualized rate of about 0.5% a year (Field 2007). TFP growth resumed after 1948 and appeared low only in comparison with the record-high pre–World War II levels. Between 1948 and 1973 the TFP growth of the US economy averaged 1.9% and the rate for manufacturing was 1.5%, with the highest sectoral rates for chemicals (2.51%), textiles (2.29%), and electric and electronic equipment (2.07%) and the lowest growth rates for leather (0.02%) and primary metal industries (0.39%) (Field 2006).

And while the higher disposable incomes of the 1950s and the 1960s led to higher imports of manufactured goods, first from Europe and later from Japan, exports of semifinished and finished products roughly quadrupled (in current dollars), from about $8.5 billion in 1948 to more than $33 billion in 1973. Consequently, the US balance of trade in manufactures declined during those decades, but it remained positive throughout the entire period. I will start my survey of the world's first mass consumption society by reviewing some of its accomplishments, then I will appraise the strengths as well as some notable problems of American manufacturing during the period of continuous growth. Finally, I take a close look at the genesis of industrial automation and the adoption of computers, greatly facilitated by the invention of the microchip.

**The First Mass Consumption Society**

The basic narrative is simple: most people prefer to amass material possessions, and only inadequate means to acquire them or the inability of producers to supply them limits this quest. During the quarter century of postwar economic expansion Americans could increasingly afford the goods (median family incomes, measured in constant dollars, had nearly doubled), and American manufacturers were eager not only to supply what was already in demand but also to create new demand by constantly introducing new consumer products and spending heavily on advertising to persuade consumers to buy.

There is an important spatial corollary to amassing possessions. Most of us also want to amass new impressions and new experiences through travel, and these possibilities became widely affordable, thanks to common ownership of automobiles and, roaming further afield, the availability of inexpensive long-distance air travel on the new jetliners. These realities dictate the content of this section. I will concentrate on three quintessential components of America's post–World War II mass consumption: first on the wide array of machines, devices, and gadgets that filled American homes during the quarter century of economic expansion; then on the ownership and use of cars; and finally on the creation and very rapid expansion of a new form of fast yet affordable long-distance travel made possible by configuring gas turbines to power airplanes of unprecedented capacity and speed.

A leading stimulant of postwar mass consumption was the combination of increasing ownership rate of increasingly larger houses located increasingly farther away from places of work. At the beginning of the twentieth century about 47% of Americans owned their homes. That figure climbed only marginally, to 48%, by 1930, then fell to less than 44% a decade later. The postwar change was rapid: by 1950 the home ownership rate had reached 55%, a decade later it was 62%, and by 1973 it stood at 65%. In 1950 a sample survey of new houses financed by the Federal Housing Administration found an average size of 983 square feet; by 1973 the median area of a new house was 1,525 square feet, the nationwide average was 1,660 square feet, and houses inside metropolitan areas reached 1,760 square feet (Grebler, Blank, and Winnick 1956; USBC 2009), or a 55%–80% increase in 25 years.

This combination of an increasing home ownership rate, increasing home size, and increasing distance from work translated first into a rising demand for both old (lumber, cement, bricks, pipes) and new (plastics, aluminum siding) construction materials and then into a mass demand for more plumbing fixtures, furniture, and carpets and for an array of household items that were either comparatively rare or entirely absent in prewar housing but that became standard in an average new house by the early 1970s. Modern prewar housing components that were expected to be part of a new home in the 1950s included central heating (either forced warm air or steam or hot water heating was in half of homes by 1950), a refrigerator (four out of five homes wired for electricity had one by 1950), a washing machine (present in two-thirds of homes by the late 1940s), an attached garage, and a telephone (by 1948 about 60% of households had one).

Television was the first expensive household item whose ownership became common only during the 1950s. The domestic production of TV sets had ramped up rapidly, from just less than a million units in 1948 to nearly 7.5 million by 1950. In 1948 only 172,000 US households had a TV, but by 1960 the total had surpassed 45 million, and sets were in 90% of all homes. During the 1960s mass ownership of appliances spread to dishwashers (in more than a third of homes by 1970), freezers (in nearly 40% of households), clothes dryers (in 1950 they were a rarity; in 1973 more than half of households used them), and color TV sets. Color broadcasts began in 1954, but the early sets were expensive, and the sales of cheaper models took off only after 1965: in that year 5% of homes had color TV, five years later the share was nearly 40%, and by 1973 the set was in two out of every three homes.

And which of the two innovations has brought greater social, economic, and political consequences, the diffusion of TV or the mass adoption of air conditioning? Sales of room (window) AC units began in 1945, but only 74,000 were shipped in 1948. This number rose to 1.5 million in 1960 and nearly 5.5 million a decade later, with the nationwide ownership rate rising from less than 1% of households in 1950 to nearly 15% in 1960, 40% in 1970, and 49% in 1973. During the same period many smaller inexpensive electrical appliances reached market saturation. By 1973 coffeemakers, hot plates, irons, radios, toasters, and vacuum cleaners were each owned by more than 90% of all households.

But a family car was often the most cherished item. The singular was the prevailing norm until the early 1960s: in 1948 only 2% of households had a second car, but by 1965 24% of households had two or more vehicles, and by 1973 that share was nearly 45%. The postwar reconversion of car factories that had been converted to military production was rapid. In 1943 only 100 new passenger cars were sold in the entire country, and in 1945 total factory sales were just short of 70,000 vehicles. But nearly four million were shipped in 1948 and 6.6 million in 1950; aggregate sales were nearly 58 million during the 1950s and 77 million during the 1960s. The prewar rate of car ownership was far higher in the United States than in any other country, but even so, by 1948 nearly half of all families did not own a car. This changed in the 25 years after 1948, when the nationwide ownership rate doubled, from 4.4 people per passenger car to very close to saturation level of 2.1 people per vehicle by 1973.

The rapid expansion of the European and Japanese car industries was steadily reducing the share of global car production originating in the United States, lowering it from about 80% in 1948 to just below 50% by 1960 and below 33% by 1973 (MVMA 1980). Inevitably, more foreign cars found their way to the world's largest car market. Imported cars were less than 1% of annual sales in 1955 and still only about 6% a decade later, when the Volkswagen Beetle was the most popular import choice. By that time VW had its first serious Japanese competition in Toyota. The company began selling, unsuccessfully, its mini Toyopet in 1958, and in 1964 it introduced the better-received Corona (Toyota 2011).

In March 1970 the Honda Car Company launched its American sales with the small two-door N600, and two years later it issued its first Civic, powered by the innovative compound vortex controlled combustion (CVCC) engine (Sakiya 1982). In 1973 these German and Japanese imports accounted for most of the 15% share imports held in the US market: with only about every seventh car made overseas, Detroit's position did not seem to be in any serious trouble. By the time Toyota and Honda began to export their small cars to the United States, the Volkswagen Beetle had what appeared to be an insurmountable lead among the imported vehicles, and it would have been a safe bet that European cars in general, and German models in particular, would continue to dominate automotive imports. To suggest that by the year 2000 the leading car model made in the United States would be a foreign subcompact, the Honda Civic, and that three out of five bestselling vehicles, the Camry, Accord, and Civic, would be Japanese would have been laughable.

The position of US companies making large commercial aircraft appeared to be similarly unassailable. The British took advantage of their wartime leadership in developing operational jet fighters and even before the war's end began to plan a postwar conquest of commercial aviation with jet-powered airplanes. The Comet was the first jetliner to enter into scheduled service, from London to Johannesburg, in May 1952 (Cowell 1976), but two accidents and three catastrophic failures caused by a fuselage rupture that propagated from small stress cracks around the square window frames grounded the remaining fleet in April 1954. By the time a redesigned Comet took off the United States had its first jetliner in international service. The Boeing 707, whose design was based on the B-47 bomber, began to fly the New York–Paris route in October 1958 (Mellberg 2003). Boeing had to compete with British, French, and Soviet aircraft builders, but the company maintained its technical lead, and during the 1960s it strengthened that lead by launching two revolutionary airplanes.

The first was the Boeing 737, launched in 1967. More than 3,800 planes, of frequently updated and expanded design, were sold by the year 2000, making it the most successful jetliner in history (Boeing 2011). The second was the Boeing 747, the first wide-body (twin-aisle) jet powered by Pratt & Whitney's JT9D turbofan engines, much more efficient prime movers than the previous turbojets (Smil 2010). The jumbo airplane was ordered by Pan Am, America's leading and the world's first truly global airline, in 1966, and its expensive but remarkably rapid development taxed Boeing's resources close to the company's financial limit. But it was a risk worth taking: the airplane flew for the first time in February 1969 and began commercial service in January 1970, carrying nearly 500 passengers in a two-class configuration. In 1972 Boeing's two domestic competitors introduced their own wide-body designs, the DC-10, by McDonnell Douglas, and the L1011 (TriStar), by Lockheed.

Within a decade, wide-bodied jetliners transformed long-distance flight from a trying and expensive experience to a fairly comfortable and widely affordable journey. The age of mass jet travel had arrived, and the American aircraft and jet engine manufacturers, particularly Boeing and Pratt & Whitney, were its foremost creators. Between 1960 and 1970 the number of passengers flown by US airlines on all routes more than tripled, while the freight-miles increased fivefold. Given their industry leadership position, US aircraft makers were not greatly concerned when in December 1970 the governments of France, the German Federal Republic, and the UK set up Groupement d'Interet Économique, which became known by a decidedly pedestrian name, Airbus Industrie. They should have been. That December agreement was the beginning of one of America's greatest, and still unfolding, manufacturing retreats.

**Automation, Computers, and Microchips**

These three great enablers of manufacturing innovation—automation, computers, and microchips—are listed in chronological order. The automation of many industrial tasks does not require electronic control, but hydraulic, pneumatic, or electromechanical techniques have limitations, and the widespread deployments of robots, now indispensable in many manufacturing sectors, would be impossible without computers. Similarly, electronic computers can be built without microprocessors (as all of them were, until Intel designed the first such device in 1971), but without microchips modern computing would be much slower, much more expensive, much less flexible, and much less portable (and "much" here means by orders of magnitude).

During the quarter century of great economic expansion, American scientists and engineers were the leaders in all three fields as they ushered in the age of automation and robotization, and then transformed electronic computers. This was a sequential process that began during the 1950s when massive and expensive machines owned by a small number of military, governmental, and research institutions and used for a variety of extreme calculations were transformed, thanks to transistorization, into compact devices that could be commonly deployed by businesses. The next step was an even greater technical revolution, as the integrated circuit made computers vastly more powerful, affordable, and truly ubiquitous components of modern economies in general and modern manufacturing in particular.

As with the assembly line, Ford Motor Company was once again at the forefront of a manufacturing innovation. In 1947 it set up a new Automation Department, charged with exploring existing electromechanical, hydraulic, and pneumatic techniques for automated manufacturing. But it soon became obvious that the best option might be to incorporate the very latest addition to these methods, the use of numerically controlled (NC) machine tools. The first step came in 1947, when John T. Parsons and Frank L. Stulen designed a milling machine controlled using IBM punch cards, but it took a while before this innovation began to make any commercial difference (Noble 1984).

Much like the first electronic computers, the first NC machines of the early 1950s were bulky and had limited capacities. Their performance improved with the introduction of the Automatically Programmed Tools (APT) computer language, developed at MIT in 1957, and as a result of work done by a new consortium of aircraft companies looking for better ways to machine such complex surfaces as wings and rotors; and by the early 1960s computer-assisted manufacturing (CAM) was an established commercial reality. Its capabilities were greatly potentiated during the 1970s with the adoption of microchip-driven designs.

Industrial robots have many highly desirable attributes, combining properties that are incompatible in the case of human labor: they are accurate yet fast, and they are able to repeat tasks endlessly without compromising the quality of the results. Multiple degrees of freedom (six for common welding robots) permit highly accurate positioning in space while maintaining high operation speed and quality (easily more than seven years between failures). Of course, robots displace humans, but they also free them from jobs that are dirty, difficult, and dangerous. Not surprisingly, the first applications of industrial robots were mostly in dirty, difficult, and dangerous areas, including the handling of hot parts, welding, and metal painting.

George C. Devol began developing his ideas for controlling machines using magnetically stored instructions right after World War II, but it was only a decade later, after he met Joseph F. Engelberger, that the two men set up Unimation (derived from "universal automation"), the world's first robot company. Their first prototype machine was ready in 1958 (Devol 1961), but the first commercially available robot was Versatran, made by American Machine and Foundry, Harry Johnson's and Veljko Milenkovic's company, in 1960. Unimation sold its first industrial robot a year later to a GM plant. The robot was designed to lift and stack hot metal parts from a die-casting machine, with the commands stored on a magnetic drum. The next breakthrough came in 1969 when the Stanford Arm, designed by Victor Scheinman, became the first computer-controlled robot, and just four years later Richard Hohn at Milacron in Cincinnati designed the world's first industrial robot operated by a minicomputer (Scott 1984).

Commercial computing advanced slowly during the first half of the 1950s, with UNIVAC machines still dominant (Cerruzzi 2003). By1954 the company had sold 19 of them, starting with a sale to the Census Bureau in 1951 and including several large corporate customers (Consolidated Edison, US Steel, Westinghouse) and various divisions and subagencies of the US Department of Defense. IBM, long established in the business of office machines, eventually responded with its first commercial designs, the IBM 701 and 650, and the two leaders were soon joined by a number of new competitors offering their own large computers and led by Honeywell, GE, and RCA. Concurrent progress was made in writing software, with FORTRAN introduced in 1957 and COBOL in 1959.

By the late 1950s transistorization had lowered typical computer costs, and by the early 1960s IBM had emerged as the leader of the large commercial sector, a position it solidified in 1965 with the introduction of half a dozen models of its IBM System/360, which became the dominant choice for companies, government and research institutions, and universities well into the 1970s. Meanwhile a different and a more fundamental development had been under way since the closing years of the 1950s: the conceptual design, first commercial offerings, and rapid success of monolithic electronic circuits, originally known as solid circuits and commonly referred to as microchips.

Their true departure point was William Shockley's 1948 design of a bipolar junction transistor, a device with three terminals whose two outer layers are doped to supply electrons in order to function much like a triode (Shockley 1964). Bell Labs started to license both of its transistor designs in 1951. In 1954 hearing aids and radios became the first transistorized devices, and the first transistorized commercial computer was built in 1956. As long as the devices were made from germanium, the obvious advantages of transistors compared to vacuum tubes—a much smaller size, a solid state ensuring reliable and low-energy operation, no need for warm-up—remained greatly underexploited because germanium transistors could not operate in high temperatures and required air conditioning.

Silicon was a superior material. The growth of large crystals was first mastered at Bell Labs during the early 1950s, and in 1955 Morris Tanenbaum succeeded in producing the first doped Si transistor. Another key invention was made at the Bell Labs in the same years when Carl Frosch and Link Derick discovered how to deposit thin $SiO_2$ film on silicon wafers. This was originally intended for their protection, but the film's selective etching could be used to control which of the chip's regions would be doped and which would remain protected. Gordon Teal produced the first grown-junction Si transistor in May 1954 at Texas Instruments, and the company became the leading supplier of transistors for the rest of the 1950s, with the US military as its largest customer, particularly after 1956, when the US Air Force began to convert instrumentation from analog to digital devices.

Texas Instruments' main competitor emerged in October 1957, when Fairchild Semiconductor opened for business. The company was established by eight young scientists and engineers, led by Gordon Moore and Jay Last, who left Shockley Semiconductor Laboratory and were financed by Fairchild Camera and Instrument (Lécuyer and Brock 2010). That was the month of the *Sputnik 1* launch, an event that led to increased military demand for semiconductors, particularly for avionics (the US Air Force began its digitalization in 1957) and for navigation and guidance computers of the United States' first intercontinental ballistic missile, the Minuteman I, which became operational in 1962. These demands made it clear that making progressively more miniaturized circuits from a variety of components would be highly impractical, if not impossible, and very costly.

Two electronic engineers working for the two top semiconductor competitors independently offered an elegant solution to this challenge. In July 1958 Jack S. Kilby, working at Texas Instruments, proposed a way to fabricate a new miniaturized electronic circuit in such a way that all of its components would be completely integrated into the body of the semiconductor material (Kilby 1964). A year later Robert Noyce, at Fairchild Semiconductor, came up with the very similar idea of making multiple interconnections on a single piece of silicon a part of the manufacturing process.

Unlike Kilby's original patent application, however, which showed clumsy wiring connections, Noyce, using Jean Horni's idea of an $SiO_2$ layer as a mask placed on top of an n-p-n sandwich, designed a true planar transistor (Noyce 1961). Noyce's planar transistor patent was granted in 1961, and a decade later his invention was given priority over Kilby's patent application, which was approved only in July 1964. But five years before this dispute was settled, Texas Instruments and Fairchild Semiconductor consented to a mutual license deal and required other licensees to make separate arrangements with both of them. Texas Instruments began to offer its "micrological elements" in 1961, but sales of devices took off only in 1965, when they began to be used by NASA's Apollo mission and in an increasing variety of military electronic devices (Hall 1996).

In 1965, when the most complex integrated circuits had 50 transistors, Gordon Moore (1965) published his famous forecast of transistor density per integrated circuit doubling every 12 months; ten years later he amended the doubling period to two years (Moore 1975). The first computer to use integrated circuits was designed by Burroughs in 1968. In that same year Gordon Moore and Robert Noyce left Fairchild Semiconductor to set up Integrated Electronics (Intel), dedicated to making increasingly more complex circuit designs. Intel's first major commercial project was a chip with more than 1,000 components for a calculator to be sold by Busicom, a Japanese company that funded the device's development. Marcian Hoff and Stanley Mazor laid out the original proposal, which used a single central processing unit (CPU) to retrieve instructions from a read-only memory (ROM). Federico Fagin was responsible for the logic and circuit design, and Mazor wrote the software (Mazor 1995).

This design made it possible to use the resulting MCS-4 chip for other applications (Hoff, Mazor, and Fagin 1974). Before Busicom went bankrupt, Intel bought back the rights for the MCS-4 and released the world's first universal microprocessor in November 1971. That tiny (3 × 4 mm) Intel 4004, which sold for $200, had 2,250 metal oxide semiconductor transistors and processed four bits of information at the speed of 400 kHz—and its 60,000 operations per second made it a functional equivalent of the ENIAC (Intel 2011). The Intel 4004 was the first computer on a chip. Four decades later it can be argued that no other devices have changed so much and so fast as those ever more powerful microprocessors did during the first four decades of their existence.

Microprocessor control opened the way not only to the two extremes of modern computing—complex, high-volume computing using expensive institutional supercomputers, on the one hand, and quotidian applications running on inexpensive personal computers on the other—but also to a massive wave of industrial automation, continuous control, and highly accurate instrumentation. The first mass-produced device containing integrated circuits was Pocketronic, a small calculator made by Texas Instruments that had been under development since 1965 and was finally released in April 1971. Its design served as a basic platform for many subsequent models (Kilby, Merryman, and Van Tassel 1974).

As for manufacturing automation, robots would never have achieved such widespread use had they remained limited to single tasks. It was the flexibility enabled by microprocessor reprogramming that made them, in less than two generations, indispensable for many kinds of manufacturing. During the early phases of this expansion the pioneer lost the top spot to a licensee: Japan began making Versatran and Unimation machines during the late 1960s, but by 1980 it had nearly 15 times as many robots in its factories as did the United States. But because that count included many simple manipulators, the totals for real industrial robots were not that far apart, 2,415 in the United States and 3,000 in Japan (Engelberger 1980).

### Manufacturing Strengths and Problems

During its quarter century of steady expansion, US manufacturing became less important in relative terms, both as a share of GDP and as a share of global output of goods, but in absolute terms the sector underwent substantial expansion: in real terms the value added by US manufacturing rose from $87 billion in 1948 to $290 billion (in constant 1965 dollars), a 3.3-fold gain, with the sectoral increase ranging from a 60% gain in primary metals to a more than fourfold rise in instrument making. Output per man-hour had doubled for all manufacturing activities, with sectoral productivity improvements as high as a fourfold rise in crude oil refining and a 2.5-fold gain in papermaking.

Fairly strong productivity gains kept the sector ahead of its foreign competitors. As noted in the previous chapter, pre–World War II US manufacturing was significantly more productive than that of any major European or Asian economy. Not surprisingly, after the war most of those countries had higher annual productivity growth rates than the United States while they were reconstituting their damaged economies: for the period between 1950 and 1973, Cobet and Wilson (2002) calculated the annualized gains in hourly manufacturing output at 10% for Japan, 6.9% for Germany, 6% for France, and 3.3% for the UK, compared to 2.6% for the United States. As a result, all of these competitors narrowed, though they did not close, the prewar productivity gap.

Estimates by Van Ark and Timmer (2001) show that in 1960, labor productivity in manufacturing, measured in terms of value added per employee, was still nearly 40% lower in the German Federal Republic, about 50% lower in France, and 75% lower in Japan—and nearly as low in the USSR. By 1973 these gaps had narrowed to, respectively, 25%, 33%, and 45%, while the gap between the United States and the USSR remained the same, with the productivity of Soviet manufacturing about 75% lower than the US performance. And for Europe's largest economies the 1973 gap was even smaller when measured in value added per hour, only about 20% for the German Federal Republic and less than 30% for France.

Notable technical and organizational advances were made throughout the entire period, and many new procedures and products that were pioneered by American manufacturers during those 25 years have had lasting impacts on global industrial production, economic growth, and social changes. Perhaps the most important (in terms of their overall socioeconomic impact) half dozen categorical advances were innovations in silicon-based transistors, commercial electronic computers, microchips, numerically controlled machines, industrial robots, and wide-body jetliners.

But during the quarter century between 1948 and 1973 US manufacturing also experienced a number of problems and had to cope with some inherent weaknesses, and those too rose to unprecedented levels, with their cumulative effect that of reducing the competitive capacities of several key industries and making much of the manufacturing sector vulnerable to a taxing combination of post-1973 changes. American mass production of consumer goods operated with two great advantages that soon changed into two serious drawbacks. First, it was, particularly during the

1950s, a producers' market, and second, it was an era of abundant and inexpensive energy.

The first reality was created by rising disposable incomes, a relatively high rate of saving, a population shift to the suburbs, and the high fertility of the baby boom era. This combination generated an enormous demand for durable goods, and US manufacturers could sell almost anything they made. Product durability, functionality, and design quality were of secondary (and sometimes, it seems, of hardly any) importance compared to the quest for quantity, a quick profit, and built-in obsolescence. Some designs were completely devoid of any functionality or any design sensibility: we need only think of those massive chrome ornaments and risible fins of large automobiles of the day.

Cheap energy was an even more important problem. A barrel of crude oil cost as much in current monies in 1965 as it did in 1950, which means that its real value was nearly a third cheaper than 15 years earlier, and the difference was even greater when set beside rising disposable incomes. As a result, durable goods could be, and were, designed as if material and energy did not matter. The best example of this easily avoidable waste of minerals and energy was provided by US automobile manufacturers, whose operation was guided by three simple objectives: make the products progressively larger, heavier, and more powerful; style them in outrageous ways; and make them rapidly obsolete.

Several trends that began during the 1950s accelerated during the 1960s, and by 1973 most of the US car models shared the following attributes: an automatic transmission (more than 90% of new cars), a V-8 engine (more than 80%), power brakes (more than 75%), and air conditioning (more than 70%). In Flink's (1985, 158) judgment, these vehicles were "overpowered, undertired, and underbraked," and Nader's (1965) well-known verdict was that they were unsafe at almost any speed. His book opened with a chapter on Chevrolet's Corvair, sold between 1959 and 1965 and called by Nader "The One-Car Accident." My personal experience with Detroit quality came with our first car—Pontiac's Astre, sold between 1971 and 1977 and distinguished by its low price and chronic difficulty even starting—and it made me a steadfast Honda buyer.

Detroit cars were also unnecessarily massive: poor body design and various add-ons pushed up the average weight to more than 1.5 t by the early 1970s, and as most of them carried a single passenger, their useful load/vehicle mass ratio was less than 5%. Even worse, the average performance of US-made cars and trucks kept on deteriorating for more than four decades. Between 1936, the first year for which the nationwide mean can be reliably calculated, and 1973, it fell from more than 15 mpg to just 13.4 mpg (Sivak and Tsimhoni 2009). This is an incredible case of technical retrogression during the two generations that saw so many impressive innovations and substantial performance gains in a variety of industrial sectors, including aviation, chemical syntheses, and electronics.

Compounding this insult were the ubiquitously poor styling and superfluous annual model changes, which were seen as more important than vehicle safety and reliability (by the early 1970s new American cars retailed with some two dozen defects). This manufacturing trend not only resulted in an enormous waste of materials and wasteful performance, it also helped raise the number of fatalities, and it was the principal cause of the country's worsening photochemical smog pollution. But America's manufacturing problems ran deeper, affecting its ability to produce steel, the most fundamental modern material. Cars are mostly steel, the quintessential metal of modernity whose use makes ours still the steel, not silicon, age (Smil 2006).

A small country would find it too costly or simply too impractical to set up its own steel industry, but it is hard to imagine how a country can remain a great manufacturing power with a weak and uncompetitive steel sector. After US steelmaking reached new output heights during World War II its postwar production declined from the 1944 peak of just over 81 Mt to 60 Mt in 1946, though by 1950 it was above the 1944 peak and, with the exception of a 1958–1963 dip, it continued to grow until 1973, when it reached its never-to-be-surpassed peak of 137 Mt. This production was essential for large infrastructural investments in transportation (the interstate highway system, airport expansions) and the energy sector (offshore drilling rigs, oil and gas pipelines, large coal-fired power plants, high-voltage transmission links).

During the first postwar decade the industry also continued to innovate. The first notable postwar innovation, coming in 1948, was the blast furnace smelting of iron ore under pressure, which resulted in substantial savings of coke. Other coke-savings techniques introduced during the 1950s included injecting natural gas or fuel oil and charging with highly beneficiated ores and oxygen-enriched blast air (Gold et al. 1984). These innovations helped maintain US leadership in steelmaking until the late 1950s, when Japan—taking advantage of a near-complete destruction of its iron and steel mills, rapidly adopting US innovations, and aggressively improving its increasingly larger operations—emerged as the sector's most innovative leader.

And the United States was even slower to adopt the latest steelmaking techniques as two replacement waves swept the industry starting in the 1950s. The first innovative wave replaced inefficient open hearth furnaces (OHFs) with basic oxygen furnaces (BOFs), and those in turn were replaced with electric arc furnaces (EAFs). OHFs began to make large gains before 1900 and produced most of the steel during the first half of the twentieth century. Their size kept pace with rising demand as the capacity of the largest US furnace increased from 42 t in 1910 to 200 t during World War II (King 1948). The postwar introduction of BOFs was not pioneered by a major steel company but came about mainly through the determination of Robert Durrer, a Swiss metallurgist, and his German colleague, Heinrich Hellbrügge. Their first small converter was ready in May 1948, and Austria's largest steelmaker, VÖEST (Vereinigte Österreichische Eisen- und Stahlwerke AG), became the first commercial user of the process in 1952.

None of the large US steelmakers was among the early adopters. The US steel industry bought its first BOF only in 1964. In 1960, 87% of American raw steel production came from OHFs, and the share was still 72% five year later. A major shift took place only in the late 1960s, with about 55% of US steel coming from BOFs in 1970—but by that time the Japanese share was up to 80% (Smil 2006). US steelmakers were also slow to adopt continuous casting, a more efficient way to produce semifinished items than the traditional casing of ingots (oblong pieces weighing 50–100 t), which had to be wastefully reheated, a process that often consumed more energy than the steelmaking itself, before making semifinished items (slabs, billets, blooms) to be subsequently turned into plates, coils, rails, or wire (Fruehan 1998; Tanner 1998). Japan installed its first continuous casting line in 1955, and 25 years later 90% of its steel came from such lines, compared to just over 40% in the United States (Burwell 1990; Okumura 1994).

The adoption of BOFs, EAFs, and continuous casting brought large productivity gains and rapidly reversed the long-standing national ranking: in 1960 the United States needed about 16.5 man-hours to produce a ton of steel, compared to Japan's mean of nearly 49 hours; by 1973 the Japanese average was less than 9.5 hours, while the US mean was just over 11 hours (USBC 1975). When the US raw steel production reached its historic peak with 137 Mt of metal produced in 1973, it was an accomplishment that owed almost entirely to the industry's past size and dynamism, and did not indicate an expansive future. The reversal was rapid as output began to plunge, and ten years later US raw steel production was halved, to less than 68 Mt in 1982, before it recovered during the late 1980s and 1990s, but it has never approached the 1973 record. In 1948 the United States was a large net steel exporter and it remained one until 1958. Afterward its net steel imports continued to increase, and by 1973 they reached about 10% of apparent consumption (DiFrancesco et al. 2010).

There were other early harbingers of US manufacturing's retreat. The production of cotton and woolen fabrics reached its highest postwar level during the early 1960s, while the value of imported clothing (measured in constant dollars) increased fivefold between 1960 and 1973; the US production of shoes peaked during the mid-1960s as the real value of shoe imports rose more than fivefold during the same period. Similar trends were seen for toys, games, and sporting goods. The domestic production of color TVs peaked in 1973, and the overall value of manufactured imports (excluding electrical machinery and cars) nearly quadrupled during the 15 years following 1958.

In 1971 the United States faced its first foreign merchandise trade deficit, thanks to imports of goods worth nearly $46 billion compared to exports of more than $43 billion. In 1972 the trade deficit for goods trade widened, from $2.3 billion to $6.4 billion, but in 1973 there was again a small surplus, less than $1 billion. And that was the last positive foreign trade balance of the twentieth century, one of many indicators marking the end of an era. Ahead were decades of endless trade deficits, soon to be joined by a deepening government budget deficit, the steady loss of production in many manufacturing sectors, and a rising dependence on imports. Many aggregate figures may have indicated a continuing rise, but a closer look shows America in retreat.

**Figure 4.1**
Large container ships are the most impressive symbols of America's large trade deficit. They come from Asia stacked high with manufactured goods and often carry back nothing more valuable than recycled paper. Color image available at http://upload.wikimedia.org/wikipedia/commons/8/86/Ever_Given_container_ship.jpg.

# 4

# The Retreat, 1974–

*America's excesses and policies have gradually undermined its greatest strengths and put in doubt its global leadership.*

The United States has had a lot of advantages—learning from defense, importing the smartest people from around the globe, having its domestic market be the largest and the most demanding and having great universities with research funding that managed to have some relationship with the private sector. . . . Over time I think manufacturing moved away because of some mixture of regulations (not all bad), high cost labor (unions), higher cost of capital (complex) and a focus on other things (comparative advantage, or misdirected cultural signals?).
—Bill Gates, 2011

Absolute numbers allow us to argue that there was no manufacturing retreat during the closing decades of the twentieth and during the first decade of the twenty-first century and that the United States has retained its primacy both as the world's largest economy and as the top manufacturing power. Of course, converting China's currency by using purchasing power parity (PPP) value (in 2010 Rmb 3.9/US$, according to the IMF) rather than by applying the official exchange rate (in 2010 Rmb 6.8/US$) would put the value added by China's manufacturing well ahead of the US total—but that would indicate merely a rapid (and long overdue) advance of modernization in the world's most populous nation, not any absolute US decline. Moreover, such a simple quantitative comparison hides a major qualitative difference: China relies overwhelmingly on deploying masses of low-paid manual workers, while US manufacturing includes a much higher share of high-value-added products. And in per capita terms, even with PPP conversion US manufacturing in 2010 was adding roughly 2.5 times as much value to the country's GDP as did China's manufacturing to its GDP.

A gradual decline in America's share of global manufacturing is another expected phenomenon. In 1974 the United States accounted for about 22% of the world economic product (measured in PPP), and for the next quarter century this share remained fairly stable at between 22% and 24% (reached in 1999 after a period of unexpectedly vigorous growth during the late 1990s), but by 2010 the share had slipped below 20%. Similarly, America's share of global manufacturing output remained high and even grew during the 1990s (from about 22% to about 25%), but by 2010 it had fallen below 20% and was virtually on par with China's manufacturing share, which accounted for less than 8% of the global total in the year 2000 and only 3% in 1990 (UNCTAD 2012).

This modest relative retreat of America's share of global GDP and manufacturing is an inevitable evolutionary shift that had to come in a world in which OPEC countries had begun to reap the benefits of their extortionary oil pricing, post-Mao China had begun its belated quest for modernity with Deng Xiaoping's economic reforms of the 1980s, India, finally, had begun to shed its counterproductive autarky, and countries from South Korea to Brazil had experienced high rates of economic growth. Claiming a less disproportionate share of the world economic product would not alone be a reason for concern, and the same could be said of manufacturing's share, particularly as the sector's overall output (measured in constant dollars) is still expanding: when measured in constant monies the value added by US manufacturing during the 1990s rose by nearly 46%, and between 2000 and 2010 it increased by nearly 18%.

But these numbers raise an obvious question: while larger systems cannot grow as fast as smaller ones, why was the relative growth during the first decade of the twenty-first century only about 40% of the rate during the last decade of the twentieth century (1.6% vs. 3.8% per year)? Was it simply due to the intervening world recession of 2008–2009? No, because even the pre-recession growth during the years 2000–2007 was down to 2.6% a year. In isolation, this unexpected deceleration in adding value in manufacturing might not be a cause for serious concern—but it becomes one once we add its impact on manufacturing jobs and set it alongside other key trends in recent US history.

Throughout the 1990s, manufacturing employment remained quite stable, with 17.64 million jobs in January 1990 and 17.32 million jobs in December 1999, but by the end of 2005 the total had dropped by nearly 18%, to 14.2 million, followed by a 20% drop to less than 11.5 million by the end of 2009. The employment figure remained essentially unchanged a year later and showed only a small, 3% increase by the end of 2011, to 11.8 million (BLS 2012). The last time the number of people employed in manufacturing was so low was in 1940, before the economy's mobilization for World War II. This is one of the major reasons why there was no net job creation during the first decade of the twenty-first century but rather a small overall job loss. In January 2000 the country had 130.78 million nonfarm jobs and in January 2010 the total was 129.28 million, but that decrement, small in both absolute (1.5 million) and relative (1.2%) terms, took place during a decade in which the country's population had increased by nearly 10%.

The last time such a loss occurred was during the 1930s, and what makes it such a concern this time is that the dismal job creation statistic has been accompanied by huge and rising budget deficits, large and persistent trade deficits, enormous indebtedness, a low saving rate, a worsening state of indispensable modern infrastructure, poor achievements in education for the masses, worrisome public health (marked by a historically unprecedented incidence of obesity)—and a grossly dysfunctional government to run it all. When seen from this perspective, the state of US manufacturing is a clear cause for concern.

Strategic considerations add to these burdens. America's military supremacy has never looked the same after the defeat in Vietnam. And although the peaceful demise of the USSR in December 1991 made the United States, as a tiresome phrase had it, the only remaining superpower, it is a superpower that just a few years later was humiliated in Somalia, then attacked by terrorists in its largest city and its capital; a superpower that spent thousands of lives and trillions of dollars on wars in Iraq and Afghanistan, whose outcomes have been anything but victories; and a country that has been strongly challenged by the economic and military rise of China. As for the mounting social problems in the United States, none is more worrisome than the perilously rising inequality of incomes and possessions, an inequality whose level is now surpassed only by China, by the most inequitable economies of Latin America and the worst kleptocracies of Africa.

The following chronology recounts fundamental turning points and thresholds that have marked the United States' economic retreat. The first broad signs of weakness became clearly evident during the early 1970s, when America's oil production began to decline, its oil imports rose even as OPEC began to increase its crude oil prices, and the country recorded its first, and growing, foreign trade deficit after eight decades of steady, often substantial, surpluses. New concerns emerged during the 1980s with record trade deficits, Japan's seemingly unstoppable economic rise and its impending dominance of advanced electronics, a weakening US currency, and the first federal budget deficits since World War II. The sudden appearance of these concerns and the need to face realities that broke a number of critical decades-long trends made them very worrisome—but in retrospect they appear tolerably mild in comparison with what followed during the two decades after 1990.

During the 1990s much of this long-term decline was masked by a surprisingly strong economic performance as the real GDP rose by 34% between 1990 and 1999. This rise, impressive for such a large and mature economy, was driven by the combination of unexpected strategic dividends (America's clear victory in the Gulf War of 1991, the nonviolent demise of the USSR before the end of that year) and the expansion of what was called at that time (and, in retrospect, with much exaggeration and without real justification) a new economy, based on the mass adoption of computers and an eager embrace of the Internet.

But after the e-bubble burst in 2000 (the NASDAQ Composite Index peaked at 5,058.62 on March 10, 2000, lost half its value within a year, and reached its lowest point in October 2002 at 1,114), and after the United States was boldly struck in New York and Washington, D.C., by Islamic terrorists, who steered jetliners into the World Trade Center and the Pentagon, the accomplishments of the late 1990s appeared to be an aberration, not a foundation for a new period of economic success. During the first decade of the twenty-first century America had transformed itself, voluntarily and deliberately, from a true economic power whose productive achievements were translated into desirable social trends (most notably demonstrated by a steady decrease in income inequality) into a debt-ridden, import-dependent state with many manufacturing sectors extinct or nearly so, and with rising inequality of incomes and opportunities: I will examine the two periods of America's post-1973 manufacturing retreat against this economic, social, and strategic backdrop.

## Signs of Weakness, 1974–1990

By the spring of 1974, as crude oil was trading above $10 a barrel, it became clear that OPEC's new pricing power was not to be easily broken, and that high oil prices would be a significant burden to any country that needed substantial imports. For the United States, this was a major cause of the expanding foreign trade deficit. The country's uninterrupted spell of trade surpluses, which began in 1895, ended in 1971; the balance turned positive again in 1973 and 1975, but it has stayed negative ever since. Before too long those rising trade deficits had another negative impact: in 1971 the US current account (the net value of imports and exports and assets owned by the United States abroad and foreign-owned assets in the United States) also showed its first negative balance, but the assets part of it made it turn positive between 1973 and 1976 and again in 1980 and 1981 before it too slipped into a continuous deficit position in 1982.

On August 15, 1971, President Nixon ended the convertibility of the dollar into gold (set at $35 per ounce), abandoning, after more than a quarter century, the Bretton Woods global monetary regime set up at the

**Figure 4.2**
Between 1906 and 1958, Packard was a leading maker of luxury cars. Its Detroit plant closed in 1958, nearly two decades before US automakers began to lose their market share and abandon their factories. Color image available at http://upload.wikimedia.org/wikipedia/commons/c/c7/Abandoned_Packard_Automobile_Factory_Detroit_200.jpg.

end of World War II. Inevitably, this move was followed by a substantial devaluation of the US currency: in 1970 a dollar was worth ¥360 and DM 3.66; five years later the rates were less than ¥297 and about DM 2.45. Geopolitics also intervened: at the end of April 1975 North Vietnamese tanks breached the gates of the former US embassy in Saigon, handing the United States its first war defeat in its 200-year history (the Korean conflict ended in a draw, with the Communist forces gaining no ground that they did not hold at the war's beginning).

This was an exceptional concatenation of fundamental turning points. In the affairs of large nations it is rare for so many key realities to change so abruptly after decades of opposite experience. What came afterward was by no means inevitable, but it was made so by the absence of any effective effort to reverse even a single one of those critical turnarounds. In 1984 the annual deficit of the US trade in goods topped $100 billion for the first time, after a fourfold rise in just five years. On September 16, 1985, the US Department of Commerce revealed that the United States, the world's largest creditor nation since the end of the nineteenth century, had become a net debtor nation. By the end of that year its overall international investment position had a deficit of nearly $28 billion, a sum that now seems trivially small.

A week later, on September 23, 1985, the finance ministers of the United States, Japan, West Germany, the UK, and France met at New York's Plaza Hotel and signed an accord that was to reduce the US deficit and help the imports-beset US economy by further extending the dollar's post-1972 decline: within three years a dollar was worth only ¥ 128 and DM 1.75. The agreement, especially when combined with the establishment of Japanese car factories in the United States, eased the trade friction with Japan, but its unintended consequence was to accelerate the emergence of a new and eventually much larger chronic trade imbalance with China. The dubious efficacy of that currency intervention can be judged by the two milestones that followed almost immediately. By the end of 1985 China had its first trade surplus with the United States, a trivial sum of $6 million that did not even register with policy makers preoccupied with Japan and its enormous trade surplus. That trivial deficit then widened to $1.66 billion; in 1987 it was about $2.8 billion; and by the decade's end, and despite the killings at Tiananmen Square, it surpassed $10 billion.

And while the number of domestic manufacturing jobs kept on increasing, the number of government jobs was rising much faster; 1981 was the first year in which the total number of people employed by all levels of government, 19.15 million, surpassed the total employment in manufacturing of 19.09 million. Two decades later the gap had widened to more than 40%. Five years later there came another notable milestone, the emergence of the financial sector (including all finance services, insurance, and real estate) as the most important source of value added to the US economy: in 1986 manufacturing's share fell to 17.4%, below the 18% for finances.

In this chapter I take a closer look at the manufacturing fortunes and misfortunes of that eventful period by examining three major developments. The first development of interest is how US manufacturing coped with the new reality of an increasingly expensive energy supply. Although the sector does not claim such a high share of overall energy demand in the United States as it does in South Korea (about half) or Japan (nearly a third), one-fifth of America's enormous primary energy use goes to manufacturing, making manufacturing highly sensitive to price changes. But the sector coped rather well, its gradual adaptive successes a result of higher energy conversion efficiencies, better production processes, and a changing mix of energies; many US companies, and particularly those whose products are highly energy-intensive, handled this challenge quite effectively and retained their competitive advantages. But it is also a story of relatively rapid failures resulting from structural shifts, above all from substantial losses in the iron and steel industry.

The second development of interest is the stumbling and failing of the country's once mighty auto industry. The origins of this process reach back to the 1950s and 1960s, when US carmakers appeared invulnerable even as they were turning out substandard and unimaginative vehicles. The obvious retreat began as foreign carmakers secured higher shares of the domestic market, and the proximate reason for a near unraveling of this key industry was the second wave of OPEC's oil price increases, which began in 1979.

Finally, I appraise the many enviable accomplishments of and challenges encountered by the country's newest key manufacturing sector, the production of electronics in general and computers in particulars, during the latter half of the 1970s and throughout the 1980s.

**Energy in Manufacturing**

One thing that US industries did not have to worry about as they rose to global dominance was gaining access to abundant and affordable sources of energy. No other country consumed as much fuelwood as did the United States during the latter half of the nineteenth century. By 1900 the United States had surpassed the UK to become the world's largest producer of coal, and except for a few years in the early twentieth century when the Baku fields put Russia slightly ahead, the United States remained the world's leading extractor of crude oil for a century, from the late 1860s to the early 1970s (Smil 2010). And those unequaled quantities of fuel supply, whether measured in absolute or in per capita terms, were available at low, even very low, cost.

All of this began to change during the early 1970s, and while the rising prices of gasoline or home heating oil received plenty of attention, the challenge of a higher energy cost was particularly great for American manufacturing, which had enjoyed more than a century of abundant and inexpensive fuel and electricity supply and now had to cope with new energy realities to stay competitive. The increase in oil prices had the widest systemic effect because it coincided with peak domestic oil extraction and with the onset of rapidly rising imports. After increasing for 110 years (starting the count with Edwin Drake's Pennsylvania well in 1859), US crude oil production peaked in 1970 at 533.5 Mt, and the additional demand had to be satisfied by higher imports.

In 1975, US crude oil output, the world's largest since the early years of the twentieth century, was surpassed by the Soviet production, and by 1977 Saudi Arabia had also begun to extract more oil. The peak in US oil output led to a momentous change whose impact was appreciated at the time by only a handful of energy experts: in March 1971 the Texas Railroad Commission, an agency that had been allotting the state's oil production quotas and hence de facto controlling oil prices in the world's largest producer, lifted all limits on crude oil extraction. This was a clear recognition of an epoch-ending loss of price-controlling power that opened the way for OPEC's price setting, with the United States itself the greatest loser.

Had oil prices continued to be as low as they were during the 1950s and 1960s, the United States could easily have afforded its higher reliance on imports. In 1970 the country's net crude oil imports of about 120 Mt were about 23% of the total demand, and were confined overwhelmingly to shipments from the country's two neighbors, Mexico and Canada, and from Venezuela. By 1980 US crude oil imports had nearly doubled, to 314 Mt, and their share of total consumption had risen to 40%, but because of OPEC's two intervening rounds of oil price increases (1973–1974 and 1979–1980), which lifted the average cost of a barrel from about $3.30 in 1970 to nearly $37 in 1980, the overall cost of these imports rose nearly 30-fold. Moreover, an increasing share of the United States' 1980 crude oil imports originated in the Eastern Hemisphere, creating new concerns about the security of the supply.

After OPEC began asserting its pricing power in 1973, all fuel prices began to rise. The average price of US bituminous coal—the fuel used to produce all of the country's metallurgical coke and to generate half of America's electricity—rose in real terms by 80% between 1973 and 1978, and natural gas prices more than doubled during the late 1970s. Rising coal prices had a particularly great impact on the iron and steel industry, and rising natural gas prices affected above all a variety of chemical industries, in which the fuel is used not only as the main source of energy but also as a key feedstock (most notably in the Haber-Bosch synthesis of ammonia and in the production of ethylene). The price of electricity, the ubiquitous energizer of modern manufacturing, was low and stable until 1973, but by 1983 it had tripled in nominal terms and risen by 50% in real terms (US EIA 2012).

US industries responded by reducing their energy intensity, the amount of fuels and electricity used per unit of economic product. Before OPEC's first price increases the United States' industrial energy use (including extractive industries and manufacturing) was growing at rates only slightly slower than the country's overall fuel and electricity consumption, with respective total gains of 42% and 50% during the 1960s and a further 10% and 12% between 1970 and 1973. Then came the first divergence: between 1973 and 1980 the overall energy demand rose by 3%, but the consumption of industrial energy declined by 2% and the demand for crude oil fell by 5%. The divergence continued during the 1980s as more industrial enterprises began to use energy more rationally. Although the country's total energy consumption increased by 8% during the 1980s, the total use of industrial energy fell by 1% and industrial oil demand declined by 13%.

Schipper, Howarth, and Geller (1990) investigated energy use in all sectors of the US economy between 1973 and 1987 and found that during that period, no other economic sector reduced its energy intensity to such an extent as manufacturing. When measured per unit of value added, energy use declined by 5% for freight shipments, 20% for passenger transportation, 24% for residential energy use, 29% for services, and 31% for manufacturing. Moreover, aggregate energy use in manufacturing fell by 21%, while residential consumption declined by only 3% and all other sectors showed overall gains in energy use. But the most interesting findings of that study concerned the importance of structural change as a key factor in the declining energy intensity in manufacturing and a relatively constant rate of average annual declines in energy efficiency.

Although the structural change (manifested above all in a reduction in the energy shares of energy-intensive metallurgical or chemical processes) had no appreciable impact on energy use in manufacturing between 1958 (the earliest year for which suitably disaggregated data are available) and 1973, it became a factor afterward. Between 1973 and 1985, structural changes lowered energy use in US manufacturing by 18%, or at an average rate of 1.6% a year, and coal, rather than crude oil, accounted for most of those savings. Its use declined by 33% during those 12 years, while the consumption of liquid fuels fell by only 16%. The decline of America's iron and steel industry was the single most important factor behind the structural change in manufacturing. This was not a specific US experience. A reconstitution of the steel industry that deemphasized traditional integrated enterprises and led to the rise of mini-mills took place in both Europe and Japan, but the loss of jobs was relatively greater in the United States, where sectoral employment fell by 77% between 1974 and 2000, than in either Germany or Japan, where the declines were respectively about 67% and 63% (Herrigel 2010).

Manufacturers in energy-intensive industries responded to higher energy prices by adopting more energy-efficient processes. Between 1972 and 1980 energy efficiency rose by 22% in the chemical industry and by 19% in oil refining, compared to 10% in aluminum smelting, another energy-intensive activity (Hirst et al. 1983). Monitoring of energy efficiency improvements by 120 large chemical manufacturers showed that their use of premium liquid and gaseous fuels declined from 56% to 45% of the overall consumption between 1972 and 1982 while their overall fuel efficiency rose by nearly 25% (Thoreson, Rowberg, and Ryan 1985). Similarly, the American Chemistry Council (2008) reported that between 1974 and 1986, the US chemical industry cut its energy consumption by 25%. Other energy-intensive sectors also had major gains. Reductions in the amount of clinker per unit of cement output and various process improvements cut the specific use of energy in US cement production by nearly a third between 1973 and 1990 (Worrell and Galitsky 2008).

But prompt and deep consumption cuts were not the norm. Schipper, Howarth, and Geller (1990) found that efficiency gains were driven primarily by long-term technical improvements rather than by short-term responses to increased prices, and a fairly pronounced price effect can be seen only in the case of crude oil. This outcome is not that surprising if we consider that for most industries, energy is a relatively small fraction of total input costs, and their energy savings arise indirectly, through reduced capital and labor expenditures. These efforts are essential components of constant technical and managerial innovation, and as a result, the post-1973 energy gains in US manufacturing were not that different from the pre-1973 period.

International comparisons of declines in the use of manufacturing energy (with data disaggregated into seven major subsectors) illustrate not only some national peculiarities but also the relative contributions of structural changes. Unander and colleagues (1999) found that between 1973 and 1986, energy use in US manufacturing declined annually by 1.9% (compared to 1.8% in Japan and Germany) and that the energy intensity in manufacturing fell by 2.8% a year (compared to 2.6% in Germany and 6.9% in Japan). The portion of the decline attributable to structural change was 1.1% a year, compared to 0.4% in Germany and 2% in Japan. Most of the structural change in US manufacturing was due to a substantial reduction of iron and steel manufacturing and a rapid rise of non-energy-intensive sectors. In a later review, Unander (2007) revisited these trends and revised the average annual US rates for 1973–1986 to –2.1% for overall energy use in manufacturing, –3.5% change in energy intensity, and –1.3% attributable to structural changes.

But the most revealing analysis of changes in the post-1973 energy intensity of US manufacturing was published by Lescaroux (2008), who performed a three-term decomposition of an intensity index to quantify the contributions of changes in industrial structure, efficiency gains at the sectoral level, and substitutions among energy sources to overall productivity improvements between 1974 and 1998. He found a total energy intensity reduction of about 40% between 1974 and 1986 (followed by years of small fluctuations with no substantial change between the mid-1980s and the late 1990s). Efficiency gains at the sectoral level drove this shift between 1974 and 1982, but substitutions among energy resources appeared to be more important than changes in industrial structure. In the long run, rising energy prices reduced manufacturing's energy intensity mainly through resource substitution, while changes in industrial structure affected the intensity in the short run (18 months to three years) but their long-term effect is secondary. This leaves efficiency gains at the sectoral level as the main source of variations.

All of these analyses agree on the relatively high importance (between a quarter and a third) of structural shifts in reducing post-1973 energy use in US manufacturing. By far the most consequential example of this structural shift was a rapid retreat of the US iron and steel industry, which was associated with significant output declines and major job losses. The United States' raw steel production was halved between 1973 and 1982, with the drop between 1981 and 1982 amounting to 38% (or three-quarters of the decadal decline). The total number of workers in the iron and steel industry was similarly halved between 1973 and 1984, to fewer than 200,000 (DiFrancesco et al. 2010).

### Problems in the Auto Industry

The first significant milestone in the retreat of the US auto industry from its commanding post–World War II position was reached in 1968, when imported cars, mostly inexpensive German Volkswagens, accounted for the first time for more than 10% of annual US motor vehicle retail sales. Even so, this was just a marginal, niche market that did not imperil the massive sales of the Big Four in general and GM and Ford in particular. Even the early Japanese car imports of the 1960s and the early 1970s were not seen as a major threat: nobody envisaged that Honda or Toyota cars would be the bestselling models just a decade after their entry into the US market.

But in retrospect, it appears that American carmakers turned into resigned bystanders simply watching their own gradual weakening; their counteractions were clearly inadequate. The retreat of the country's largest manufacturing industry began in earnest in the mid-1970s as imports captured more than 15% of all retail sales in 1973, then surpassed 20% in 1979 as 2.3 million cars (including 1.85 million from Japan) were shipped from abroad (MVMA 1985). This was a result of four independent but symbiotic trends. The oldest one was the lack of appropriate innovation and inertial development of American car designs. For too long the machines stayed too large, too inefficient, and, on average, too unreliable.

The second one was the relatively high prices of American cars, attributable mainly to the combination of high wages and generous benefits that the United Auto Workers, the union representing all workers in Detroit's factories, secured through strikes and bargaining since the 1950s—in 1979, hourly wages in the US auto and parts industry were twice the Japanese average (CBO 1980)—and the higher productivity (as much as 40%–50% above the typical US level) of Japanese car manufacturing, largely a result of better assembly processes and superior workforce management (Abernathy et al. 1982; Smil 2006). This gave Japanese companies a significant cost advantage of at least $750 but more likely $1,200–$1,500 per vehicle.

The third one was a combination of good value, rapidly improving quality (in 1977 the first imported Honda Accord had serious body rust problems, but five years later the car was judged at the top of its class), and the relatively high fuel efficiency of imported (overwhelmingly subcompact and compact) Japanese cars. Japanese cars of the late 1970s and the early 1980s came with fewer defects, most of them were more appealingly designed than their US counterparts, and they quickly earned millions of loyal buyers (Womack, Jones, and Roos 1990). By 1980 owner surveys were putting only one US model among the 11 top-rated small cars, and nearly 90% of buyers rated imported vehicles as better than, or much better than, average (CBO 1980). After switching from Fords and Chevys to Hondas and Toyotas, most customers stayed with the imports and were rewarded by driving well-built, reliable vehicles.

The most shocking was the fourth change, two sudden OPEC-driven increases in oil prices, the first one in 1973–1974, which quintupled the world oil price, and the second one, precipitated by the fall of the Iranian monarchy, in 1979–1981, which more than tripled the world oil price and led to a worldwide economic slowdown and rising unemployment—and to increasing demand for smaller, more efficient vehicles, the category neglected by Detroit for decades. The shift was rapid: in 1978 compacts claimed 48% of US car sales, but by April 1980 their share was up to 66% (CBO 1980). The average performance of American cars kept on declining for 40 years, with the lowest gas mileage in 1973 at 13.4 mpg (Sivak and Tsimhoni 2009; Smil 2011).

Besides the obvious waste of energy, this poor performance was also a key cause of high levels of photochemical smog in most of America's large urban areas, a harmful form of air pollution that began to be addressed in earnest only in the early 1970s with the introduction of three-way catalytic converters, which greatly reduced emissions of carbon monoxide, nitrogen oxides, and volatile hydrocarbons. Only after the first round of oil price rises did the US Congress enact the Corporate Average Fuel Economy (CAFE) regulations in 1975, with the first efficiency increases taking place in 1978 (for cars) and 1979 (for light trucks). CAFE rules mandated a minimum performance for new vehicles of 20 mpg for passenger cars (and 16 mpg for two-wheel-drive light trucks) in 1980 and 27.5 mpg (19.7 for light trucks) by 1985.

These were not onerous specifications as cars of similar or greater efficiency were routinely produced in Europe and Japan—but in light of Detroit's long-standing preference for large, fuel-wasting vehicles, their achievement required considerable adjustment of the vehicle mix (and hence new designs and retooling) to meet the mandated corporate averages. This, along with compliance with other newly mandated environmental and safety regulations, led to higher costs and many new designs of low quality precisely at a time when lower prices and high quality were in unprecedented demand. Detroit was unprepared to deliver fuel-efficient, well-built, inexpensive vehicles that would offer excellent value for the money—and it paid a high price for this failure.

Between 1979 and 1981, sales of US-made cars dropped by 25%, while sales of imports remained steady at 2.3 million vehicles a year, and by June 1980 accounted for nearly 30% of all sales. And 1980 was also the first year when Japan produced more cars than the United States (roughly 11 million vs. eight million). The resulting decline of the US auto industry was swift and substantial. In 1978 the sector employed just over one million people, but two years later the total was 22% lower, and the drop was even greater, 26%, or 270,000 jobs, for production workers

(MVMA 1985). The industry's high multiplier effect meant that loss of jobs resulted in additional job losses in other industries, above all in the steel and aluminum sectors. Chrysler was bailed out in 1979 with $1.5 billion in federal loan guarantees; there was no profit realized on the average vehicle sold in 1980, and only minimal gains in 1981; and everybody agreed that the US automobile industry was in crisis.

The chosen way out was a wrong strategy to follow. Voluntary export restrictions (VER) was the euphemism chosen to describe the converging interests of two antagonists, US politicians responding to demands by unions and companies to ease the pressure on domestic carmakers (even as public opinion polls showed continued support for imports) and the Japanese government and car exporters, who preferred to avoid a greater backlash (and possibly deeper cuts) by resorting, judo-like, to a partial retreat. The imposition of any export restrictions was against the open-market principles promoted by the United States in the General Agreement on Tariffs and Trade (GATT, the WTO's precursor) and was also contrary to US antitrust law; hence, only by pretending it was voluntary and unilateral could it avoid violating existing regulations (Sousa 1982). There is no better illustration of how far and how fast the US auto industry had declined by 1980 than the need to resort to this arrangement.

The VER agreement, made on May 1, 1981, was to limit Japanese exports to 1.68 million vehicles a year for three years, but in 1984 it was extended at the higher figure of 1.85 million vehicles a year. Its eventual effect was to raise Japanese car prices (by an equivalent of about 8%), improve sales of domestic cars, and increase substantially the profits of Detroit carmakers (Berry, Levinsohn, and Pakes 1999). Japanese carmakers protected their earnings by shifting the composition of exports toward higher-priced vehicles (this shift accounted for about two-thirds of the price increases caused by the VER), and Feenstra (1984) calculated that the agreement was responsible for adding only 19,000 jobs, eliminating only one-tenth of the car industry's unemployment, by late 1981. Similarly, Crandall (1987) concluded that the VER added substantially to the cash flow of US carmakers but had a small effect on employment, and that overall welfare losses were unlikely to be recouped through higher productivity and quality gains.

Japan remained committed to a voluntary quota of 2.5 million passenger cars until 1992, but actual imports stayed well below that level ever since 1987 as a result of rising car output from US-based Japanese plants. Consequently, US car imports peaked at 30% in 1987 and then began to decline: by 1994 they were below 20%, and two years later they fell temporarily below 15%—not because of any resurgence of American carmaking but because every major Japanese car company set up new assembly plants in the United States, and some also did so in Canada, with the 1988 North American Free Trade Agreement guaranteeing access to the US market (Russ 2009).

Honda, originally a maker of motorcycles, began its American car manufacturing in 1982 with a factory in Marysville, Ohio. Toyota set up its first American factory as a joint project with GM (New United Motor Manufacturing Inc., or NUMMI) in Fremont, California, in 1984. Nissan followed in 1985 with a plant in Smyrna, Tennessee, and Mazda in 1987 with an assembly plant in Flat Rock, Michigan. In 1988 came two new plants, a Mitsubishi-Chrysler operation in Bloomington, Illinois, and Toyota's factory in Georgetown, Kentucky. This brought the total capacity of US-based Japanese plants to 1.53 million cars a year. Obviously, these new plants helped prevent substantial labor losses in domestic car manufacturing, and as the economy recovered during the 1990s, overall employment in US car and parts manufacturing rose once again, to one million people by 1999, but neither the VER nor the post-1982 Detroit recovery was able to increase the market share claimed by US automakers.

Japanese imports had 19% of all domestic sales in 1980, but by the end of the 1990s Japanese firms (manufacturing in the United States and importing from Japan) had increased their share to 30%. Meanwhile, the world's largest automaker was getting steadily weaker: GM's share of the US car market peaked around 1960 with a nearly 50% share; by 1970 it was below 45%, in 1980 it was 41.4%, by 1990 it had declined to 33%, and by the end of the 1990s it had slipped below 30%. More important, the US shift toward smaller, more efficient vehicles was largely abandoned once the world oil price collapsed in 1985. Small car sales peaked in 1983 at almost 39% of the total and by 1999 had declined to just 23%; concurrently, the share of midsized vehicles rose from about 41% to nearly 53%. And, mostly as a result of the first wave of incongruously named SUVs (where is the sport in driving them to a shopping mall?), larger luxury models went up from less than 10% to almost 17% of all sales (Ward's Communications 2000).

Because SUVs were exempt from CAFE standards, many models averaged less than 20 mpg, and some even less than 15 mpg. Nobody appeared to be bothered by this. In 1985, when the steadily rising CAFE standards for passenger cars reached 27.5 mpg, the United States abandoned its decade-long effort to make ordinary cars more efficient and left the standards unchanged for the next 25 years. And because of an intervening shift to much less efficient SUVs and light trucks, which were subject to much lower CAFE limits than passenger cars, the overall efficiency of the entire US vehicle fleet was no higher in 2005 (at just below 25 mpg) than it was in the early 1980s.

**Electronic Triumphs and Defeats**

During the 1970s and 1980s American inventors, engineers, and entrepreneurs created not only new electronic products but entirely new manufacturing sectors whose revenue soon rose to rival, then surpass, many long-established industrial activities. The era's key innovations were the first personal computers, which had limited market reach and appeal (1974–1980); the widespread adoption of personal computers, driven above all by the success of IBM's PC and Apple's Macintosh (1981–1984); and the gradual introduction and improvement of key hardware and software components that by 1990 had coalesced into the Internet.

In the last chapter I briefly described the first Intel microprocessors and the first commercial successes of its more powerful designs. The company's success in following closely Gordon Moore's prediction of performance doubling every two years received a great deal of popular attention (Intel 2011). In 1974 came the 8080 microprocessor, with 5,000 transistors. Five years later the 8088 had 29,000 transistors, and the choice of the 8088 as the CPU of IBM's first PC made it the first microchip with an annual production run of more than 10 million units. The fabrication of microprocessors moved from large-scale integration (up to 100,000 transistors on a microchip) to very large-scale integration (up to 10 million transistors) in 1980 and then to ultra-large-scale integration (up to a billion transistors) in 1990.

But personal computers could not become quotidian consumer items without integrating those more powerful and less expensive microprocessors with other hardware components and without animating them appropriately with reliable software. Only the symbiotic development of hardware and software could create a new manufacturing sector and transform computers from expensive machines for special uses to cheap devices produced by the tens of millions. This technical symbiosis is also a perfect example of a new kind of manufacturing in which the hardware cannot function without laboriously designed components whose creation would normally be classed as a service category. In fact, the interdependence is even greater, as complex software has routinely been used to design new microprocessors and guide their fabrication. In no other industry it is less possible to separate hardware, the manufacturing and operation of devices and machines, from software, the intellectual service component of designing and guiding their functions.

Remarkably, nearly all other critical components of the entire hardware-and-software package needed to make user-friendly personal computers were created and deployed during the 1970s by the Xerox Palo Alto Research Center (Xerox PARC 2011). PARC came up with a WYSIWYG—what you see is what you get—editing and graphical user interface (using icons and pop-up menus). It also introduced the combination of text editing and graphics, offered spell checking and a thesaurus option, and made editing, file servers, and printers easily accessible by the point-and-click ability of an ergonomic mouse, an older invention by Douglas Engelbart that was patented in 1967.

But Xerox leadership lacked the imagination to turn these advances into commercial products (Smith and Alexander 1988). Xerox had actually come close to disappearing, and it was left to others, including computing enthusiasts and hobbyists, to turn these prototypes into commercially successful designs. This was an almost exclusively American affair, with new designs introduced in rapid succession and with performance rising and prices falling. The first programmable calculator, the HP-65, came in 1974. It was quickly followed by the Altair, the first personal computer (initially sold without any keyboard or display and programmed by toggle switches), which was featured on the January 1975 cover of *Popular Electronics*.

The second innovation wave, in 1977, brought several designs that became ephemerally successful, but only one marked the beginning of a longlasting series of machines. The Apple II was the commercial breakthrough by a company that famously originated in a Cupertino garage, and Steve Wozniak's design took advantage of PARC's inventions (Moritz

1984; Ceruzzi 2003). By 1980 the annual sales of personal computers had surpassed one million units, with the TRS-80, Atari 400 and 800, Commodore PET, and Apple II accounting for most of the sales, and in 1981 Adam Osborne introduced the Osborne 1, the first portable computer. As important as these designs were in the evolution of personal computers, the single greatest impulse for their large-scale adoption came with IBM's development of a machine that became known simply as the PC.

The design took only about a year to develop, and in physical terms it was not a true IBM product, as it consisted of readily available parts (made by a variety of electronics companies in several countries) and was connected to a previously developed IBM monitor. In 1982, *Time* made the computer its Machine of the Year, and in 1984 IBM sold two million units. Unlike Apple, IBM made public the machine's complete circuitry, source code, and programming information.

The IBM PC initially had a strong competitor in the Commodore 64, which captured 40% of the market in 1984, but IBM PCs and their clones ranked first the next year, and by 1990, when US sales of personal computers reached 20 million units, they accounted for nearly 85% of the total. By that time every one of the other surviving early designs, including the Atari, Amiga, and Apple, had only a few percent of the maturing market, and attention shifted from new hardware designs to new computing capabilities, particularly the ability to act as an instant means of communication and information retrieval.

The original proposal of an Internet-like web was made by Joseph Licklider in 1962, and the Pentagon's Advanced Research Project Agency (ARPA) began to operate the ARPANET (initially restricted to just four sites) in 1969 (Waldrop 2001). In 1972 Ray Tomlinson wrote the first programs that made it possible to send messages, and even chose @ as the locator symbol for e-mail addresses (Tomlinson 2002). Two years later Vinton Cerf and Robert Kahn made it possible to communicate across a system of networks, and by 1983 the Internet was in place. In 1988 NSFNET linked more than 170 networks, and in 1989, when the connections grew to more than 100,000 hosts, the first commercial Internet services were offered by CERFNET, UUNET, and PSINet. The World Wide Web followed a year later.

But even as American innovators were riding this wave of e-triumphs, the industry making these achievements possible found itself in considerable trouble. This anxious chapter in the history of America's manufacturing has been superseded by many greater worries but deserves a closer look, not only because it was the first major challenge of its kind but even more so because of the way it was resolved. The anguish about the future of the semiconductor industry that preoccupied so many American leaders during the 1980s seems incomprehensible when viewed from the vantage point of the second decade of the twenty-first century: since 1990, American manufacturing has given away so much more with little publically voiced concern.

Right after the second round (1979–1981) of OPEC's oil price increases, with a recession, relatively high unemployment, and another spell of deteriorating relations with the USSR, the United States had no shortage of economic and political challenges. But it was still a net creditor state, its trade deficit was tolerably low, and although its previously unchallenged automobile and aircraft industries had to deal with new Japanese and European competitors, they faced no imminent danger of becoming second-rank players. That was not the case with the country's semiconductor industry. Solid-state electronics in general and the large-scale fabrication of semiconductors in particular were thoroughly American inventions. US manufacturers were the only silicon transistor makers during the 1960s, and, after the release of Intel's first microchip in 1971, they dominated that most advanced field of solid-state electronics for the rest of the decade (SIA 2011).

In 1976 US makers had 65% of the global market, compared to 4% for Japan; in 1980 the shares were 55% and 4%. But in the second half of the decade US primacy in making certain types of devices came under pressure from Japanese makers: in 1974 the US-Japan split of the global 4k microchip market was a worry-free 83 to 17, but just three years later the United States had no more than 59% of the 16k market and Japan had 41%. By 1982 Japan was producing 92% of 256k chips; in 1984 it had 32% of the overall global market, compared to 43% for US companies; and by the end of 1985, the year in which Japan captured 96% of the global market for the first 1M microchip, it was ahead with 38%, compared to the US 35%. By 1987 the US market share had declined to 30%, while the Japanese share had reached 42% (SIA 2011).

This was a threat different from the one faced by the auto industry because its repercussions extended across all economic sectors and had obvious effects on US military capabilities. In May 1986, responding to this rapid reversal of US fortunes, the Semiconductor Industry Association and Semiconductor Research Corporation called for the creation of a nonprofit consortium to pool the resources of US companies and the financial aid of the US government in order to regain the global leadership in microchip making. In 1987 14 US-based semiconductor companies formally established SEMATECH (SEmiconductor Manufacturing TECHnology), and in December of that year the Reagan administration approved the first $100 million in matching funds as part of a Defense Advanced Research Agency program (SEMATECH 2011).

In 1988 Robert Noyce of Intel became the first SEMATECH CEO, and the first fabrication facility opened in Austin in November. By 1990 the difference between US and Japanese shares of the world semiconductor market had reached its greatest extent (less than 27% vs. 42%), but in 1992 the order was reversed as the revenues of US manufacturers were nearly 2% higher. By 1996, when the consortium members voted to discontinue the federal subsidies, the gap had grown to more than 25%, and the United States kept its leading position in semiconductor fabrication for the rest of the decade, claiming 31% of the global market in the year 2000, compared to 24% for Japan.

In retrospect, it would be wrong to credit all, or perhaps even most, of this reversal of fortune to SEMATECH. Irwin and Klenow (1996) concluded that the federal subsidies did not induce more semiconductor research than would have taken place otherwise. SEMATECH eventually expanded to an international consortium of semiconductor manufacturers and now works as a collaboration of chipmakers, suppliers, research organizations, and governments. It has recently introduced new lithography techniques, identified new transistor materials, and worked to maximize the productivity of fabrication facilities and reduce production costs (SEMATECH 2010).

When American businesses and politicians of the late 1980s were marshaling defenses against Japan's economic might, they did not know they were mobilizing against a challenge that was about to implode. After years of a rapid stock market rise, a speculative climb in property prices, currency appreciation, and unrealistic expectations, there came the economic reversals of the 1990s, which demoted Japan from the feared position of an unstoppable economic superpower. That threat receded—but in the early 1990s American manufacturers did not realize it would be China, not Japan, that would pose by far the greatest challenge to the US economy of the twenty-first century.

But even as US hardware makers worried about their future, the country's software designers were setting down solid foundations for the industry's progress and for the continuing dominance of their products in the new e-world. Manufacturing has greatly benefited from computer-assisted design (CAD), whose tentative beginnings go to the 1960s and whose real ascent (in both 2D and 3D forms) began during the 1980s, thanks to such programs as AutoCad, introduced by Autodesk in 1982, and Pro/Engineer, introduced in 1986 (the most recent products of the Massachusetts-based company is Creo, launched in 2010).

But general-purpose software has been no less important for management and communication in the manufacturing sector, and a few other applications have made such a contribution as spreadsheets. Their success began timidly with VisiCalc, in 1978. By 1980 the field had progressed to a successful Lotus 1-2-3, but it was Microsoft's Office Excel (released in 1985, and thus predating Windows) that proved the ultimate winner and that, more than a quarter century later, remains the world's leading spreadsheet. During the 1980s Microsoft also introduced and gradually improved a key product that has become indispensable for efficiently using the increasing capabilities of new computers. The Windows operating system became first available in 1987 and by 2008 was installed on more than one billion computers worldwide. Another ubiquitous design, one much helped by an explosion of cell phone ownership, is Java, launched in 1991 by Sun Microsystems. And all of the three other leading computing platforms—Linux, the Mac OS, and UNIX—are also American.

For most people, computer use is synonymous with word processing, and here again, US software designers led the innovation wave during the 1980s with programs such as Word, WordStar, Multimate, and WordPerfect, but Microsoft's Word gained an early dominance, and by the late 1990s its market share had surpassed 80%; it is now above 90%. America's software designers have thus done an outstanding job in pioneering a new industry and bringing it to a rapid maturity—but strong and rising worldwide sales of their products have not been able to make up for the country's massive purchases of electronic hardware, and the United States thus has a large trade deficit in the high-tech sector.

## Multiple Failures, 1991–2012

The 1990s were, deceptively, much kinder to the United States than the 1980s. A triumphal victory in the Gulf War in February 1991 was followed by the peaceful dissolution of the Soviet Union in December 1991. Crude oil prices had stabilized within, in retrospect, an amazingly narrow and affordable band between $15 and $20 per barrel, and the country's economy appeared to have been rejuvenated by the dizzying rise of its new, e-based economy, which was rapidly driving the stock market to record heights. The Dow Jones Industrial Average rose from 2,800 in

**Figure 4.3**
American flag made in China. Color image available at http://nova100.typepad.com/.a/6a00d8341c684553ef012875b19cef970c-800wi

January 1990 to 11,400 in December 1999; during the same period the NASDAQ Composite Index soared by an order of magnitude, from about 450 to just over 4,000.

This new wealth rapidly spilled into excessive consumption, and two items became icons of this excess. In 1992, American Motors General began retailing a civilian version of a high-mobility, multipurpose wheeled vehicle (HMMWV). GM bought the brand in 1998 and eventually produced three models of the Hummer, a vehicle its website called "like nothing else"—as indeed it was, with a mass up to 3 t and an extravagant fuel consumption (fuel waste would be a better term) of 6 mpg. The second icon of excess was the McMansion, which can be characterized as a sprawling, ostentatious, yet rather shoddily built house with so many rooms that some remained unvisited for months and with at least three garages, an outdoor pool, indoor Jacuzzis, and a dubiously furnished great room with a cathedral ceiling.

Amid this e-boom and excess consumption, US manufacturing seemed to be doing well: its total value added to the country's GDP rose (in real terms) by 46% between 1990 and 2000, and overall employment in the sector not only held but actually rose slightly, by about 3%. But underneath this veneer of good news the trends that had begun weakening the foundations of the country's economy during the 1970s and 1980s were only accelerating. In 1996 crude oil imports supplied for the first time more than half the total demand. A significant decline in the trade deficit that began in 1988 lasted only until 1992, after which the rise resumed, and new records were reached in rapid succession: in 1999 the country still had a (diminishing) surplus in service trade, but its deficit in trading goods had surpassed $330 billion, for an overall net outflow of nearly $265 billion.

By the year 2000 the country's net international investment position had fallen to a deficit larger than $1 trillion, and it continued to slide, surpassing $2.7 trillion in deficit by the end of 2009. A new energy dependence record was reached in 2001 as US imports of crude oil and refined petroleum products rose to 60% of the total consumption—and then grew to 66% just four years later. The terrorists who attacked on September 11, 2001, succeeded in damaging the US economy: the direct losses were a small fraction of the enormous sums that the United States began to spend on massive new bureaucracies (the Department of Homeland

Security), on much expanded information gathering, and on waging wars in Afghanistan and Iraq that, in the absence of any new taxation—indeed, at a time of large tax cuts—had to be funded by increased borrowing.

And then the country was hit by the global economic crisis of 2008–2009, the worst downturn of the entire post–World War II era. The effects of the crisis were fought by the US government with huge bailouts of financial institutions and auto companies and with federal spending aimed at stimulating the economy. The federal budget deficit began to multiply. After four years of budget surpluses (1998–2001), the deficit rose to nearly $320 billion in 2005, then quadrupled to $1.293 trillion in 2010; it remained even slightly higher in 2011 ($1.3 trillion) and 2012 ($1.327 trillion) (White House 2012). As a result, the accumulated US debt increased from $5.7 trillion in December 2000 to $13.5 trillion by the end 2010; it was $14.8 trillion a year later, and well over $16 trillion by the end of 2012.

This massive debt load has required repeated lifting of federal debt ceilings and led to the downgrading of the country's AAA rating as Standard and Poor's lowered it to AA+ in August 2011. Incredibly, during this period the country showed no signs of voluntary austerity as it continued its extravagant purchases of foreign goods: in 2006 its trade deficit reached a new record of nearly $753 billion, a sum larger than the annual GDP of all but the world's 13 largest economies in that year, and the deficit remained close to $700 billion in 2007 and 2008. The economic downturn cut the deficit to less than $400 billion in 2009, but by 2011 it had risen to $560 billion, and in 2012 it came even closer to $600 billion (USBC 2012a).

Meanwhile, American manufacturing, which began the twenty-first century with nearly 17.2 million workers, saw that total plunge by 17% in just five years. Another depressing milestone was reached in 2003: 22 years after government workers became the largest category of the country's employees, the retail sector rose to second place, surpassing the manufacturing labor force by more than 600,000 people. By 2005 this gap had widened to more than 1.2 million, and by 2009, despite the decline in consumer spending brought on by the greatest economic downturn since World War II, the difference between jobs in manufacturing and in retail had reached nearly three million workers, a depressing reality of a failing economy where most new opportunities were low-paid, part-time positions to sell Chinese apparel and electronics bought on credit. The losses of manufacturing jobs continued when another 2.7 million workers were let go between 2005 and 2010, a 10% cut in five years that brought the total decadal loss to 5.7 million workers, or almost exactly a third of the manufacturing labor force in the year 2000.

This loss was worse than the loss of manufacturing jobs during the worst years of the Great Depression, which saw a 30.9% cut between 1929 and 1933. By 2010, 13 out of 19 manufacturing sectors were producing (in real terms) less than in 2000. Mass layoffs in manufacturing reached their peak in the last quarter of 2008 and the first two quarters of 2009: during those nine months there were nearly 4,000 such events around the country, and about 710,000 people lost their jobs (BLS 2012). The job loss of the first decade of the twenty-first century was not just another episodic decline in manufacturing employment that accompanies all recessions. Atkinson and colleagues (2012) showed that during the period from 12 months prior to the recession to the end of it, the average manufacturing job loss in all post–World War II recessions was 6.7%, and that the job rebound amounted to 6.4% 30 months after the recession. In contrast, the manufacturing loss during the period between 2000 and 2010 was 12.4% (nearly double the long-term mean), and by the end of 2011 manufacturing had recovered only about 200,000 jobs, less than 4% of the decadal loss.

By the end of 2010 manufacturing employed only 8.2% of US workers, compared to about 19% in Germany and 18% in Japan. After adding directly affected family members and the jobs lost in manufacturing-dependent services, this decline in manufacturing employment changed the lives of more than 20 million people. No wonder that the nationwide unemployment rate in early 2011 was above 10% and that the underemployment rate (including all part-time workers who wanted to work full-time) was 19.9% and rising (Gallup 2011)! These nationwide figures do not convey the misery of job losses at the state level: between 2000 and 2010 Michigan lost nearly 47% of its manufacturing jobs (mostly in the auto industry), and North Carolina lost almost 44% (mostly in textiles). The losses were in excess of 35% in such populous states as Ohio, New Jersey, and New York, and only 10 states had losses below 20% (BLS 2012).

Even so, many economists remained unconcerned, seeing manufacturing's retreat as just an obverse of the rising knowledge and service economy and deindustrialization as just a natural stage of economic development, a sign of a country getting richer. Atkinson and colleagues (2012) collected more than a dozen such representative quotes, many of them also claiming that productivity growth was the major reason for the post-2000 job losses and that these productivity-driven employment cuts, accompanied by rising output, should be seen as entirely desirable. But Atkinson and colleagues (2012) calculated that the official data greatly overstated increased labor productivity in manufacturing: it rose by no more than 32% (less than in the UK, Japan, and South Korea) rather than by the claimed 72%. They also calculated that when properly adjusted, the overall manufacturing output did not rise by 15.5% between 2000 and 2010 but actually fell by 11% during a period when the GDP rose by 17%. Among the major economies only Italy and Canada did worse, while the manufacturing's growth rate was 3.2% in Japan and 9.5% in Germany.

At the same time, the world recession hardly dented the post-1986 dominance of the financial sector. In 2009, despite the setbacks caused by the sector's often criminal mismanagement, an imploding housing market, and a shrinking economy, the sector added nearly twice as much value to the US economy as did all manufacturing, nearly 22% versus 11%. Stock market valuations reflect this manufacturing retreat. By the year 2000 three out of the five largest NYSE-listed companies were manufacturers: General Electric (number 2, including its huge nonmanufacturing involvement in finances and banking), Intel, and Merck (numbers four and five). By 2010 none of these was among the top five (GE had fallen to 10th place), and the only manufacturer in that group was Apple (second after Exxon), a company that did not make a single unit of any of its products in the United States but employed tens of thousands of workers in Asia. These are stunning statistics, but even more stunning is how the major manufacturing sectors fared between 1990 and 2010.

I will look first at those industries that suffered not only the largest employment losses but whose products either are no longer made in the United States or whose domestic production has been reduced to minority shares. These manufacturing categories include not only such long-lost cases as virtually all electric and electronic gadgets (ranging from irons and microwave ovens to flat-screen TVs and personal computers), low- and medium-priced textiles, and clothing and shoes but also furniture (a new post-2000 addition) and (since 2007, when foreign models, including those made in the United States, captured more than half the domestic market) passenger cars. A decline, or a complete demise, of domestic manufacturing has become no less common in the high-tech sector, where the United States was supposed to have a lasting comparative advantage. After appraising that weakening category I focus on the counterpart to this economic retreat, the new world of "Made in China" and sold by Walmart, a great symbiosis that has weakened US economic leadership in general and seriously undermined the country's manufacturing capabilities in particular.

**Sectoral Losses and Capitulations**

What happened to America's labor force in most sectors of manufacturing since 1990, and especially during the first decade of the twenty-first century, can be only partially described as a process of continuing losses: in some categories it amounted to nothing less than outright capitulations as closures of US plants and the offshoring of domestic capacities resulted in a nearly complete loss of industries that had dominated the lives of many cities and regions for generations and now appear to be irretrievably lost. These losses range from TVs (until 1992, Zenith Electronics had a small assembly plant in Springfield, Missouri) to cutlery: the last US maker of stainless steel flatware, Sherrill Manufacturing in New York, closed in 2010 (Sherrill Manufacturing 2010). And yet these losses have been seen by many economists as both inevitable, part of a continuing shift to an ever-widening array of services, and beneficial, because American consumers pay lower prices for clothes, electronics, furniture, and a myriad of other goods now made abroad, particularly in China.

Perhaps the best example of a manufacturing sector that is very close to total capitulation is leather-based manufacturing, embracing activities from tanning hides to making expensive handbags: between 1990 and 2010 this sector saw an 82% drop in total employment. Labor decline in this once large and diverse American industry—in 1850 it employed about 15% of all manufacturing labor—began during the late nineteenth century with the mechanization of tanning and shoemaking that continued during the twentieth century; even so, in the mid-1950s the industry still employed more than 300,000 workers (Ellsworth 1969). The subsequent large-scale imports of shoes and other leather goods from Europe, led by Italian and Spanish exports, and later also from Brazil reduced the total number employed to less than 100,000 by the mid-1990s; a wave of Chinese imports beginning in the late 1990s then cut the total to 25,000 by the end of 2011 (BLS 2012). The United States still slaughters every year more cattle—more than 30 million head—than any other country, and at more than 100 million animals its pig kill is second only to China's, but more than 90% of these hides and skins are now exported (earning more than $2 billion a year), with, predictably, China as their largest destination.

But the process that has advanced faster and gone further since 1990 than the losses in any other major manufacturing sector has been the great retreat of American textile and apparel production. Jobs in those two sectors have been disappearing since the late 1960s, but even so, the extent of job losses during the two decades between 1990 and 2010 is shocking. In those two decades employment in textile mills and textile product mills fell by 67% as apparel-makers let go 82% of their 1990 labor force, for an aggregate disappearance of more than 1.2 million workers in 20 years. Moreover, these losses often had an extraordinarily deep impact on smaller communities, where large fabric or apparel factories were the largest or the only substantial employers for generations, in many cases for more than a century.

While the deindustrialization of America has been widely seen and often studied as a problem of the northern Rust Belt, the largely southern phenomenon of textiles-related job losses (roughly half of all pre-collapse textile jobs were traditionally located in the Carolinas and in Georgia) has received much less attention. Minchin's (2009) inquiry into the effects of losing 4,800 jobs in Kannapolis, North Carolina, the site of America's largest textile mill, which closed in 2003, is one of few detailed appraisals of such events. The mill was established by James W. Cannon in 1908, and its area eventually surpassed that of the Pentagon. By the early 1970s Cannon Mills made more than half of all towels and more than a fifth of all American bedsheets. Besides the standard excuse about inability to compete, Pillowtex, the company's owner since 1997, also had excessive debt at the time it closed the Kannapolis plant—giving workers a two-hour notice—and shipped some of its looms to Pakistan.

A little appreciated fact is that, mainly because of its yarn and fabric sales, the United States remains the world's third largest exporter of textile products, with exports valued at $19.7 billion in 2010 and $22.4 billion in 2011, but massive imports of textiles and apparel have created a huge and increasing sectoral trade deficit (NCTO 2012). The deficit total reached $93.3 billion in 2010 (after rising by 15% above the 2009 value) and $101.3 billion in 2011, with China accounting for 40% and Vietnam a distant second at just over 7%, followed by India, Indonesia, and Mexico (OTEXA 2012). Another traditional manufacturing sector that has suffered heavy job losses is furniture making: in a decade it lost 43% of its workers, with only 350,000 remaining by the end of 2011 (BLS 2012).

Such impacts are never evenly distributed, and towns in southern states with larger plants specializing in wooden case goods were hit most by job losses to China (Drayse 2008). Sofas, wall units, large dining tables, beds, and dressers are relatively heavy and bulky, and hence the cost of shipping them from overseas is fairly high, amounting to 15%–25% of the product's value, compared to just a few percent for electronic gadgets. But that has not prevented Chinese furniture makers from dumping their products on the US market. They aggressively targeted wooden bedroom furniture, raising the category's share of US imports from 26% in 2001 to more than 50% by 2003, a gain leading to the loss of more than 35,000 jobs.

John Bassett, chairman of the largest US wooden bedroom furniture maker, Vaughan-Bassett Furniture of Galax, Virginia, led a successful fight against this dumping, and in 2004 a ruling by the Department of Commerce and the US International Trade Commission (USITC) confirmed that unfair pricing was injuring domestic furniture companies. Duties were placed on Chinese imports, subject to review every five years. A lengthy USITC ruling in November 2010 found that ending the duties would lead "to continuation or recurrence of material injury within a reasonably foreseeable time" (USITC 2010), improving the survival odds for the remaining domestic furniture makers.

Besides textiles and apparel, the only other sector with recent employment losses surpassing half a million jobs was the production of motor vehicles and parts. This sector employed nearly 50% fewer people in 2010 than it did in the year 2000. I noted earlier how the establishment of Japanese factories in the United States ended a further increase in market share claimed by imported vehicles. But while making Hondas in Ohio and Toyotas in Tennessee created new manufacturing jobs, other jobs were lost in existing plants of the US automakers, whose market share continued to fall steadily, from 72% in 1995 to 68% at the beginning of the year 2000 and to 59% five years later. By that time the Japanese car companies had claimed about 20% of America's light vehicle market. A crossroads came in the summer of 2007 when the Detroit Three began to sell less than half of all passenger cars and light trucks bought in the United States (Morgan and Company 2011). In 2010 the split was roughly 45% American and 55% foreign makers, with Japanese companies accounting for nearly 85% of the latter share; in 2011 the Detroit Three managed to increase their share to 47.1%.

In 1950 about 95% of cars sold in the United States were made by US companies. Sixty years later the country that invented mass automobile production bought most of its cars from foreigners and, surpassed by China, also ceased to be the world's largest car market. All US automakers lost market share, but GM fared worst. Its fall from the sector's dominance has been largely self-inflicted. The list of blunders is long: complacency born of being the world's largest automaker, the production of too many models sold under too many contrived brands, unappealing vehicle design, defect rates chronically higher than those of the Japanese imports, distracting and costly diversification (above all the GM Acceptance Corporation offering mortgages and getting involved in subprime loans), excessive costs (largely due to high health and pension benefits negotiated with the United Auto Workers union, and by 2005 prorating to at least $1,600 per vehicle), inadequate capital investment (about half the rate of the Japanese companies), and the reluctance of top managers to make radical changes.

Repeated promises of turnarounds and plans for regaining market share came and went with new executives even as the company's performance, and its market value, kept on declining. Why have American automakers lost more than half their domestic market? The high quality, excellent reliability, and great value of Japanese imports were obvious by the mid-1980s; why was no effective response evident even two decades later? Several factors combined to bring about this avoidable outcome. The most important original driver behind the market share losses was the poor quality of US-made cars. No less important was the inexcusable reluctance of Detroit's automakers to break with the past: for too long they believed that cosmetic changes would see them through what they considered just a period of aberration.

Two mitigating factors can be argued: at least until 1985, foreign carmakers had the benefit of undervalued currency, and once they began making vehicles in the United States, they were not burdened by excessive labor costs. Both are true, but the currency advantage disappeared with the Plaza Accord, and both Honda and Toyota paid their American workers well without committing themselves to such excessive health and retirement benefit packages as those won by the UAW. As a result, the UAW never succeeded in unionizing any Japanese plant (Russ 2009). I would argue that a key reason why any resolute fix was postponed was the abandonment of CAFE standards for passenger cars after 1985, a move that led to the rise of SUVs, vehicles that gave Detroit a period of increased earnings and a false feeling of long-term prosperity but that in reality only worsened its unavoidable crisis.

Because of the sector's traditionally high concentration in Detroit, this deindustrialization has had a truly devastating impact on the city (Leary 2011). Short of driving through what was once a real city, there is no better way to realize this than with a view from space. Satellite images show block after block of disappeared housing and the ruins of large factories. In 2009 the Detroit Residential Parcel Survey (2011) found that more than 91,000 lots and nearly 34,000 houses were vacant, which means that 26.5% of the city's nearly 344,000 lots had either no structures or no inhabitants. In several parts of the city more than 50% of residential lots are empty, with many abandoned structures damaged by arson. This is perhaps the most powerful retort to the inane claim that the United States is not losing manufacturing, only manufacturing jobs: obviously, Detroit would look different with most of its former jobs still intact.

The consequences of deindustrialization have also been all too obvious in such former centers of steelmaking as Youngstown, Ohio, where the retreat of the steel industry led to a more than 15% population decline per decade in every decade since the 1970s, or Gary, Indiana, a city whose economy was dominated by US Steel and whose population was more than halved between 1960 and 2010. But the repercussions have been felt throughout the US economy as laid-off workers began to miss their mortgage payments and as many corporations (led by car parts and steel companies) defaulted on their pension plans and transferred the liabilities to the Pension Benefit Guaranty Corporation, whose 2010 deficit was more than $20 billion (PBGC 2011).

Of course, foreign automakers have gradually become largely American as they are not merely assembling cars from imported parts but have come to rely on extensive networks of US-based suppliers and, in aggregate, are now significant employers, particularly in the southern states. They have invested $44 billion in 300 facilities employing directly 80,000 workers and have created another 500,000 supply and dealership jobs (Global Automakers 2012), but the profits go back to Japan, Germany, and South Korea, and virtually every one of those factory jobs has been made possible by often extremely generous infrastructural and tax subsidies offered by states competing for the location of new manufacturing plants.

### The Myth of High-Tech Dominance

Defenders of unlimited imports of consumer products do not see unconstrained importing as a problem because, they claim, America's proven high-tech prowess gives the country an unassailable competitive advantage in the global market, and exports of expensive advanced manufactures can pay for imports of inexpensive clothes, toys, and TVs. This mantra may sound soothing, but it is not true. The genesis of this mistaken impression is easy to understand: after all, US researchers and companies did invent and commercialize a disproportionately high share of what the US Census Bureau labels "advanced technology products" (ATPs), a category that includes modern goods made by the following manufacturing industries: information and communication, electronics, flexible manufacturing, advanced materials, aerospace, weapons, nuclear power, optoelectronics, biotechnology, medical diagnosis, and manufacture of drugs (USBC 2012b).

Unfortunately, these great pioneering efforts did not confer any commercial advantage during the closing decade of the twentieth century and the first decade of the twenty-first century. In 2000 the United States exported $222.5 billion of ATPs and had a very slight trade surplus in that trading category (about $5 billion). By 2002, however, the balance of ATP trade had turned negative. By 2005 the annual deficit had reached nearly $43 billion; in 2010 it surpassed $80 billion; in 2011 it reached almost $100 billion ($99.6 billion); and in 2012 the deficit was only slightly smaller (USBC 2012a). The only sector that has seen a strong recent increase in exports is electromedical equipment (including CT and MRI equipment), while sales of semiconductors, computers, and office equipment have declined by about a third in 10 years, hardly a trajectory inspiring hope for a continuing US high-tech leadership (in contrast, we are told, to China's leadership in low-tech assembly).

During the past two decades nearly all American ATP manufacturing has followed one of two trajectories, with neither one pointing upward. The first one has been a total sectoral capitulation; that is, the United States does not make a single unit of those products. The second one traces a substantial retreat from what was once a position of undisputed dominance and has resulted in a state that could best be described colloquially as no better than "hanging on" and facing even more daunting challenges in years to come. The best examples of the first trajectory are most of the goods belonging to a broad category of computers and electronic products. Not a single flat-screen, laptop, or tablet computer, not a single cell phone, not a single digital camera (to say nothing of TVs, DVD, and Blu-ray players, and electronic games) is now made in the United States, although many parts (above all microprocessors and other semiconductor products) from which some of these items are assembled in China, Taiwan, South Korea, Malaysia, or Indonesia come from US-based plants or from American-owned factories abroad.

Those who argue that the employment losses in low-tech manufacturing will be more than made up by gains in high-tech industries have not noticed that computers and electronics formed the manufacturing sector with the highest absolute job losses during the past two decades: with 760,000 workers gone between 1990 and 2010, it surpassed the total of 719,000 jobs lost in apparel-making. Not surprisingly, the entire sector has become more dependent on imports: between 2005 and 20011 the deficit in the computer trade more than doubled, from $19.4 billion to $48.1 billion (USBC 2012a).

One industry within this sector seems to be doing well, but a closer look reveals major concerns. American makers of semiconductors—some 24 companies, including the three pioneers, Fairchild Semiconductor, Texas Instruments, and Intel—remain the world's leading producers of these now ubiquitous products. Their share of global sales has been in the upper 40s since 1996 and in 2009 rose to nearly 51%

(compared to 20% for Japanese companies, 13% for South Korea, 12% for Europe, and 4% for Taiwan), and US makers are particularly dominant in microprocessors (producing more than 80% of worldwide output) and weak in memory chips (just over 20%). Despite this share gain the total nationwide employment in the production of semiconductors and electronic components fell from about 575,000 in December 2001 to 375,000 a decade later, with chipmakers employing about 185,000 people (SIA 2011).

And the surplus in the semiconductor trade declined from $21.2 billion in 2005 to just $5.9 billion in 2011 (USBC 2012a). This means that in 2011, US semiconductor producers netted the country less money than it cost to import toiletries and cosmetics! Moreover, the future of US semiconductor producers appears to be more uncertain than it was in the panicky years of the late 1980s because the expensive (multibillion) semiconductor fabrication facilities are increasingly located abroad: for example, Intel has three fabrication plants in Ireland and one each in Israel and China, as well as a number of assembly and testing plants in Asia. During the late 1990s, 30%–35% of all new semiconductor fabrication equipment was shipped to the United States, but by 2004 the share had declined to just 15%, and although it has recovered a bit it was below 25% in 2009, and investment in new semiconductor equipment was higher in both Japan and Taiwan and almost as high in South Korea, all considerably smaller economies (SIA 2010).

By 2009 only one of the 16 new plants under construction was in the United States, compared to six in China and five in Taiwan (SIA 2011). This shift can be largely attributed to the capital grants and tax benefits offered by Asian competitors; these advantages make it 10%–15% cheaper to locate outside the United States, for an absolute difference of close to $1 billion (Wilson 2011). By 2010 only 16% of the world's chip manufacturing capacity was located in the United States. That is why Intel's decision to build another fabrication plant at its Hillsboro, Oregon, site and to locate its most advanced fabrication plant (costing $5 billion) in Chandler, Arizona (to be ready in 2013), came as such welcome news. In 2010, the Semiconductor Industry Association called for a doubling of semiconductor exports in five years, to $76 billion, but achieving that goal would require some substantial changes to increase US competitiveness (SIA 2010).

America's aerospace industry in general, and the manufacturing of commercial aircraft in particular, is the most worrisome example in the other, "hanging-on" ATP category. The United States became the world leader in commercial aircraft designs during the 1930s as McDonnell Douglas and Boeing introduced, respectively, the revolutionary DC-3, the most successful propeller design in history, and the Clipper (the Boeing 314, the first machine to make transoceanic passenger flight a commercial reality). The wartime experience with designing and building superior fighters and bombers became a great asset for pioneering the era of jet flight, and by 1970 the United States was its undisputed leader. Its fighter and bomber planes had capabilities superior to all but a few Soviet designs, its production of small (general aviation) craft included dozens of models by such famous makers as Beechcraft, Cessna, and Gulfstream, and three companies—Boeing, McDonnell Douglas, and Lockheed—offered a large line-up of jet-powered aircraft.

That was the high point of the trajectory. Aerospace manufacturing then entered such a relentless decline that in 2002, when the Commission on the Future of the US Aerospace Industry issued its final report, the executive summary contained this rather worrisome statement (Walker et al. 2002, vi):

> We noted with interest how other countries that aspire for a great global role are directing intense attention and resources to foster an indigenous aerospace industry. This is in contrast to the attitude present here in the United States. We stand dangerously close to squandering the advantage bequeathed to us by prior generations of aerospace leaders. We must reverse this trend and march steadily towards rebuilding the industry.

This was always to be a difficult challenge, given the average age of the US aerospace workforce (45 years in 2009, 54 for Boeing's engineers), an ongoing wave of retirements, and increasing competition from foreign aircraft builders (Platzer 2009). Unfortunately, nearly a decade after the 2002 report there are no signs of any reversal in US aerospace fortunes. As the following summary statistics indicate, the industry is actually weaker than it was two decades ago. Its total product shipments, expressed in constant monies, were 18% lower in 2009 than they were in 1991 (and only 6% above the 2000 level), while the employment (overall as well as for production workers) was 40% lower (ITA 2011b).

And while the value of total aerospace exports had increased by nearly 70% since 1990 the value of imports had grown even faster. Still, the surplus (in current monies) in 2010 was still 60% above the 1990 level. But for the largest segment of the aerospace market, sales of commercial jetliners, the trend has been discouraging. Although 589 large commercial aircraft were delivered in 1991, the total was only 481 in 2009 and 462 in 2010 (and as few as 281 in 2003), a result of losing the global competition to Airbus (Platzer 2009; Airbus 2011). In 1971, when Airbus made its first sales, Boeing sold nine times as many jetliners (90 vs. 10). By 1980 the Boeing/Airbus ratio was nearly 12 (753/32), a decade later it declined to less than two (556/289), and in 1997, when Boeing merged with McDonnell Douglas, its edge was less than 25% (568/460). The year 1999 was the first year that Airbus sold more planes (476/392) than Boeing, and between 2001 and 2010 Airbus ended second only in 2006 and 2007. As for the actual deliveries, Airbus has led since 2003: that year the difference was just 24 planes (305 vs. 281), but by 2010 the gap had increased to 48 planes (510 vs. 462), and in 2011 it reached 57 planes (534 vs. 477).

Boeing was to reassert its primacy with a revolutionary new design. In late January 2003 it announced its plan to produce a plane for 210–330 passengers. The craft was originally designated the 7E7 Dreamliner; two years later it was numbered Boeing 787 (Boeing 2011). The aim was to build an aircraft to be used primarily for point-to-point connections (unlike the Airbus 380, which was designed for hub-to-hub flights) using 50% of composite materials by weight (80% by volume) and offering a more comfortable interior (larger windows, better air quality) at an operating cost 20% below the cost of the comparably sized Boeing 767. By the time the plane was rolled out in Seattle on July 8, 2007, it had captured a record number of orders, 677, for a new aircraft, but little has gone right afterward.

The original date for entering commercial service was May 2008, with All Nippon Airways (ANA) as the launch carrier, but a series of construction problems kept moving back the target day as the company was forced to announce a series of postponements. The maiden flight took place only in December 2009, and 11 months later the first test plane had to make an emergency landing in Texas because of smoke and fire aboard. The first 787 was finally delivered to ANA in September 2011, but the company still has many problems turning the innovative design into a quotidian mass-scale operation that will keep turning out the more than

800 planes already ordered. Airbus also faced many delays in launching its super-jumbo jet, but in the end it beat Boeing's 787 delays: the plane was announced in December 2000 and first flew commercially in October 2007, on a Singapore Airlines flight.

When the balance of aircraft trade is seen in a wider perspective, the impact of this US high-tech success appears discouragingly modest. Between 2006 and 2010 the United States exported annually about $35 billion and imported roughly $15 billion worth of airplanes, resulting in an annual surplus on the order of $25 billion (ITA 2011b). For comparison, that is less than the annual import bill for TV sets (nearly $30 billion in 2009) or for baby carriages, toys, and sporting goods, and about as much as the import bill for seafood and alcoholic beverages—or only about 1.5% of total US imports in 2009. Could there be a more disheartening testimony to the fallacy of a high-tech comparative advantage than the fact that the US surplus in aircraft trade could not even buy the annual imports of TVs?

The overall verdict is clear: during the two decades between 1990 and 2010, America's manufacturing retreat combined the gradual losses of domestic market shares to foreign makers in almost every major sector with what might be termed full sectoral capitulations. In large categories of goods, it is now either exceedingly difficult or simply impossible to find a single US-based manufacturer. As a result, no other powerful country in history has ever been as dependent on chronic deficit–inducing imports of basic manufactured products as the United States is today. And although US exports of ATP products rose by 20% between 2000 and 2010, its imports of ATP merchandise increased by 60%, leaving the country with a rising deficit in what was supposed to be its dominant manufacturing category.

And instead of comparing numbers and checking the statistics we might illustrate the changing fortunes of US high-tech manufacturing by looking at some of the sector's leading companies. Although Boeing remains a prosperous global player it lost its dominance, and between 2003 and 2012 it had received fewer orders than Airbus; Xerox nearly went out of business, and by the end of 2012 the company that invented and dominated the market for copiers was trading lower than in the late 1970s (and only at about a tenth of its peak value in the spring of 1999); and Kodak, the inventor and a leading maker of film and cameras, went bankrupt in 2012 after 131 years.

**"Made in China" and the Walmart Nation**

The United States had its first trade deficit with China in 1985, but the total was the negligible sum of $6 million. In just five years the trade deficit grew by three orders of magnitude, to more than $10 billion, and in the year 2000, at $83.3 billion, it surpassed the deficit with Japan, which stood at $81.5 billion (USBC 2011b). In September 2001 China joined the World Trade Organization, and by 2004 the US-China trade deficit had doubled, to $162 billion. The recession of 2008–2009 caused it to dip by about 15%, but in 2010 it reached another record high, $273 billion, a figure that was surpassed in 2011, when the deficit reached $295.5 billion. But China's Custom Statistics show different values: they put the surplus with the United States at $181.3 billion in 2010, about 35% lower than the official total published by the US Department of Commerce (MOFCOM 2012).

This is nothing new. Compared to US data, Chinese statistics chronically overvalue imports from the United States (usually by less than 10%, but some years by almost 20%) and underestimate exports to the United States by a much larger margin, anywhere between 20% and 45% (22% in 2010, 33% in 2005, 45% in 2002). This phenomenon consistently reduces the value of US trade deficits with China as reported in Beijing and arises from differences in official definitions of exports and imports, goods in transit, and exchange rates, and above all from intermediation (substantial Chinese shipments go to Hong Kong before being exported to the United States) and deliberate misidentification of the country of origin, and underinvoicing (Martin 2009). I will use US data that show that despite the global economic crisis of 2008–2009, the US trade deficit with China grew by 35% in just five years, and reached new records in 2010 and 2011.

Few comparisons indicate the magnitude of this lopsided trade. US imports from China now account for about 20% of all imports, far surpassing (by about 31% in 2010) even imports from Canada, traditionally the United States' largest trading partner. The disparity is even greater in terms of imbalances: in 2010 the US deficit with China was nearly ten times larger than with Canada. And China's exports to the United States are heavily skewed toward manufactures: in 2010 about 97% of their value was in industrial goods. Computers and computer accessories, peripherals, and parts add up to the largest imported group by value because of none of these machines and devices are now made in the United States, not even a single mouse. Other merchandise groups with recent imports exceeding $10 billion a year include toys, sporting goods, apparel, shoes, furniture, and miscellaneous housewares.

Who would have guessed in 1976, when Mao died, or a decade later, when China was in the early stages of Deng Xiaoping's modernization, that by 2010 the United States would have its largest ever trade deficit with a state still firmly controlled by its Communist Party, whose leaders see America as their principal strategic enemy and who are in the habit of lecturing the United States on its failings? Given these huge trade imbalances it was not surprising that in September 2008, China surpassed Japan as the largest foreign holder of US Treasury securities, and those holdings rose to more than $1.3 trillion by June 2011 and stood at almost $1.2 trillion at the beginning of 2012, about 23% of the total US foreign debt of $5.1 trillion and a total larger than the annual GDP of all but the world's three largest economies, the United States, China, and Japan.

To some, the story of US-China trade is a welcome example of globalization at its best as two great economies realize the mutual benefits of free trade. To others, the story of American trade with China is a tale of ineptitude, dissembling, the toleration of massive intellectual property theft, and impotent pleas to change the setup, which has been nearly perfectly rigged by China, with the enthusiastic cooperation of large US companies, to prevent any correction of the enormous trade imbalance. The symbiosis has indeed been remarkable. China's ruling party, as firmly in control of the government as ever, attracts foreign companies and enormous direct investment by guaranteeing the stability of a police state and by supplying a docile workforce that labors with minimum rights, commonly for extended hours under severe discipline, and is housed in substandard conditions.

In return, it gets to run excessive trade surpluses and to amass trillions of dollars that can be used to expand the country's military and police might, to use for unprecedented resource-buying sprees around the world, or to start acquiring US companies. America's corporate giants can further expand their profits while shedding American jobs and weakening the country's technical leadership. Many find it easy to argue that these trade and economic policies have undermined America's economic and strategic security and should be urgently reformed (Mann 2007; McMillion 2009; Prestowitz 2010a).

Quantifying the effect of the symbiosis on America's manufacturing jobs is not a simple task, but using a model of labor requirements developed by the US Bureau of Labor Statistics makes it possible to estimate not only the direct effects of any changes in output but also the indirect effects on the subcontracting manufacturers. Scott (2010) used the input-output table for the year 2006 to estimate not only the job losses caused by trade with China during the years 2001–2008 as a nationwide aggregate but also at the state level and for all congressional districts. His aggregate finding is that 2.4 million manufacturing jobs were lost during those eight years, with the biggest losses in California (370,000), Texas (nearly 194,000), New York (140,500), and Illinois (105,500).

Three revealing comparisons can be made. First, if those 2.4 million jobs had remained in the United States, the total number of unemployed at the end of 2008 would have been 8.9 million rather than 11.3 million, and the unemployment rate would have been only 4.6% as opposed to the actual rate of 5.8%. Second, insofar as about two-thirds of all jobs lost to Chinese imports have been in manufacturing, that loss of roughly 1.6 million jobs between 2001 and 2008 would amount to nearly 40% of the 4.3 million factory jobs that disappeared from the United States during those eight years. Third, if only half those jobs had remained after the world recession of 2008–2009, the manufacturing unemployment figure at the end of 2010 (1.6 million people, averaging 40 weeks out of work) could have been cut in half. Little else is needed to show the price paid not only in chronic trade deficits but also, and more important, in disrupted and broken lives.

I will briefly recount the most common Chinese manufacturing and trade practices and offenses, as well as the incomprehensible US failures that have made this quarter-trillion-dollar imbalance possible. The two items that must be at the top of any such list are China's manipulation of its currency's exchange rate and a large variety of open and hidden subsidies. The third great advantage is the pitiful wage paid the country's workers as repressed labor rights have kept wages at a fraction of their fair level (AFL-CIO 2006). Average earnings in the year 2008 were 16.5 yuan in urban factories but less than 6 yuan in township and village enterprises, or less than $1.40 (Banister and Cook 2011).

Since that time some manufacturing wages have risen rather steeply, and even the average urban wage increased by nearly a third between 2008 and 2011, but the gap between Chinese and American earnings remains huge: in 2008 China's mean compensation in manufacturing was just 4% of the US average, and hence even two successive doublings would still leave it at less than 20% of the US rate. But low wages have not been the main reason why America's largest companies have been so eager to manufacture in China. Many other countries offer even cheaper labor but not the promise of such a large new market; an obsession to claim a share of it led many US companies to produce goods in China even if it meant incurring years of losses, being forced by joint venture arrangements to transfer know-how and specialized machinery to Chinese partners (who often proceeded to take over and become new exporters themselves), and tolerating the theft of intellectual property.

There can be no doubt that many American companies became active participants in the deindustrialization of the US economy as they went out of their way to kowtow to China in order to maximize their profits (Carey and Kelleher 2011; Lipscomb 2011). This drive for excessive profit has been well illustrated by the already noted analysis of the major cost components of Apple's iPhone, assembled in China (Rassweiler 2009). But it cost Foxconn, a Taiwanese company making the phone in Shenzhen in Guangdong province, only $6.50 (or only 3.6% of the total cost of $178.96) to assemble the phones in China, with the rest of the shipping cost accounted for by components (memory, display module, baseband, camera, etc.) supplied from abroad—but with a retail price of $500, Apple's profit margin in 2009 was 64%.

Xing and Detert (2010) showed that assembling the iPhone in the United States would still have left a 50% profit margin for Apple—and, of course, it would have created a large number of American jobs. Capozzola (2012) pointed out that Apple could easily make its products in the United States not only because labor costs are such a small share of the overall cost but because its famed i-gadgets compete on quality, not price, and because the high productivity and top quality of US-based manufacturing would offer its own cost savings. But in its quest to maximize profits, Apple prefers China. So much for the social responsibility of that much-admired e-company! Chinese workers get paid a very small fraction of the realized sale price, but at least they have jobs.

And while it is true that a large share (one-half to two-thirds) of well-paid engineering and professional jobs involved in the design and upgrading of e-gadgets have remained in the United States, this quality-for-quantity shift works well only for those Americans who have high-tech qualifications; it has reduced the country's pool of potential lower-paying manufacturing jobs by hundreds of thousands. But it has been a boon to Apple and its shareholders: the company's gross profits have soared, from $4.33 billion in 2005 to $26.71 billion in 2010 and $54.56 billion in 2011, and the company became the world's richest in 2011, after surpassing Exxon.

But the corporation that has emerged as a great symbol of China's conquest of American market for the most often purchased consumer goods is not in the business of making anything; rather, it is the United States', and the world's, largest retailer. In 2011 Walmart (Wal-Mart before July 2008) had 4,413 stores in the United States (and 4,557 stores in 15 other countries, including China), and its annual net sales approached $420 billion, including $260 billion in its US stores (Walmart 2012). In terms of capitalization, it was the world's 16th largest company. That Walmart has played such a key role in the deliberate American plunge into deep trade deficits is ironic because during the 1980s Sam Walton, the company's founder, advocated maximum reliance on American products, stating that "our company is firmly committed to . . . buying everything possible from suppliers who manufacture their products in the United States" (Walton 1985).

And in 1993, Walmart's president promised to the company's shareholders and employees to "buy American . . . more aggressively than ever" (AP 1993). How things have changed! In the mid-1980s only about 5% of Walmart's products were foreign-made; two decades later more than 80% of the company's suppliers were in China (Wal-Mart Watch 2007), and Scott (2007) calculated that between 2001 and 2006, Walmart's China imports displaced nearly 200,000 US jobs. After some investigative reports (by PBS's *Frontline*, CBS, and the *New York Times*) in 2003 and 2004 showed the role of Walmart in the China trade—if Walmart were a nation it would have been China's eighth (or perhaps even sixth) largest trading partner, importing as much as $30 billion of goods a year and creating a de facto Walmart-China joint venture—it has become impossible to get the latest figures on the company's Chinese transactions.

In Walmart's 2011 annual report there is not a single line or figure referring to the origins of the company's merchandise, and China is mentioned only as a country targeted for further business expansion (Walmart 2012). The word "imports" does not appear once in the entire report. Walmart claims that "we save people money so they can live better," and its defenders see China and Walmart as "champions of equality" that have increased the purchasing power of the poor (Broda and Romalis 2008). Those would be good arguments if economic inequality in America were actually declining rather than increasing.

**Figure 5.1**
The Douglas DC-3 is an enduring symbol of US manufacturing prowess. The airliner was the most durable propeller-driven aircraft in history, with some planes in service 75 years after its introduction in 1935. Image available at http://www.museumofflight.org/files/imagecache/lightbox/dc-3-1_Filler_P2.jpg.

# 5

# The Past and the Future

*Long-term perspectives on the successes, failures, and challenges of American manufacturing show a complex mix of inherent advantages, solid achievements, inexplicable neglect, and self-inflicted defeats.*

"I'd love to make this product in America. But I'm afraid I won't be able to."

"Wages?" I ask. "Wages have nothing to do with it. The total wage burden in a fab is 10 percent. When I move a fab to Asia, I might lose 10 percent of my product just in theft." I'm startled. "So what is it?" "Everything else. Taxes, infrastructure, workforce training, permits, health care. The last company that proposed a fab on Long Island went to Taiwan because they were told that in a drought their water supply would be in the queue after the golf courses."

So begins my education on the hollowing-out of the American economy, which might be titled: "It's not the wages, stupid."

—Carl Pope, "America's Dirty War Against Manufacturing," *Bloomberg View,* January 18, 2012

Modern manufacturing has evolved from manual work—unaided or made easier by simple tools—to often highly complex operations that rely on automated design, electronic controls, and completely mechanized production. Making things remains a quintessential human endeavor without which there can be no prosperous large economies and no socially stable populous societies. Dematerialization, understood as a reduction of material use per finished item or per unit of economic product, has been a widespread trend in modern manufacturing, whose quest for higher productivity and lower prices cannot ignore the often expensive cost of requisite material inputs—but there has been no dematerialization in absolute aggregate terms even as far as the world's most affluent economies are concerned.

At the same time, even in affluent countries many citizens still have not attained a minimally acceptable standard of living. The EU's quantification of "material deprivation" (including lacking a color TV, telephone, and a car and living in structurally unsound dwellings or in an accommodation without a bath, shower, or indoor flushing toilet) shows that in the continent's poorer nations, particularly Spain, Portugal, and Greece, as many as 20%–50% of inhabitants are deprived in terms of lacking two or more durables and 20%–40% have at least one housing inadequacy (EU 2005). Taking the poverty rate as the best proxy measure (in the EU it highly correlates with the two indicators of material deprivation), the analogical shares in the United States would be close to 15%, just over 20% for Hispanics, and more than 25% for African Americans (USBC 2011c).

Most of the world's population is much worse off, and in the low-income countries of Latin America, Africa, and Asia material deprivation as defined by the EU would likely affect on the order of 80%–95%. Moreover, in the affluent world large manufactured inputs continue to be needed not because of any massive increase in personal consumption but because of the increasing need to maintain and upgrade an aging and poorly functioning infrastructure. As a result, in absolute terms worldwide manufacturing is expected to reach new heights during the twenty-first century, and great benefits will accrue to those countries that succeed in supplying most of their domestic needs for durables and are also able to tap the immense foreign demand for manufactured goods.

The potential needs are thus substantial, but I will not close this book by offering any formal forecasts. Rather, I wish to compare the past achievements of American manufacturing, which created the world's largest economy and the world's first truly prosperous mass consumption society, with its state today, and examine some of its notable recent failures, the source of many economic, social, political, and strategic concerns, eventually appraising the existing limits and future possibilities of the sector. There should be no illusion that the globalization of manufacturing, the rising value of international trade, and the activities of such supranational entities as the World Trade Organization have, as a well-worn but apt expression has it, created a level playing field for the production and sales of manufactured goods. I will illustrate continuing inequalities and biases by focusing on America's three principal manufacturing competitors.

## Successes and Challenges

The rapid elevation of the US economy to global dominance, maintenance of this status for more than a century, and the creation of the world's first mass consumption society have been the most obvious accomplishments of American manufacturing. During the extraordinarily inventive decades of the late nineteenth century these achievements (while we do not forget

**Figure 5.2**
Apple's iPhone symbolizes both American inventiveness and the retreat of American manufacturing, particularly in its once dominant electronics sector.

the hardships of industrial workers) appeared astonishing even to contemporary observers and created a long-lasting image of America as a land of accomplishment and opportunity. The power of these advances carried into the twentieth century, and even the setbacks of the 1930s could not prevent America from emerging as the first true global power after the Allied victory in World War II, an achievement that would have been impossible without greatly expanded and accelerated manufacturing. Afterward, and despite the anxieties created by the protracted Cold War, American manufacturing completed the process it began before the 1930s by creating a society in which a large majority of citizens enjoyed lives of unprecedented material comfort.

When in July 1959 Richard Nixon argued the merits of capitalism and communism with Nikita Khrushchev, there could have been no better setting for the debate than a model American kitchen—built by All-State Properties for the American National Exhibition in Moscow, with the room cut in half for easy viewing—full of the latest furniture and electric appliances, all adding up to a direct, confident, and appealing advertisement for the American way of life, defined by manufactured goods (video of the debate has been archived; YouTube 2009). Three decades later the Soviet version of communism was on its way out, in no small measure because the superpower able to amass rockets could not satisfy the desires of its citizens for manufactured consumer goods, be they ordinary blue jeans or small passenger cars.

But by that time, during the late 1980s, American manufacturing was itself in trouble. Although its aggregate output continued to grow and although new products found new consumers, a new economic era began during the 1970s. Its proximate initiators were the two rounds of large oil price increases imposed by OPEC—a fundamental change after decades of stable or decreasing energy costs—and its fundamental underlying cause was the impossibility of sustaining the high postwar rates of economic growth (real GDP had more than doubled between 1945 and 1970) for another generation. While the moderation of economic growth was inevitable, the substantial retreat of several key manufacturing sectors—most prominently cars, steel, textiles, and electronics—was not. Those sectors lost large shares of the market to foreign competition as the deindustrialization of America became sadly evident in abandoned factories, lost jobs, and depopulated and decaying towns and cities.

The 1990s offered only a temporary resurgence, aided by the end of Japan's vigorous economic growth and the demise of the USSR, and the first decade of the twenty-first century was in many ways a repeat of the 1980s: the aggregate volume of US manufacturing kept growing, but some key sectors came close to obliteration; the unprecedented consequences included the largest ever loss of manufacturing jobs, record levels of merchandise trade deficits, and truly stunning budget deficits. Moreover, there is not now and never will be a truly undistorted foreign trade. A closer look at America's three major competitors, China, Germany, and Japan, makes it clear that some of their particular strengths will further complicate any attempts at the future growth of US manufactured exports. An overall verdict regarding the balance between the successes and failures of American manufacturing depends, as is usually the case in assessing the state of complex systems, on subtle shifts of emphasis as a multitude of indicators makes it easy to support a preconceived argument.

Those who deny there is anything wrong with US manufacturing point to the rising value added by the sector—in real terms, the value added by US manufacturing to the country's GDP was roughly 2.5 times higher in 2010 than it was in 1950—and see large job losses as just an inevitable consequence of the dual process of impressively rising productivity and the migration of low-value-added work to low-income countries. They argue that American manufacturing thrives in different ways and with different kinds of labor force than it did two or three generations ago. But the economic, social, environmental, and strategic consequences of America's manufacturing retreat make any comparison based on just the total value added highly incomplete.

Those growing aggregate numbers are only a part of the story because they ignore the realities of offshoring, outsourcing, the loss of entire manufacturing sectors, and the huge labor shifts that left behind many unemployable workers, boosted income inequality, and depopulated cities and towns, which were left to decay and be reclaimed by grass and trees (Cowie and Heathcott 2003; Hira and Hira 2005; Buffington 2007; High and Lewis 2007; Paus 2007; Ramrattan and Szenberg 2007; Bivens 2011). These realities support an opposite claim, namely, that many manufacturing sectors have been experiencing a protracted decline, and little can be done to avert further losses.

Both these arguments can find support in selected statistics, but neither offers an adequate basis on which to appraise the real state of affairs. The first view ignores the breadth of American deindustrialization (including the loss or near disappearance of entire industries once dominated by the United States) and the declining capacity of even some of the most advanced US manufacturers to compete. The second view does not emphasize that most of that decline has not been an inevitable outcome of either unstoppable economic forces or an equally unstoppable mechanization and robotization of modern manufacturing but a matter of deliberate choices, the self-inflicted weakening of America's productive capacities resulting from companies' dubious quest to maximize profits and individuals' and households' desire to maximize the consumption of cheap goods. Many economists argue that the overall outcome has been beneficial. A more complete perspective recognizes the economic, social, and environmental toll of American deindustrialization.

## The Achievements of American Manufacturing

The contributions of manufacturing to the transformation of the United States from a preindustrial economy dependent on European imports to the world's dominant power are self-evident. Before the Civil War the country's manufacturing remained outclassed by the British performance, and in some ways it was also weaker than France's and (un-unified) Germany's. During the last four decades of the nineteenth century the rise of US manufacturing was the key reason the country became established as the leading economic power of its day, a position it retained throughout the entire twentieth century. The breadth of achievements was founded on an unprecedented (and so far unequaled) burst of innovation, on what I called a great saltation, a huge leap, of technical advances during the late nineteenth century (Smil 2005). There were, of course, notable contributions by other nations, particularly Britain, Germany, and France, but no other country contributed so much and was able to convert ideas and prototypes into commercial realities as fast as the United States did after its Civil War.

During the 1870s and 1880s the United States became the world's largest producer of most categories of durable manufactures, and by the 1890s its products were successfully competing against goods from European countries. These achievements were consolidated during the first four decades of the twentieth century with the maturing of new large manufacturing sectors, above all steel and aluminum production, electricity generating and transmission equipment, electricity converters (motors, lights, and appliances), telephones, and transportation machinery (passenger cars, trucks, and locomotives).

At the same time, continuing innovation led to the emergence of entirely new manufacturing activities, most notably the rapid post–World War I expansion of the aircraft, telecommunications, and plastics industries. And although the overall level of manufacturing was greatly affected by the Great Depression, the 1930s turned out to be one of the most innovative decades of the twentieth century. This designation is justified because of the combination of a large cluster of fundamental inventions, ranging from radar to nuclear fission; an unprecedented rise in manufacturing productivity; and the commercial emergence of new industrial sectors, including those outputting affordable televisions and household refrigerators, a large group of new plastic materials, locomotives and ships powered by diesel engines, and gas turbines for flight and electricity generation, whose mass-market development defined the post–World War II world.

Contrary to a commonly held impression, the wartime years were not particularly innovative as the focus had to be on the rapid mass production and deployment of existing designs and prime movers, a need that favored even some obsolete but well-proven designs. The development of nuclear weapons and wartime advances in the design of electromechanical computers, radar, and jet engines were the most important exceptions as their continued postwar development ushered in the era of nuclear armaments, ubiquitous computing, and affordable long-distance commercial aviation. The enormous size of the wartime manufacturing mobilization was predicated on unprecedented rates of factory and housing construction and labor migration, and the country's unmatched production of military matériel was a decisive factor in the Allied victory.

During the post–World War II period US manufacturing extended its global dominance, thanks to continuing innovation and productivity growth in established industries such as metals, chemicals, automobiles, and airplanes and the rapid development of entirely new industries based on solid-state electronics. These advances were driven by invention and the rapid commercialization of solid-state devices and machines that incorporated semiconductors, starting in 1954; integrated circuits, adopted during the 1960s; and microprocessors, which were introduced in the early 1970s and made possible the spread of personal computing during the 1980s and the Internet during the 1990s. Today, microchips are embedded in most machines and complex devices.

Cars offer an excellent example of this progress. By the late 1960s all American cars had some electronic components, and by the century's end a typical vehicle had microprocessors controlling everything from spark timing and the air/fuel ratio to the recirculation of exhaust gases, antilock braking, and audio and panel displays. By 2010 the electronic controls for a typical sedan required more lines of software code than the instructions needed to operate the latest Boeing jetliner. American manufacturing has thus turned modern cars into remarkable mechatronic machines. The first decade of the twenty-first century also brought innovations ranging from the deployment of new materials (carbon composites in aviation, nano-structures) to wireless electronics.

After its rise during the late nineteenth century, US manufacturing has remained a remarkably stable component of global production. Its share of the world's output was less than 10% after the end of the Civil War but then rose rapidly to nearly 24% by 1900 and remained at close to that level during the entire twentieth century; in 2010 its share was 19.4%, compared to China's 19.8%. In personal terms, the achievements of US manufacturing can be illustrated by tracing the rise of objects owned by an average household: by the end of the twentieth century such ownership was higher than in any society in history, and the following realities are perhaps the most telling indicators of this status not only because of the values themselves but because those possessions and energy flows have come to be seen as fully expected norms rather than as signs of globally unmatched excess.

In 2000 the average size of a new house was more than double the mean of 1950, and filling it with furniture and other goods required relatively even more manufactures because of the desire to own so many new electronic gadgets. Virtually all new houses in colder regions used natural gas or fuel oil for central heating (the only exceptions being some houses heated by wood-burning stoves), and 85% of them had central air conditioning, including those in the northernmost continental states, where the figure was 88% by 2009. This has made them into major users of fossil fuels and electricity, claiming about a fifth of all the primary energy supply.

In the year 2000 the United States had 80 motor vehicles per 100 people, with 55% of families owning two or more vehicles (and 17% having three or more), each of them driven on average nearly 20,000 km a year (roughly twice as much as in the EU); this use has been largely responsible for an extraordinarily high per capita demand for crude oil (more than 20 barrels per year in 2010). Until the 1960s American manufacturing had supplied all but insignificant fractions of all these durable material riches; afterward came many notable sectoral retreats as imports, or products made by foreign companies in the United States, began to claim rising shares of the US market. The results of this still unfolding process range from roughly halving the market share of US products—cars are the most consequential example—to marginalization of domestic production in sectors ranging from shoes to furniture, to a complete elimination of previously large (in terms of both employment and value added) manufacturing sectors, most notably consumer electronics.

But in aggregate terms, the upward progress of US manufacturing was interrupted only during the Great Depression and, briefly, by a few recession years. In real terms the value added by manufacturing rose about 14 times during the twentieth century, with a 2.4-fold gain between 1950 and 2000. Because of better product designs, the electrification of manufacturing operations (which must be singled out as the most important innovation of the twentieth century), and the mechanization and automation of the vast majority of manual tasks, these large output increases were achieved through higher labor productivity: historical data for labor and the value added (inflation adjusted) by manufacturing indicate that the sector's average annual output per worker doubled between 1900 and 1950 and then more than doubled again by the year 2000.

Historical reconstructions and regular statistics tracing labor productivity in terms of output per hour show impressive improvements during the entire twentieth century. International comparisons show that the United States had a large pre–World War II productivity lead, leaving even Germany far behind, and that—counterintuitively—the 1930s were the best decade for manufacturing productivity gains. Not surprisingly, the reconstructing economies of Japan and Europe showed impressive productivity gains during the 1950s and 1960s: between 1950 and 1973 both Japan (with an annual average growth rate of 10%) and West Germany (averaging 6.9%) outperformed the US rate of 2.6% (Cobet and Wilson 2002).

But for the three decades between 1979 and 2009, US manufacturing productivity was again in the lead, averaging 4.2% annual gains, compared to Japan's 3.0% and Germany's 2.3%; only Taiwan and South Korea, countries at different stages of economic development, have done better, and the difference between the United States and Germany and Japan grew wider during the first decade of the twenty-first century (BLS 2012). An important caveat is that all of the US productivity growth rates are most likely overstated because of outsourcing and offshoring. Houseman (2007) estimated that outsourcing accounted for about half a percent of the officially stated annual growth rate, lowering it from 3.71% to 3.17% for the years 1990–2000, but she found offshoring's impacts more difficult to quantify. In any case, such corrections should be applied to all economies that have been outsourcing to a significant degree, including Japan and, to a lesser extent, Germany.

And although all of America's competitors have narrowed the gap in productivity, the official statistics, questioned by Atkinson and colleagues (2012), still have the United States as the leader: in 2010 its average hourly manufacturing output was about 15% ahead of both its two main competitors' output (BLS 2012). An interesting corollary is that between 1950 and 2000 the average number of working hours declined in both Japan and Germany but stayed the same in the United States. Productivity improvements translated into relatively low price increases—since 1960, the average price of manufactured goods has increased by only 2% a year, compared to 3.7% average annual price increases for the entire economy—and made many classes of consumer goods, particularly household durables, easily affordable.

Manufacturing employment nearly doubled between 1900 and 1929 (from almost 5.5 to 10.7 million), the pre-Depression peak was surpassed only in 1940, with the wartime peak reaching 17.6 million in 1943. After the postwar plunge an undulating rise (accelerating since the mid-1960s) brought manufacturing employment to a peak annual figure of 19.4 million in 1979. A year later, in the midst of a recession, the total was still 18.7 million. After the recovery of the late 1980s there was a relatively small drop, to 17.7 million in 1990, and this total had declined by only a bit more than 2% a decade later, to 17.3 million, or nearly as many employed in manufacturing as in 1970.

Productivity improvements have been the key reason for producing so much more with an unchanged or slightly declining labor force during the 1970s and 1980s. Rowthorn and Ramaswamy (1997) calculated that between 1970 and 1994, 65% of the decline in US manufacturing employment (from 26.4% to 16% of the total labor force) was due to productivity growth, 10% to trade deficits, and the remainder to other factors. But matters were different during the first decade of the twenty-first century, which saw a plunge in manufacturing jobs: an 18% drop to 14.3 million during the first five years, followed by a 19% drop by December 2009 to just 11.5 million (BLS 2012), a loss that was too large and too rapid to be attributed mostly to higher productivity.

Manufacturing has been one of the most potent forces creating America's unusually broad middle class. Before World War I it provided ready employment opportunities for tens of millions of skilled and unskilled immigrants. During World War II it was the great social integrator of women and southern blacks, and after the war its affordable output of durables fostered the widespread ownership of goods that came to define, for better or for worse, the standard of new middle-class living. Although there were always many poorly paid manufacturing jobs, the sector as a whole has paid more than the average for the entire US economy: by the end of 2010 the average rate was 21% above the earnings for all private jobs, nearly twice the rate for retail labor, and only 3% less than for professional business services (BLS 2012). Moreover, 99% of workers in manufacturing companies with more than 200 employees have been receiving health care benefits (Duesterberg 2009).

For more than a century, US manufacturing enjoyed virtually unlimited access to inexpensive and high-quality energy supplies: the United States was the world's largest producer of coal until 1985 (when it was surpassed by China), of crude oil until 1975 (when it was surpassed by the USSR), and of natural gas until 1983 (also yielding to the USSR), and relatively low efficiencies of energy use were an unfortunate corollary of this generations-long, low-priced self-sufficiency. The importance of energy in the US economy is perhaps best illustrated by an analysis by Ayres, Ayres, and Warr (2003), who considered the useful work (the product of overall energy inputs multiplied by prevailing, and changing, energy efficiencies) performed by all productive sectors as its growth engine. Their calculation showed that during the twentieth century, that aggregate rose more than 150-fold and had an enormous impact on economic growth as rising efficiencies led to lower costs and to increased demand, which called for more useful work.

That is why the sudden post-1973 increases in world energy prices (coinciding with rising energy imports) were more worrisome than in countries whose high reliance on energy imports fostered better conversion habits. But US manufacturing coped with these new realities far better than did households or the transportation sector. Between 1973 and 1987 the entire manufacturing sector reduced its energy intensity by nearly a third (Schipper, Howarth, and Geller 1990), and since 1987 its energy efficiency has risen by 43%, compared to 33% for the rest of the economy (Duesterberg 2009). Moreover, energy-intensive industries, particularly chemical synthesis and crude oil refining, have achieved even greater relative savings in individual processes and products. A notable example is the iron and steel industry, a leading energy user, which reduced its total energy input per tonne of hot steel by 45% since 1975 (NEED 2011).

**Failures and Problems**

Among the many sector-specific failures already noted in the book, perhaps none has been more consequential—being a key reason for the United States' now chronically large bill for imported crude oil—than the retrogression of the country's automotive performance. For four decades, while virtually every other technical parameter kept on improving, the efficiency of the country's light vehicle fleet declined between the early 1930s and the mid-1970s, then roughly doubled within a decade, before staying flat for another quarter century. This poor performance and decades of low production quality explain why US auto companies do not make even half the vehicles sold in the United States.

In 1950 about 95% of cars sold in the United States were made by US companies. Sixty years later the country that invented mass automobile production bought most of its cars from foreigners, and the crossroads came in the summer of 2007, when Detroit's three remaining carmakers began to sell less than half of all passenger vehicles and light trucks bought in the United States (Morgan and Company 2011). Ford eventually improved its performance, but GM lost its primacy and had to be salvaged by public funds. And while 2011 and 2012 were good years for all three automakers, they have a long way to go: GM still owed the government $25 billion, Ford's bond regained an investment grade rating only in April 2012, and Chrysler's 2011 return to profitability has been built not on offering more efficient vehicles but on the resurgence of the Jeep Grand Cherokee and the Dodge Durango SUV, and on expansion of the company's SUV lineup into Europe and Asia (Payne 2011).

And as a long-term technical perspective shows (US EPA 2012), fundamental design problems remain. Light-duty vehicles are now using a number of techniques that improve their performance, such as variable valve timing, gasoline direct injection, and a continuously variable transmission, but these gains have been negated by increasing weight and power. Average vehicle weight declined by 20% between 1975 and 1987, but then all of it, and more, came back, so that in 2011 the mean mass of an American vehicle is 1.85 t, roughly twice as much as is necessary for a safe, well-designed four-seat passenger car. Moreover, the average power of new vehicles was 66% higher in 2012 than in 1975, and as a result, the average fuel economy in 2011, 22.8 mpg, was less than 4% higher than it was a quarter century before (22 mpg in 1987). The obvious question is, will US automakers ever learn?

Meanwhile, the most depressing consequence of this long-term mismanagement, the shrinking of Detroit, is now reaching new heights of desperation as the bankrupt city, which is more than $12 billion in debt, plans to cut the number of its street lights by nearly half, from 88,000 to 46,000 (Christoff 2012). This decision will leave entire sparsely populated areas unlit (blocks with only 10%–15% of all houses occupied and with no commercial activity), a move that may finally force the remaining residents of these distressed areas to relocate or to face becoming particularly attractive targets of criminals operating in the dark.

A combination of the same three factors contributed to the decline of both the automobile and the steel industries: unionized labor repeatedly striking for higher wages, even though the auto and steel workers were already the highest paid in the world; management ignoring the long-term quest for a profitable business and willing to buy short-term labor peace by granting these increases while unwilling to take the radical modernization steps needed to remain competitive with foreign producers; and the federal government extending its support, whether through tariffs or loan guarantees, to struggling producers, who used it only to delay instituting the necessary changes. As result, by 2011 there was not a single US steel company among the world's top ten producers (US Steel was 13th, Nucor 15th), and at less than 400 kg per year the apparent average per capita steel use in the United States during the first decade of the twenty-first century was well below the German rate of about 500 kg per year (WSA 2012).

And while a common impression is that the United States has a strong comparative advantage in producing high-tech manufactures (the US Census Bureau classifies them as ATP, advanced technology products), the reality is that in this sector the United States has had a trade deficit since 2002; moreover, between 2006 and 2011 ATP exports rose by 18%, but imports increased by 35%, and as a result, the ATP deficit grew by 77% in just two years between 2009 and 2011, when it reached $99.3 billion (USBC 2012b). And the fate of sectors that have experienced production and employment declines or total capitulations, such as apparel, consumer electronics, kitchenware, and wooden furniture, has not been an inevitable outcome of globalization but has resulted primarily from the deliberate and eager pursuit of offshoring by profit-maximizing US companies. But when appraising the prospects for US manufacturing, the most worrisome challenges are those that lie beyond any particular economic sector.

Because manufacturing is such a critical part of any modern economy, much more important than its share of GDP would suggest, and because it has so many links and feedbacks to its every component, its fortunes are critically affected by a number of factors that shape the country's overall political, economic, legal, educational, social, and health care situation. Unfortunately, even a brief review of some of these key overarching influences demonstrates that on many of these counts, America's recent performance has been at best undistinguished, often mediocre, and even inexplicably poor. Naturally, these failures have put US manufacturing at a disadvantage when compared with some of its leading competitors.

Dysfunctional governance and growing partisan polarization are the country's most persistent political problems. Key economic challenges include excessive government debt and internationally uncompetitive taxation. The legal system has become a drag on innovation rather than its enabler. America's famous universities attract students from around the world, but the country's educational system falls far short of preparing a competitive labor force. The country has underinvested in its infrastructure, and growing income inequality and a highly skewed wealth distribution are at the root of many social challenges, even as the United States remains the only modern state without universal health insurance.

All of these problems have well-recognized solutions, but the record of the past few decades shows acrimony, discord, delays, and delusionary arguments rather than a strong and persistent commitment to effective action. There are many options for reducing the debt burden, ranging from allowing past, temporary tax cuts to expire and raising taxes on income and capital gains to adopting a value-added tax, but a solution will have to include some form of higher taxation because almost all government revenues are already spoken for through mandatory programs or interest costs (Cembalest 2011). The country's legal maze is beyond any rational navigation (the *Federal Register* has grown from 2,600 pages in 1936 to more than 80,000 pages), and only a radical tort reform could limit America's litigiousness.

But the likelihood of reform is low, as is the likelihood of any resolute steps taken toward debt reduction. Perhaps the only much-needed legal change with a better than even chance to be enacted in the near future is the long overdue simplification of rules for inventors, and particularly changes that reduce the frequency of expensive interference lawsuits (E. S. Reich 2011). All of these factors are, obviously, beyond the control of manufacturers, but they have a long-term impact on manufacturers' decisions and prosperity. I will return to some of these challenges when reviewing the major points of some recent suggestions for strengthening US manufacturing output and performance, and will close this recounting of failures by calling attention to what in the long run might be the most damaging consequence of the retreat of US manufacturing from its post–World War II heights, namely, the effect that the decades of manufacturing job losses have had on the country's rising income inequality.

Its striking increase became noticeable right after the first major wave of deindustrialization during the early 1980s, and the publications by Piketty and Saez (2003) and Saez (2010) now provide a nearly century-long (1913–2007) perspective on this worrisome phenomenon. Naturally, there is no such worry if you agree with Reynolds (2007) that these findings are largely misleading artifacts arising from comparing incomparable tax returns (owing to companies' switching from filing under corporate to individual tax system, to the growth of tax-favored savings plan, and to the exclusion of transfer payments), but while some of his critique is undeniably correct, his outright dismissal of the phenomenon is not.

Consequently, there is a valid argument about the actual extent of this shift, but not about the shift itself. Before World War I the top decile income share in the United States was about 40%; by 1929 it had risen to almost 50%. During the 1930s the share fell and stagnated around 45%, then it took a steep wartime tumble, and for the next four decades it fluctuated within a relatively narrow range between 32% and 34%. Its rise began right after the economic downturn of 1981–1982. By 1990 the share was back up to 40%, and by 2007 (after a brief dip between 2000 and 2003) it stood at 50%, equaling the 1929 level. The income share for the top percentile has followed a very similar trend, ending up at 23.5% in 2007, and even within this rarefied group the recent gains have been extremely concentrated, with the share of the top 0.01% (the top 15,000 families making at least $11.5 million in 2007) up to 6%, the highest share ever.

Inevitably, wage trends were a major factor in these shifts. Goldin and Margo (1992) showed that the 1940s were a decade of exceptionally rapid narrowing of wages. World War II and the rules laid down by the National War Labor Board explain some of this great compression, but the main reason was a rapid increase in the demand for unskilled labor concurrent with increases in educated labor, the two factors that prevailed until the 1970s: by 1985 the wage differential had expanded back to its 1940 level. This pushed up the country's Gini coefficient of inequality to just over 40—far above the level of other affluent countries (rounded values for Japan, Germany, and Canada are, respectively, 25, 28, and 33) and uncomfortably close to China's, at 41 now perhaps the most notorious paragon of rising income inequality (UNDP 2011).

As result, by 2010 one in six Americans was in an antipoverty program, with about 50 million people relying on Medicaid and more than 40 million people receiving food stamps, but perhaps the most worrisome outcome of this process is the proportion of American children living in poverty. By 2009 their share had risen to 18.2%, or nearly every fifth child (USBC 2011c). Wilkinson and Pickett (2009) showed that levels of inequality also correlate highly with low social mobility, teenage births, incarceration rates, mental illness, and lack of trust. Rising inequality prompted a Nobelian economist to write about a nation "of the 1%, by the 1%, for the 1%" whose disparities have reached the level that "even the wealthy will come to regret" because of "one thing that money doesn't seem to have bought: an understanding that their fate is bound up with how the other 99 percent live" (Stieglitz 2011).

Stieglitz admits that economists do not have a full explanation of America's growing inequality and lists labor-saving advances (reducing the demand for manufacturing jobs), globalization (pitting American workers against lower-paid foreign labor), and the decline of unions as major factors, but singles out particularly the US tax policy that "has given the wealthiest Americans close to a free ride." Schmitt (2009), who writes about inequality as policy, attributes this "sharp and sustained" rise in economic inequality not to a changing demand for skilled labor resulting from the diffusion of computers and associated innovation (a trend that drives up the wages of better-educated employees and depresses those of unskilled workers) or to the impacts of globalization but to a shifting balance of power between workers and employers (manifesting in industrial deregulation, a low and falling minimum wage, the privatization of many government services, and the decline of unionization).

The shift is undoubtedly a multifactorial phenomenon, but both Stieglitz and Schmitt recognize the loss of manufacturing jobs as an important cause of the deterioration. This must have been particularly the case with losses of millions of jobs that provided above-average remuneration in the steel, automotive, and aerospace industries. Another indicator whose undesirable trend is largely explainable by the loss of manufacturing jobs and the inability of low-skilled workers to find adequate alternatives has been the falling rate of labor force participation among American men between 25 and 54 years of age. Between 1990 and 2009 that share declined from nearly 94% to 90%, while in Japan it is still above 96% and in Germany above 93% (OECD 2011).

No wonder that the combination of declining employment in the manufacturing sector and rising inequality has led to talks about the hollowing of the middle—because the trend toward employment polarization has been disproportionately affecting middle-skilled white- and blue-collar jobs (Autor 2010), with destruction of jobs in between—and to concerns about the future of the middle class (as it was known during the five post–World War II decades). By 2005 the richest 1% of US households earned annually as much as the total earned by the poorest 60%, and the wealth of those wealthy families was as much as the total for the bottom 90%, a state of affairs that Kapur, Macleod, and Singh (2005) called plutonomy. At the same time, serious writers do not just worry about the state of the middle class, they ask whether it can be saved (Peck 2011).

**Global Competition: Never a Level Playing Field**

Globalization has not had an equal impact either on individual countries or on specific economic sectors. The great openness of the US economy, the propensity of Americans to save little and spend readily, inadequate defense of domestic production, and the eagerness of major companies to transfer their plants abroad have combined to make America the richest playground for importers while challenging those American enterprises committed to exports. By far the most common complaint of industries affected by inexpensive imports, as well as those trying to find new markets for their imports, has been the absence of a level playing field. This has been a naïve expectation.

Although most of the world's countries eventually acceded to the General Agreement on Tariffs and Trade (GATT, set up in 1947 and lasting until 1993), and although all major economies (Russia was last to join in 2012) are members of the WTO (set up in 1995), these arrangements have always coexisted with a multitude of tariff and nontariff barriers to trade and with numerous government policies favoring domestic producers.

For decades, the United States had its largest trade deficit with Canada, but that total shrinks substantially after subtracting what has always been its two single largest components, exports of cars made by the Big Three US automakers in Canada and car parts made by numerous subcontractors in Ontario and Quebec and traded since 1965 under the Auto Pact. And because of Canada's exports of all forms of energy to the United States, the two economies have been more closely tied than those of any other two Western trading nations; the North American Free Trade Agreement, enacted in 1988, made them even more complementary. Consequently, when US manufacturers worry about a level playing field, they worry primarily about the largest overseas competitors, Japan, Germany, and China.

Worries about Japan are now only a fraction of the anxieties and fears that were unleashed by the flood of Japanese exports during the 1980s. The burst of Japan's bubble economy in 1990 and the two subsequent decades of low growth, stagnation, and deflation (all made worse by the March 2011 Tōhoku earthquake, the ensuing tsunami, and the Fukushima nuclear plant disaster) have relegated Japan to a well-tolerated competitor. Further, recent realities have changed even that worshipful attitude to what was supposedly Japan's greatest overall manufacturing innovation, the development and assiduous application of Toyota's *kaizen*, the process of continuous improvement combined with total quality control whose key components are not just the automatic detection of defects and, if needed, the shutdown of an assembly line, and the supposedly infallible prevention of errors (Fujimoto 1999).

Such measures were widely admired when they became known in the West, but their origins are thoroughly American, going back to Ford Motor Company's training and William Deming's advocacy of statistical quality control (Deming 2000). Key admonitions from Deming's 14-point plan for quality improvements—"Cease dependence on inspection to achieve quality; understand that quality comes from improving processes. . . . Processes, products, and services should be improved constantly; reducing waste. . . . Drive out fear of expressing ideas and concerns"—became *kaizen*'s key mantras. Although the measures were soon copied abroad, many observers believed they were not really transferrable. Even after Detroit spent two decades trying to assimilate them, Maxton and Wormald (2004, 112) concluded that truly implementing the Toyota system was beyond the American ken, because while GM or Ford can fairly "claim that they have adopted or adapted the Toyota manufacturing system for their own use . . . they have often not fully grasped the thinking which goes behind it."

But it turned out that this was not a case of some permanently elusive Oriental advantage after all. By 2010 Toyota was recalling millions of vehicles to fix manufacturing defects. In its pursuit of quantity to surpass GM as the world's largest automaker, Toyota had ceased to be a paragon of high-quality car manufacturing (Ohnsman, Kitamura, and Green 2001). More important, in surveys conducted by the RDA Group between September 2009 and May 2010, 85,000 American drivers found the quality of the Ford Fusion, a fuel-efficient midsize sedan, unsurpassed by that of the Honda Accord and better than that of the Toyota Camry (Media.Ford.Com 2010), and the result was repeated in 2010 when the website ReviewCars.com rated the Ford Fusion at 4.0 overall and 4.2 on performance; comparable scores for the Camry were 3.9 and just 3.6 (ReviewCars.com 2011). And in 2010, worldwide semiconductor sales of Intel (global number one at $40 billion) were far ahead those of Toshiba (number three at $13 billion), as five of the top ten chipmakers were American, compared to just two Japanese firms.

But these new realities have not translated into a better trade balance. In 1985 the US trade deficit with Japan stood at $46 billion; a decade later it was $59 billion (USBC 2011b). By that time a fairly stable trading pattern had emerged, with the United States exporting on the order of $60 billion and importing about $120 billion annually, and hence incurring an annual deficit of $60–$65 billion, the second or third highest in its global trade (after China and Mexico) over the past 15 years. Prestowitz (2010b, 36) is correct: "The numbers aren't lying: It's time to realize that the United States never really beat Japan." The composition of this deficit shows that it is overwhelmingly due to machinery and transport equipment (mostly cars by Toyota, Nissan, and Honda), while in the broad ATP category Japan continues to have an overall surplus that is mostly due to its exports of information and communication goods and electronics, with the United States ahead in aerospace and manufactures (mostly diagnostic devices) used in health care (USBC 2011b).

The US trade deficit with Germany increased from just $9 billion in 1995 to $50 billion a decade later, then moderated a bit, reaching just short of $35 billion in 2010. As with Japan, most of the deficit has been due to imports of machinery and transport equipment, and in the ATP category the United States had a surplus in the aerospace sector (USBC 2011b). While the recent trade deficits with Germany have been only a fraction of those with Japan and China, the United States has no greater global competitor in the category of high-quality manufactured goods. German manufacturing excellence has a long tradition, but post-unification Germany (the German Democratic Republic ceased to exist in October 1990) was no model economy, with low GDP growth and relatively high unemployment. German fortunes began to change in the new century, and the country's economic situation kept on improving even as the rest of the affluent world was affected by the worst economic downturn since the 1930s.

During the first decade of the twentieth century Germany had a higher average annual growth in per capita GDP and a lower government budget deficit than any other affluent country, with the unemployment rate lower only in Japan and with low household debt, and by 2010 the business confidence index was higher than at any time since the unification two decades earlier. And, as the only country defying China's trade expansion, it also had a rising share of world exports and trade surpluses, accounting for some two-thirds of the overall GDP growth. No wonder that the *Economist*'s headline of February 5, 2011, declared the country "A machine running smoothly."

Some commonly acknowledged general German socioeconomic advantages include a high domestic saving rate, a strong preference (be it by households or governments) for balanced fiscal books, worldwide respect for the country's high-quality products, and the benefits accruing from being the largest economy in an economic union of half a billion people. Perhaps the most important specific advantages are the widespread family ownership of *Mittelstand* manufacturing plants (which can operate free of the burden of quarterly profit reports), effective training of a skilled labor force, and the dedicated pursuit of manufacturing exports. As a result, Germany has many hidden champions, companies that fit Simon's (2009) definition of highly successful manufacturers and exporters, whose products claim large shares of their specialized markets.

This specialization is particularly evident as far as the German machine industry is concerned (VDMA 2011). In 2009, 17 of its 32 sectors that can be compared internationally were the global export leaders; they included such diverse industries as power transmission engineering, materials handling, agricultural machinery, machine tools, food processing and packaging, and industrial furnaces and burners. German manufacturers also had eight second places and three third places, while US producers were the global export leaders in only four subsectors, construction equipment, power systems, and mining and firefighting equipment, and second in nine categories.

Less appreciated advantage includes the country's long tradition of a strong and well-organized social democratic movement and allied labor unions with a considerable influence on the government. The Sozialdemokratische Partei Deutschlands was the strongest party in the Reichstag before World War I (it received nearly 35% of all votes in the 1912 elections) and a leading party in pre-Nazi Germany, and since 1966 it has been a coalition partner in several federal governments (between 1966 and 1988 and again between 1998 and 2009). Strong labor unions may be a problem for manufacturers, but they may also make some challenges easier. During the recent economic downturn the acceptance of smaller wage increases (or even wage freezes) by German unions in return for guaranteed employment, as well as a decision of many owners not to fire workers during a time of slumping demand but to retain a skilled labor force in anticipation of an economic recovery, helped make the country the only economy with falling unemployment.

But in 2010 the US trade imbalance with China was more than twice as large as the combined deficit with Japan and Germany, making China the United States' most worrisome competitor and presenting the most formidable challenge because the Chinese have felt least constrained to adhere to international norms, both in domestic production and in foreign trade. As far as unfair trading practices are concerned, China has done it all, from implementing directives to buy only domestic goods to mandating lengthy tax-free periods, from assessing punitive taxes on imports (imposing, for example, a 17% VAT on imported semiconductors vs. a 3% VAT on domestic production) to dumping goods on the US market, such as quadrupling the exported value of tires between 2004 and 2008. And it is small consolation that between 2004 and 2008, the United States won all of its seven complaints to the WTO, with four more pending in 2011 (McMillion 2009; Morrison 2011).

This is also a suitable place to repeat that Chinese companies have been unsurpassed masters of the theft of intellectual property and the allied art of knocking off counterfeit products. In 2005 American businesses lost $2.6 billion owing to China's copyright piracy, and counterfeits now make up 15%–20% of everything made in China (adding up to about 8% of GDP). The country accounted for 79% of pirated goods seized by US agents in 2009 (Morrison 2011). Nor should we forget the health and safety concerns that have come with Chinese manufactured products, ranging from contaminated toys and children's jewelry to drywall emitting hydrogen sulfide and substandard medicinal ingredients (McCormack 2010).

Many Americans observers consider China's practice of keeping the value of the yuan renminbi artificially low as the greatest cause of imbalanced trade. There is perhaps no greater reminder of the weak hand played by America than the repeated pleas of the US secretary of the treasury to change this reality, pleas that are swiftly dismissed by China as the worst examples of an unwelcome interference in its sovereign affairs. Before June 2005 the currency was fixed at 8.3 to the dollar, between June 2005 and August 2008 it was allowed to appreciate by nearly 19% in trade-weighted terms, then it remained fixed once again at 6.83 yuan to the dollar until June 2010. By the middle of 2011 it was trading at about 6.5 to the dollar, and a year later it was around 6.35 to the dollar, with the usual Chinese promises of further gradual appreciation in years to come.

What the real value of the yuan should be has become, not surprisingly, a matter of dispute. The merry-go-round of America buying Chinese exports and China buying US treasuries used to turn ever faster, but it has shown clear signs of saturation. In 2000 China held about $50 billion, a small fraction of the Japanese holdings. By 2005 it was about $300 billion, and by the end of 2010 the total had surpassed $1.1 trillion. It reached a peak of $1.315 trillion in July 2011 and a year later was reduced to less than $1.2 trillion, with China just ahead of Japan and far ahead of oil exporters as the United States' largest foreign creditor (US Department of the Treasury 2012). Obviously, this is an unsustainable situation, but while it lasts it makes a huge difference. Cline and Williamson (2010) estimate that the subsidy effect of this intervention makes Chinese exports 40% cheaper while raising the cost of US imports by a similar margin.

On the other hand, there are those who argue that the exchange rate has not been seriously misaligned, that China's growth has not been led by exports made possible by an undervalued currency, and that there are no convincing indicators of the yuan's undervaluation (Keidel 2011). What is hard to dispute is that even a significant revaluation of the yuan would not make a substantial difference in the cost of the more expensive electronic goods that are assembled from mostly foreign-made parts in China and sold by US companies at a very high profit. But a closer look at the cost structure in the furniture industry shows that the low yuan is a large part of the overall advantage: US labor and overhead add up to 45% of the total cost, compared to just 7% in China, and even after higher transportation costs are included Chinese wooden furniture is easily 30% cheaper, but that advantage would be much reduced or totally eliminated by a properly valued yuan.

Another well-documented practice that gives China an unfair trade advantage is the widespread use of massive subsidies and low-cost loans to export-oriented enterprises. Haley (2007) calculated that between 2000 and 2007, such subsidies added up to $27 billion for China's steel industry, and even greater subsidies ($33 billion between 2002 and 2009) made much-deforested China the world's largest producer of paper and, incredibly, an increasing net exporter of paper products to the United States (Haley 2010). As for the highly touted high-tech exports to China, in 2005 the United States had a $47 billion deficit in that trade, and by 2010 the gap had doubled to $94.2 billion, after growing 40% in a single year. The trend has thus been going in the wrong direction, and fast. The future looks even bleaker as the category with the largest (if absolutely rather small) US surplus (just over $5 billion in 2010), aerospace exports, will not see any strong growth (and may see large losses) because of strong gains that Airbus has been making in China and because of the introduction of China's own commercial jetliners.

Selling to China also means encountering numerous nontariff barriers (Japan, too, used to be a master of this game) and putting up with routine violations of intellectual property rights, the production of counterfeit goods, and illegal reverse engineering of complete machines and industrial processes. At the same time, the risks associated with some of China's exports have been high enough to elicit a US response: a tougher Consumer Product Safety Improvement Act followed massive merchandise recalls, which reached their peak in 2009, when 472 different products were recalled, including 20 million toys and 175 million pieces of children's jewelry (Morrison 2011).

In addition to being the world's leading counterfeiter and open infringer of intellectual property rights, China also operates what amounts to the world's largest network of industrial espionage, with only the proverbial tip of that iceberg appearing above the surface of normal trade relations. I will note just one remarkable recent incident. On February 28, 2007, Hanjuan Jin, a software engineer who worked for Motorola since 1998, was arrested in Chicago as she was about to board a flight to China with more than 1,000 electronic and paper documents, including proprietary information and trade secrets belonging to Motorola. This followed a number of previous thefts of intellectual property from Motorola on behalf of Huawei, China's largest telecommunications company (Anderlini 2010).

None of these realities are surprising to those who have never entertained serial wishful thinking about China. Contrary to the claim used to promote China's WTO membership, the US trade deficits have ballooned since China joined in the year 2000. And contrary to a common post-1990 mantra, China has not become capitalist, and the presence of markets and economic exchange does not make it so as long as all of its important industries are still firmly controlled by the state (Blumenthal 2011). The claim of inevitable political liberalization that has been promoted by multinational corporations to justify their kowtowing to China and their large-scale investment in the country, as well as by many US politicians to defend their inaction when confronted by Beijing's affronts, is simply wrong.

This is a critical point because, as Mann (2007, 6) has stressed, "without the claim that trade would open up the Chinese political system, trade legislation probably would not have been enacted. It is difficult if not impossible to find an American president or congressional leader who said, 'China has a repressive political system and it's not going to change, but let's pass this legislation anyway.'" Obviously, as long as the state (read: the Communist Party) bans the formation of any organizations and institutions it does not control, rising trade with America and Europe will not make it more democratic. And the control is now stronger than ever: in 2011 China publicly acknowledged that for the first time ever the budgeted spending on its internal security (including a huge secret police force, an armed militia, jails, and massive Internet censorship) would surpass the spending on China's military (Buckley 2011).

Given these realities, a trading nation must be prepared to retaliate when confronted by indisputably questionable, illegal, or discriminatory practices pursued by its trading partners. It must be also ready to carry on vigorous advocacy efforts on behalf of its exporters, matching its sellers with foreign buyers, removing trade barriers and enforcing trade rules, and providing export assistance. The United States has been a weak player in these recurrent conflicts and a comparatively poor exports promoter, partly because of its inherent domestic weaknesses, partly because of its lack of assertiveness and an incredible naïveté when dealing with China.

Moreover, US companies have been enthusiastic participants in deindustrializing America by outsourcing and by closing domestic factories and opening new ones abroad, above all in China.

For one of America's leading manufacturers and exporters, it took nearly a generation to have its epiphany. Speaking at an event organized by GE to promote the competitiveness of the US economy, James McNerney, Boeing's CEO, admitted that "we, lemming-like, over the past 15 years extended our supply chains a little too far globally in the name of low cost. We lost control in some cases over quality and service when we did that, we underestimated in some cases the value of our workers back here" (Malone 2012). Comparing the behavior of the leading US companies to the primitive instinct of a rodent is an astonishing admission of failure on the part of America's top-level management. Is it just possible that this kind of behavior has had to do at least as much with the relative deindustrialization of America as the exchange value of China's currency has, or the unfair business subsidies given by foreign governments to their companies?

## Should Anything Be Done?

Nothing at all should be done, say many prominent economists who have not been concerned about the country's manufacturing retreat. Either they are quite comfortable with the fact that many of the country's manufacturing sectors have been reduced to small fractions of their previous size or have ceased to exist entirely, or they simply deny (quoting the overall rise in annual value added by the sector to the country's GDP) that any retreat has taken place. Management guru Peter Drucker (2001) saw it all as a natural economic evolution, with manufacturing "following exactly the same path that farming trod earlier" as the sector's employment and share of GDP, as well as the prices of manufactured goods, decline while the overall physical output rises. "In America, this transition has largely been accomplished already, and with a minimum of dislocation," as "even in places that relied heavily on a few large manufacturing plants, unemployment remained high only for a short time."

Drucker predicted that by 2020, manufacturing output in affluent countries would at least double, while the sector's employment would shrink to 10%–12% of the total labor force (Drucker 2001). In the United States, such a shrinkage was accomplished in just a decade: would

**Figure 5.3**
Caterpillar has been one of America's leading machinery exporter, and the 797B has been the company's largest off-highway dump truck (weighing more than 620 t, able to carry more than 300 t). The truck is used at large surface mines around the world. Color image available at http://www.autogaleria.hu/autok/caterpillar/797b/caterpillar_797b_r1.jpg.

Drucker—he died in 2005—have rejoiced? And what would he have to say about the unemployment rate, which has not remained high "only for a short time"? When introducing the report on the competitiveness index for the Council on Competitiveness, Michael Porter concluded that "America is better positioned than perhaps any country to benefit from the forces that are reshaping the global economy," although he admitted, in remarkably oblique language, that that process "is especially challenging to those at the lower end of the skills ladder" (Porter 2007, 9). In plain English, read "multinational US companies" for "America" as the great beneficiaries, and "chronic unemployment and underemployment" for "especially challenging."

At a press conference held to release the report, Porter claimed that the United States "is not losing manufacturing, it is losing manufacturing jobs. . . . That is a fundamental distinction," adding that US multinationals sell through their foreign affiliates three times more than they export, shattering irrevocably "the old model where we exported stuff" but doing so "not at the expense of the US" (McCormack 2006). And thus the unemployment/underemployment rate of nearly 20% is just an inevitable downside of this new way of engaging in the global economy. And does not the fact that the ten years ending in 2010–2011 were the first job-loss decade since 1928–1938 have something to do with the loss of nearly five million manufacturing jobs during that period?

But Porter is no exception, as most of the country's leading economists are cheerleaders for offshoring and have no concerns about the massive disappearance of jobs in US manufacturing. Jagdish Bhagwati, perhaps the most aggressive proponent of these notions, uses catchy comparisons, facetious statements, twisted arguments, irony, and condescending remarks when attacking anybody who might suggest that manufacturing jobs may be of importance, and accuses such misguided advocates of succumbing to "the new fetish of manufacturing" and being promoters of "a quasi-Marxist fallacy," assigning the critical role to the means of production (Bhagwati 2010a, 2010b). Some of his arguments are truly exasperating, For example, when rebutting Cohen and Zysman (1987), who dared to argue that manufacturing matters and that without manufactures, service sectors are untenable (in my opinion, a simple truism), he calls this a specious argument because "one can have a vigorous transportation industry, with trucks, rail, and air cargo moving agricultural produce within and across nations" (Bhagwati 2010b).

Obviously, if a nation produces enough bananas (to stick to Bhagwati's produce example) to buy all the requisite machinery and to import all the other merchandise and food and energy it needs in order to prosper, it does not have to manufacture anything. But the United States is not a small banana republic, and for a generation it has not been able to sell enough of its services and goods to buy all the manufactures, energy, and food it needs to import to support its high standard of living. This situation has resulted in rising trade deficits, now surpassing half a trillion dollars a year, that have been mostly incurred by the purchases of goods and cannot be supported indefinitely. Would not this add up to a good argument for either consuming less—or manufacturing more?

Moreover, Bhagwati (2010b) questions the fact that manufacturing is more innovative than the service sector by citing FedEx, faxes, mobile phones, and the Internet as great innovations in communication. This is a monumental categorical error that ignores first causes and consequences: all of these innovations in communication—next-day package deliveries, the instant transmission of printed matter, and rapid access to information—had to be preceded by fundamental innovations in manufacturing, the construction of jetliners and gas turbines, the development of xerography, and the design and mass production of ever more powerful microprocessors and higher-resolution screens.

Clyde Prestowitz, a consistent advocate of manufacturing's importance, responded to Bhagwati's dismissal of any special concerns about the sector by making the same point in a slightly different way, noting "a great conundrum." Virtually all economists call for global rebalancing, the need that arises primarily from a huge US deficit in trading goods, mostly with China, Japan, and Germany. Rebalancing would necessitate a large drop in US imports of goods and a large increase in US manufactured exports (as service exports are not enough to erase the deficit), a hard thing to do "unless the US actually begins producing more manufactured goods. So, in fact, it seems that we must after all have some special concern for the fate of US manufacturing" (Prestowitz 2010c). Bhagwati (2010b) remains unmoved: "The case for a shift to manufacturing remains unproven, because it cannot be proved."

Bhagwati is not alone in welcoming the sequential failures of American manufacturing. Perhaps the most quotable encapsulation of this attitude comes from Alan Blinder, an economist who actually has some doubts about the unbounded offshoring of US jobs and whose concerns were disparaged by Bhagwati (Blinder 2009, 49):

> The TV manufacturing industry really started here, and at one point employed many workers. But as TV sets became "just a commodity," their production moved offshore to locations with much lower wages. And nowadays, the number of television sets manufactured in the US is zero. A failure? No, a success. Like the cowboy hero, the leader innovates and moves on.

The mantra about an automatic progression to more and better-paying jobs in ever more advanced manufacturing or service sectors contrasts with the realities of deepening deficits in the trade of advanced manufactured products and with the country's nearly 20% real unemployment. There is no categorical difference between making "just a commodity" and creating a new high-tech future. Andrew Grove, Intel's founding chairman, offers what I think to be the best counterargument: "I disagree. Not only did we lose an untold number of jobs, we broke the chain of experience that is so important in technological evolution . . . abandoning today's 'commodity' manufacturing can lock you out of tomorrow's emerging industry" (Grove 2010).

And that is precisely what has happened. For example, when some three decades ago the United States stopped making virtually all "commodity" consumer electronic devices and displays, it also lost its capacity to develop and mass-produce advanced flat screens and batteries, two classes of products that are quintessential for portable computers and cell phones and whose large-scale imports keep adding to the US trade deficit. In contrast to those who see these realities as welcome confirmations of economic progress, those who do not feel that things are just fine or who do not believe the current situation is an inexorable outcome of economic evolution have been able to find a great deal of common ground when arguing for new departures.

## Calls for Change

Recent programmatic papers, reports, and books offer systematic lists of recommendations for restoring and boosting manufacturing in general and manufactured exports in particular. There is no shortage of analyses of what went wrong and recommendations for how to make it right again. Some of these appraisals—including the Milken Institute's report on jobs for America (DeVol and Wong 2010) and Fallows's (2010) evaluation—took broader economic and social perspectives. Others have focused on the entire manufacturing sector (Pisano and Shih 2009; Lipscomb 2011; Liveris 2011; NAM 2011a), on such of its key components as electronics (Dewey & LeBoeuf 2009; Grove 2010; Tassey 2010) or energy (Freed at al. 2010), and on the need for greater exports (National Export Initiative 2010; Katz and Istrate 2011).

The complex dynamics of factors shaping the manufacturing success preclude dividing them unequivocally into distinct categories, but there are clearly three kinds of changes of increasingly wider scope and hence commensurately decreasing likelihood of rapid implementation: changes specific to the manufacturing sector or its subsectors, broader reforms within the economic realm, and fundamental shifts in those primary social and political drivers that shape any effective long-term national transformation. One of the most comprehensive and carefully outlined lists of desirable policies and actions has been prepared by the National Association of Manufacturers in its strategy for creating jobs and a competitive America, and exemplifies this mixture of fairly specific actions and general appeals for fundamental socioeconomic changes (NAM 2011a).

The list of items, presented in no discernible order, includes a taxation regimen that does not put US producers at a disadvantage in the global marketplace; the preservation of a dynamic labor market and investment opportunities through limiting further expansion of federal mandates and regulations; legal reforms to eliminate costs arising from excessive (the world's most frequent) litigation (the aggregate burden is now equal to almost 2% of GDP); stimulation of R&D activities through appropriate tax credits and to encourage continuing federal participation in this work; a push for international safeguards for US intellectual property; means to attract a talented labor force from abroad; promotion of fair trade practices; the modernization of outdated export controls and export-assistance programs for small and medium-sized producers; less dependence on imported energies; promotion of environmental protection; investment in infrastructure and in improved education at all levels; and support for cost-reducing health care reform.

Variants of this list can be found in other reports and publications calling for the (choose your noun) rejuvenation, renaissance, revitalization, or return of US manufacturing, and some of the more specific steps are invariably stressed in assessments that focus on the prospects for individual sectors. Perhaps the least contentious and most commonly encountered suggestion is the strategic promotion of exports. This desirable and eminently realistic quest can bring both immediate returns and long-term rewards, and I explain its rationale and potential separately in the next section. In this section I look at perhaps the most common call for change, the one for reducing the US corporate income tax and increasing the R&D credit, and at the state of US education, health care, and infrastructure.

A generation ago there was nothing inexplicable about the way the United States taxed its companies: in 1990 the top US marginal corporate tax rate of 38.7% was actually slightly below the average of 41.2% for 31 OECD countries. In the intervening years the United States lowered its already fairly low income tax rates, and it remains the only affluent nation without a federal consumption tax (equivalent to the value-added tax in the EU or the general sales tax in Canada)—but its manufacturers are now taxed excessively. After 1990 every OECD country except the United States began to lower the top marginal corporate tax rate in order to make its industries more competitive in the global marketplace: by 2010 the OECD mean was just 25.5%, whereas the US rate had risen marginally, to 39.2%, second only to Japan at 39.5% (OECD 2010).

But in December 2010 Japan moved to cut its rate to 35%, leaving the United States in a dubious first place as the undisputed leader in corporate taxation. In other major manufacturing countries the rate ranges from 30.2% in Germany and 28% in the UK to 24.2% in South Korea and just 19% in China. Supporters of the high US corporate tax rate argue that the tax rate doesn't actually disadvantage manufacturing firms, and point to companies like General Electric, which has avoided paying US taxes for two years in a row. But GE—unlike Daimler or Fujitsu—is as much a finance company as it is a manufacturing forum, and it uses the write-offs it gets from its overseas lending divisions to offset taxes owed on its American manufacturing. The example of GE proves that it has been extraordinarily adept at tax avoidance, not that the level of taxation is irrelevant.

DeVol and Wong (2010) calculated that reducing the corporate income tax to the average level of the OECD countries would boost US GDP by more than 2% by 2019, create an additional 350,000 manufacturing jobs, and raise overall employment by 2.13 million, a most desirable combination of impressive incomes in return for what should be a rather simple legislative action. They also estimate that increasing the R&D tax credit by 25%—to encourage more of these activities to take place in the United States rather than to be, as is now increasingly common, outsourced abroad—would have similarly beneficial effects by boosting GDP by 1.2%, raising manufacturing employment by 270,000, and adding more than half a million of new jobs within a decade.

Whatever the actual specific gains might be, there is broad agreement that the United States must maintain a high level of industrial R&D. Despite the recent rise of Asian capacities it is still the leader: with $369 billion in 2007 it accounted for a third of the total $1.1 trillion spent globally on R&D, ahead of the Asian total of $338 billion and the EU total of $263 billion, with American industry funding about 67% of all expenditures, compared to 55% in the EU (70% in Germany) and over 60% in Asia (NSF 2010). And because foreign competitors have been adept at offering entire baskets of benefits (low tax rates, tax deferrals, R&D tax credits, location grants, prepaid infrastructure, low-interest-rate loans) to the semiconductor industry, it is not surprising that the calls for its American revitalization cite similar measures (Dewey & LeBoeuf 2009).

The United States used to be proud of its educational achievements as a generation of World War II veterans took advantage of the GI Bill, its top universities became global academic leaders, and its population achieved the world's highest rate of post-secondary education. But it has become increasingly clear that the country's educational system is doing both too much (requiring compulsory high school education even though large shares of students never graduate, and many of those who do perform far below the expected level) and too little (especially in terms of vocational training), and that it compares poorly with the rest of the affluent world.

The results of the latest round of the Programme for International Student Assessment (PISA) rank the United States 19th of the 33 studied countries, behind Ireland, with South Korea ranking second (after Finland), Japan third, and Germany ninth (OECD 2009). In terms of the share of students performing at an advanced level in math proficiency, the United States (with 6%) placed 49th, barely beating Spain, while the rates for Germany were 13.1% and for South Korea 23.2%; even after using the data for individual states the best performer, Massachusetts, ranked 17th (behind Austria and Germany), while the last one, Mississippi, did hardly better than Thailand (Hanushek, Peterson, and Woessman 2010). And Ripley (2010) stresses that even relatively privileged American students do worse than their foreign counterparts.

These concerns have been around for a long time, and this is precisely why Wildavsky (2011) maintains that ever since the launch of *Sputnik* in 1957 the United States has been going through periodic cycles of panic and self-flagellation, and that such exercises are unwarranted, as neither the Chinese math whizzes nor the Indian engineers are stealing American kids' future. But would he dismiss a high correlation among PISA scores, share of manufacturing, and level of manufactured exports? Germany, Japan, South Korea, the Netherlands, Switzerland, Finland, and Belgium are all among the top PISA ten. Would he disagree with US plant managers, who often find large numbers of job applicants unprepared by their previous education to take up the position?

The challenge extends from basic vocational training all the way to elite universities. Compulsory high school attendance and the entrenched belief that there is no comfortable future without a university degree have clearly undermined America's ability to train the skilled labor force needed in modern manufacturing. The German model offers the greatest contrast, with most pupils (about 70%) never attending *Gymnasium* (up to grade 13) but, after *Hauptschule* or *Realschule* (ninth or tenth grade), entering a *Berufsschule* for a wide variety of vocational training in apprentice programs (Clarke and Winch 2007). Germany has a long tradition of this training, and a law passed in 1969 (*Berufsbildungsgesetz*) defines the shared responsibilities of the state, labor unions and associations, and private companies in carrying on with this rewarding practice. These programs produce highly skilled workers familiar with the latest manufacturing processes.

In contrast, one of the most common complaints of both American employers and foreign managers eager to locate their new factories in the United States is the lack of a qualified labor force: even with a high unemployment rate it is often difficult to find qualified workers. Andrew Liveris, CEO of Dow Chemical Company, has been complaining about such labor shortages for years (Liveris 2011). The CEO of Siemens USA has complained about the mismatch between the jobs his company can offer "and the people we see out there," and noted that the company has to invest in education and training, including apprenticeship programs of the German kind, to address this shortage of skills (Singla 2011). Martinez (2011) quoted the head of Daimler Trucks North America, who felt that workers at his plants in Mexico were more skilled than in the United States, where some had to be taught math and writing skills.

The *Economist* of September 10, 2011, noted the great mismatch: unemployment is high, yet skilled and talented people are in short supply. Predictably, workers with adequate math and science skills who can operate advanced machinery are in high demand. But such a demand for creative and analytic skills cannot be satisfied by a system whose schools turn out semiliterate teenagers. And the overall situation will only get worse, given the high median age of the labor force in many manufacturing sectors: for example, in aerospace, the median age of workers in 2008 was 45 years and the median age of engineers was 54 years (Platzer 2009).

And while America's universities made enormous and fundamental contributions to the country's scientific and technical accomplishments during the twentieth century (Cole 2009), a closer look reveals their many weaknesses (Greene 2010; Hacker and Dreifus 2010). Almost without exception they are excessively expensive (in no small part owing to bloated administrations), with the tuition rate increases far surpassing even the country's notoriously runaway health care costs. The massive influx of students has, necessarily, created quality problems: drop-out rates are up, degrees take longer to finish. Research is all too often solipsistic, return on investment is poor, and while the great American "PhD factory" keeps producing excess numbers of overqualified people (Cyranoski et al. 2011), science and engineering faculties, the key places to train future manufacturing innovators, enroll declining numbers of Americans. No wonder the *Economist* (September 4, 2010) dared to ask, "Will America's universities go the way of its car companies?"

And there are problems at the opposite end of the labor spectrum as both employers and employees have to face many new realities of what Bernhardt and colleagues (2008) call the "gloves-off economy," the workplace conditions and standards at the bottom of America's labor market. These realities include a continuing influx of illegal immigrant workers (whose labor has become indispensable in several manufacturing sectors, particularly in meatpacking), high shares of workers with criminal records (with more than 700 inmates per 100,000 people, the United States has the world's highest incarceration rate), and rising numbers of single mothers in the labor force. America's failure to manage its health care costs, deliver adequate health services to all of its citizens, or redesign and reform its existing (utterly unsustainable) system of Medicare has become one of the signal examples of the country's dysfunctional policy making. In this case, American exceptionalism is nothing to be proud of: US spending on health care is nearly 2.5 times the average for OECD countries ($7,290 per capita in 2007), while the rate for Germany is less than $4,000 and for Japan less than $3,000 per capita—and yet it is Japan that leads the global life expectancy ranking (more than 82 years), with the United States ranking only 24th of the 30 countries (OECD 2010).

The state of America's infrastructure is regularly appraised by the American Society of Civil Engineers in their biannual report card (ASCE 2011). The grades for 2009 were uniformly poor, with the best ratings for the management of solid waste (C+) and for bridges (C). Public parks and recreation and rails received C– (and I would greatly dispute the latter grade, particularly in comparison with the EU or Japan), energy (transmission, pipelines) was the only D+, while aviation, dams, roads, schools, and transit got a D, and drinking water, inland waterways, levees, roads, and wastewater treatment got a D–, for an overall grade of D—and an estimated bill of $2.2 trillion needed between 2009 and 2014 to eliminate the worst inadequacies.

And there is no shortage of blame to be placed on American manufacturing companies themselves. Complacency, a slow reaction to market changes and nimble foreign competitors, and lack of determination to export have been all too common. A generation ago Hayes and Abernathy (1985), when describing how America manages its way to economic decline, quoted an observer who noted that "the US companies in my industry act like banks. All they are interested in is return on investment and getting their money back. Sometimes they act as though they are more interested in buying other companies than they are in selling products to customers." Those comments would not be out of place today as short-term concerns overrule long-term commitments and as recent record profits have been used to buy back stock or simply to amass reserves rather than to train a new labor force or boost investment in R&D.

### Exporting Goods

For more than a century the world's largest manufacturing economy was an efficient mass-maker of industrial products for its huge domestic market, but in relative terms, the United States has been always a rather inferior exporter. In 1870 the country's total exports (of goods and services) amounted to only about 8% of its GNP. That share spiked to 12% during World War I, only to dip to just 4% during the economic crisis of the 1930s and to a mere 2% during World War II, followed by a fluctuating climb to more than 11% by 2009. For comparison, 2009 exports per GDP shares were 13% in Japan (contrary to a common perception, Japan is not such a massive exporter), 23% in France, 27% in China, and 41% in Germany, with some smaller EU countries (the Netherlands and

Czech Republic) having the highest rates (around 70%) among affluent nations (World Bank 2011). But in both Japan and Germany more than 85% of all exports were manufactured goods, while the U.S share was about 75%.

Although undistinguished in relative terms, US exports of goods and services have been providing for millions of families. In 2008 they supported 10.3 million jobs, with exports of goods accounting for nearly three-quarters of that total (7.5 million jobs), or 5% of the country's labor force (Tschetter 2010). But their importance for manufacturing has always been much higher, with the sectoral shares at 7% for finances, 19% for agriculture, 23% for transportation, and 27% for manufacturing. There is yet another employment benefit tied to exporting. Bernard and Jensen (2004) found that exporting plants have a substantially higher productivity, and while exporting may not increase their productivity growth rates it does help them increase employment and overall sales faster than among nonexporting enterprises.

The relatively modest contribution of American exports made little difference for nearly four generations, as long as the country was also a relatively modest importer of manufactured goods, energy, and food and hence able to run solid trade surpluses, a state of affairs that lasted between 1896 and 1970. This long spell was followed by five years of alternating small deficits and surpluses, and in 1976 the country's trade deficit was still just $6 billion. But since 1976 the United States has experienced the unenviable combination of an unbroken run of deficits in the trade of goods; a huge crude oil import bill, which reached a record $342 billion in 2008; and a declining surplus in its food trade (USBC 2011b). Although the country has had a positive (and, since 1986, generally rising) balance in service trade, those earnings have been able to erase only a fraction of the merchandise deficit and cannot prevent a chronic annual shortfall.

By 1990 the trade deficit was more than 13 times larger than in 1976 (at $80 billion in nominal terms), and every year since 1999 it has been in excess of $250 billion, with a maximum of nearly $760 billion reached in 2006. Although the economic downturn reduced the annual balance to –$375 billion in 2009, it increased again in 2010 to nearly –$500 billion. Indeed, in 2010 the US trade deficit was larger than the GDPs of all but 19 countries in the world. The need for higher exports of manufactures is all too obvious. Encouragingly, their nominal value increased by nearly half between 2000 and 2008 before dropping by 25% in 2009 as a result of the economic downturn—and then almost recovering in 2010. But the imports of manufactures have also kept on rising, by about 46% between 2000 and 2008. As a consequence, in 2009 the United States had a massive manufacturing trade deficit of $322 billion, which increased further to $377 billion in 2010 and to $425 billion in 2011 (USBC 2012a). Many American economists see no problem with these deficits and actually consider them a sign of wealth: America can afford to buy more than it sells.

Such a rationalization makes sense only in a country that values its consumption above anything else, and that needs a plausible excuse for its excessive habits. The only reason the United States has been able to sustain such a long period of high trade deficits is because it holds the world's reserve currency and can finance the deficits by continuous sales of US bonds to foreigners. Other arguments ascribe the principal cause to a low domestic saving rate or to China's manipulated currency. Both of these claims are partially right, but that still does not justify such a blasé attitude toward the US trade deficit. Saving rates have been falling throughout much of the industrial world (including in Japan, a former big saver), and a rapid and substantial reversal of this trend is unlikely. Similarly, China's overvalued currency is a major problem, but China's slow revaluation may not help the United States reach a desirable level for another 15–20 years, not soon enough to prevent substantial devaluation of the dollar.

In contrast, America's two main affluent competitors, Germany and Japan, have experienced decades of large manufacturing trade surpluses: the totals for 2009 were, respectively, $290 and $220 billion, and both of them grew in 2010 to $323 and $ 333 billion (WTO 2012). Although Japan—the country that a generation ago was seen as the greatest threat to America's economic primacy in general and its manufacturing dominance in particular—now hardly registers as a major strategic concern, it has not ceased to be a winning trade competitor. Since the burst of its bubble economy in 1990, Japan has experienced nearly two decades of stagnation, and the world recession had a great impact because of the combination of the country's high dependence on exports of cars and high-tech products and its deteriorating domestic demand (Sommer 2009; Fackler 2010). Even Sony, the company whose name was synonymous with the modern world of small electronic gadgets, has lost most of its appeal.

One might say that Sony was the original Apple. From its miniature transistor radio in 1955 to the planet-sweeping Walkman in 1971 and the PlayStation, launched in 1994, Sony's sleek designs were envied but, for a long time, rarely successfully copied or surpassed. But in 2009 the company lost more than $2 billion; in 2010 the annual loss grew to more than $3 billion; and in the fiscal year ending March 31, 2012, the loss was more than $2.5 billion, with Sony's TV division a large money-loser for the eighth straight year. Not surprisingly, Sony, after cutting it global workforce by 16,000 people in 2008, announced 10,000 more layoffs in April 2012. The problems go far beyond corporate Japan, and as the long-awaited economic renaissance failed to materialize, the government kept on borrowing, turning Japan into the world's most indebted affluent economy: in 2012 Japan's net government financial liabilities were about 135% of nominal GDP, compared to about 52% in Germany, 66% in France, and 80% in the United States (OECD 2012).

A new study on sovereign fiscal responsibility that defined the fiscal space and fiscal path of 34 major economies put Japan in 31st place, just behind Ireland and ahead of Iceland, Portugal, and Greece (Walker et al. 2011). Japan—until recently the world's second largest economy, admired for its high-tech innovative drive and product quality, and, in some views, even a presumptive heir to the US global economic primacy—thus finds itself with a perilously diminished fiscal space, on par with Portugal, with just five years left before it hits its maximum feasible debt ceiling (for the United States, this point presently appears to be in 2027). Sovereign debt downgrading has already begun—in May 2009, Moody's cut Japan's rating from AAA to Aa2, and in January 2011 Standard and Poor's posted an AA rating, while the United States and Germany retain their AAA ratings—and the governor of Japan's central bank keeps repeating the mantra of no country being able to run deficits forever.

Moreover, for years Japan has not had a government able to make significant decisions. Politically the country now resembles postwar Italy, with five prime ministers coming and going during the five years between 2006 and 2010. The historic shift in September 2009 from more than a half century of nearly uninterrupted Liberal Democratic Party rule to control by the Democratic Party has brought neither improvements in policy clarity nor more resolute management of the nation's affairs. Add to this the country's already highly aged population and the enormous economic shock and human impact of the March 2011 Tōhoku earthquake, and even the best outlook is for a struggling economy preoccupied with domestic challenges. All of this adds up to a remarkable story of an economic reversal unprecedented in its scope and rapidity—but as far as trade is concerned, Japan still comes out as a huge winner and the United States remains a continuous loser in the bilateral exchange.

Germany is now in a much more enviable position. During the 1980s and early 1990s US trade deficits with Germany were much lower than with Japan ($11 billion in 1985, $9 billion in 1990) but afterward they rose to $29 billion by the year 2000 and $34 billion in 2010, with transportation equipment (mostly passenger cars) making the largest difference (nearly $15 billion in 2010). But in several other key categories, including machinery, chemicals, and computers and electronic products, the trade has been remarkably balanced. The challenge is thus not an excessive trade imbalance but rather Germany's exceptionally strong manufacturing success effectively translated into unrivaled exports, a situation that makes it much more difficult for US companies to compete globally.

Most Americans are not aware that the country with a GDP only a quarter of the US size had a higher share of global merchandise exports in 2009 than the United States (9% vs. 8.5%); in 2010 the United States was ahead, but only by $1 billion (WTO 2011). Undoubtedly, German manufacturing success has its deep historical roots, a part of sometime excessively revered German genius (Watson 2010), and it has been helped by specific features of what Albert (1993) called "Rhenish capitalism," a combination of long-term bank-oriented financing of corporations, cooperative industrial relations as well as cooperative relationships between firms, and a highly specialized training system (Busch 2004). German manufacturing has benefited from its famous *Mittelstand*, midsized companies typically employing 100–500 workers and often located in small towns, whose managers—commonly members of a family that set up the business a long time ago—are much less preoccupied with quarterly earnings and much more with the long-term survival of their enterprises.

These companies have cornered large shares of the global market for their highly specialized metal, plastics, and chemical manufactures. These realities served the country well during the 2008–2009 financial crisis, when companies were able to retain sufficient financing and did not have to resort to mass layoffs, thanks to the combination of strict employment protection regulations, the adoption of flexible employment, and *Kurzarbeit*, or the reduction in work hours to spread work around. During the sharp demand downturn of 2009, the German machine industry reduced its workforce by less than 3.5% as the number of *Kurzarbeit* workers rose from just 6,000 in 2008 to 190,000 in 2009 (VDMA 2011). Work hours declined by about 4%, and so did labor productivity because the jobs were preserved, but, unlike in all other major affluent economies, the German unemployment rate actually declined from 8.6% in 2007 to 7.9% at the start of the recession to 7% by May 2010 (von der Leyden 2011).

This led *Time* to wonder whether Germany knew the secret to creating jobs, and to pay a backhanded compliment by asking how the country became the China of Europe (Schuman 2011). But there is more to the recent German success than an unwavering and consensual pursuit of manufacturing excellence. After all, the country's economic performance during the last two decades of the twentieth century was hardly distinguished. The German unemployment rate, including the critical long-term version of it, was much higher than the annual US mean during most of the 1980s, throughout the 1990s (affected by the unification), and then until 2006. Mean unemployment during the years 2000–2006 was 10% in Germany and 4%–6% in the United States. In 2010 the German rate was 7.1%, compared to 9.6% in the United States; in 2011 the difference widened to 5.9% versus 9.0%, and by spring of 2012 it had shrunk a bit, to 5.6% versus 8.1% (OECD 2012).

What has worked in Germany's favor was that its industries benefit from the "made in Germany" cachet, appreciated in the Middle East and throughout Asia (particularly when selecting expensive automobiles), and from the dominance of many manufacturing niches by German companies, whose products found rapidly expanding markets in those fast-growing economies. With export markets in most affluent countries at or close to saturation level, the future growth of manufactured exports will have to come from Asia, Latin America, and Africa, and in many categories the success of US companies will depend primarily on how well they are able to compete with their often better-established and highly skilled German competitors.

And the United States is lagging even further behind not only its main G7 competitors but even the global mean as far as export intensity is concerned. This simple measure, rarely used in popular discussions of manufacturing, is the ratio of a nation's exports to its total manufacturing sales. In 2009 the United States was exporting only about 45% as much of its output of manufactured goods as was the global average, a poor performance that placed it 13th out of the 15 largest manufacturing countries, ahead of only Russia and Brazil (NAM 2011b). Japan's export intensity was 20% higher and China's about 38% higher; the global average is about 2.1 higher, and the leading EU countries had export intensities 2.5 times (Spain) to four times that of the United States. Per capita comparisons of the value of manufactured exports are even more dramatic: in the United States they added up to only $2,400 in 2009, compared with $3,700 for Spain, $4,000 for Japan, $4,600 for Canada, and $11,200 in Germany.

If the US export intensity had matched only the global average, the country would have sold abroad more than $700 billion worth of additional goods in 2009, twice the amount needed to eliminate that year's overall trade deficit. If they had equaled the average export intensity of the EU's four largest economies (Germany, France, the UK, and Italy), US sales of manufactured goods would have more than tripled and the country would enjoy a large trade surplus even in the absence of any steps to address its large volume of frivolous imports of consumer goods and its excessive dependence on foreign crude oil. This is also a good place to stress that it is primarily the United States' low export intensity rather than its high level of manufactured imports that explains the country's large trade deficits. Contrary to a common perception, when measured in relative terms the United States has not been an extravagant buyer of foreign manufactures. In 2009 they accounted for about 65% of total imports and prorated to about $4,600 per capita, while Germany had an identical import share of manufactures but its imports were more than twice as high as in the United States, at about $9,600 per capita—but the US exports were, as already noted, only about a fifth of the German level (UNCTAD 2012).

The potential for expanding manufactured exports is indicated by gains that took place during the eight years between 2000 and the onset of the economic downturn: worldwide US exports of medicinal and pharmaceutical products expanded nearly threefold, those of industrial chemicals grew 2.4-fold, those of primary plastics 2.2-fold, and sales of power-generating machinery equipment and equipment rose by 70%—and after recession-induced dips they reached new highs at 10%–15% above the 2008 level by 2011 (USBC 2012a). These gains should continue as companies that were formerly uninterested in exports realize that the increasing numbers of newly rich middle-class consumers, particularly in Asia, are eager to buy high-quality American products (Rohde 2012).

But the well-established exporters will keep making the greatest contribution. The US aerospace industry has been the largest exporter for many years; no other trade in manufactured items has had such a large and reliable annual surplus as the large category of aircraft, aeroengines, and parts, and foreign sales in this category have been supporting more domestic jobs than any other industrial activity. Aerospace exports, dominated by sales of Boeing's jetliners and GE and Pratt & Whitney jet engines, grew from less than $37 billion in 1990 to $81 billion in 2010, a 120% increase in two decades, and even though the imports of aircraft, engines, and parts grew at a faster rate (from $10.9 billion in 1990 to almost $32 billion in 2010, a 190% rise), the surplus nearly doubled in 20 years, from $25.8 billion in 1990 to $49.5 billion in 2010.

Maintaining the sector's competitiveness must be a key component of efforts to boost US exports, and the exports will have to be a large part of the sector's sales because the world's largest aerospace market of the next two decades will be in Asia, above all in China and India, and American aircraft and aeroengine makers should benefit from this expansion. Moreover, many other companies providing aviation security equipment and a multitude of components for airport infrastructure could also benefit from the concurrent expansion of Asian airports, with China adding 80 new terminals by 2020 and India planning an increase from 80 to 500 commercial airports (ITA 2011a).

Further, the US semiconductor sector has maintained its global lead by becoming overwhelmingly dependent on exports. In 2010 the sector accounted for 48% of worldwide sales (with Japan producing less than a quarter and China producing less than 1% of the total); it is still spending some three-quarters of its R&D monies domestically; and it is still coming up with new and superior designs, including 3D interconnects that bond semiconductor wafers to produce multilevel chips (SEMATECH 2011). During the early 1980s American manufacturers bought half of all semiconductors made worldwide. By 1990 that share was halved, and by 2003 the value of products sold to Asian producers (led by Taiwan, South Korea, and China, but excluding Japan) was twice the US total (SIA 2011).

By December 2010 the United States was buying only 18% of all shipments, compared to 16% for Japan and 53% for other Asian countries, whose industries now dominate the production of all kinds of consumer electronics. As a result, by 2010, 82% of US semiconductor sales were abroad, making them (in terms of value) the country's second largest export, following aircraft, aeroengines, and parts. While few US manufacturing sectors could ever match such a high dependence on exports, most of them have underperformed as exporters when compared with their major competitors, and hence most of them have a huge potential to increase their foreign sales.

But even the impressive export gains of the past decade could not prevent a further increase in overall US trade deficits and did nothing to change the lopsided trade with China. Here is, obviously, the greatest export opportunity. US sales to China more than doubled between 2005 and 2010, to $91.9 billion, but as imports rose by more than $120 billion the deficit gap actually widened, from $201.6 billion to $273.1 billion, and in 2011 it increased by more than 8%, to $295.5 billion (USBC 2012a). More containers cross the Pacific, but little has changed, as they go eastward crammed with high-value-added electronic products, apparel, and other consumer items and go back either empty or filled with wastepaper, to be remade in China into cardboard to package more goods for sale in the United States or turned into more durable products.

Things are not (yet?) as bad as Prestowitz (2010a) would have it: wastepaper and scrap metals are not America's largest export to China, but they have been large enough. In 2010, US exports of waste and scrap (NAICS category 910) reached nearly $9 billion, and in 2011 they surpassed $11 billion (USBC 2012a), less than transportation equipment, electronics, or agricultural products but more than the exports of all nonelectric machinery and more than five times as much as the sales of all electrical equipment, appliances and components. Of course, the proponents of globalization would see this as a perfect example of a comparative advantage, but I fail to see how a country can maintain its high standard of living by running huge and chronic trade deficits that would have been even greater if not for its copious exports of waste.

**Encountering Limits**

Any attempts to stabilize, or perhaps even to reverse, the fortunes of US manufacturing will face many obstacles and limits, some country-specific, the self-inflicted products of neglect, failed vision, and questionable management, others universal realities that shape the manufacturing fortunes of every nation—and I am not sure whether the latter challenges are more intractable than the former. The first category of limits that will affect the quest for strengthened US manufacturing is the magnitude of the domestic economic and social reforms needed to repair the country's fiscal situation.

The magnitude of required key interventions is easily illustrated. In 2011 the federal budget deficit of $1.4 trillion amounted to about 40% of government spending, or the total spent on social security and on defense: cutting these two items is about as likely as getting rid of the deficit by raising taxes, as that would require a 64% increase in the federal take. Even if taxes were to go up by a third there would still be the need to cut nearly $700 billion, that is, either all defense or all social security payments (Medicare/Medicaid claimed nearly $820 billion in 2011). Not surprisingly, some published deficit reduction plans do not balance the books before 2030. An IMF review of US economic policy illustrated the challenge in a similar way: it concluded that closing the huge fiscal gap would require a permanent annual fiscal adjustment that would have to be equal to about 14% of the country's GDP (IMF 2010).

Insofar as federal revenue in 2010 was about 15% of GDP, such an action would essentially demand an immediate and permanent doubling of all taxes but would yield a surplus equal to about 5% of GDP, which would be needed to pay the enormous uncovered federal liabilities arising from pensions and the health care costs of the country's aging population, whose annual cost totals about $4 trillion a year (in 2010 monies). The very magnitude of this problem has been a key reason why no effective steps have been taken so far. The Patient Protection and Affordable Care Act was enacted on March 23, 2010, with provisions to be phased in between 2011and 2018, but it will not reverse the country's excessive and rising spending on health care—and the reform of social security programs has not progressed even that far.

There are also some severe limits to what can be achieved in reforming America's education; indeed, hoping for any near-term returns resulting from improved education is almost delusionary. In this particular instance near term cannot be shorter than a complete educational cycle, that is, at least between 12 and 16 years. But the past two decades have seen many attempts at reforming education that ended in near-complete failures; their recent review by Klein (2011) makes for depressing reading. These are perhaps the most telling conclusions: the United States has doubled (in real monies) its spending on K–12 public education without anything to show for it as only a third or so of eighth-grade student are proficient in math, science, or reading, the high school graduation rate remains below 70%, and nearly 80% of graduates are not adequately prepared for university study.

When seen through a prism of international comparisons the taxation reform should be much less contentious than putting heath care and social security on sustainable bases. Americans are taxed no more than the Japanese (government taxes accounting for about 28% of GP) and much less than Canadians (35%) and Europeans (typically 40%–45%), but the structure of taxation is different: in the United States it comes mostly from income and capital (48% in the United States vs. 31% in Germany), whereas elsewhere it comes from the consumption of goods and services (16% in the United States vs. 26% in Germany) and from social contributions (41% in Germany vs. 25% in the United States). As the United States is now the only affluent country without a nationwide consumption tax (an equivalent of the goods and services tax in Canada or the value-added tax in EU countries) while having the highest corporate income tax, there is a logical appeal to enacting the first tax and lowering the second one.

A close look at America's manufacturing prospects suggests the two most important realities limiting its resurgence are the extent to which the domestic productive capacities of many industries have been compromised, reduced, or eliminated and the success of foreign competition in many remaining sectors. The most consequential example of the first process is the US automobile industry, which has lost more than half of its domestic market and whose profitability and quality remain questionable. The most worrisome example of the second reality is the country's once globally dominant aerospace industry and still America's strongest remaining exporter, though now besieged by competition from an increasing number of countries.

Despite some improvements in earnings and product quality, it is far from clear that US automakers have finally, after more than 30 years of failures, learned their lessons. In 2010, after decades of missed opportunities, and with Toyota sliding from its seemingly unassailable position, US automakers began to return to profitability, largely thanks to much improved quality. On June 20, 2011, Bob Lutz, the former CEO of GMC, published an opinion piece extolling the rise of Detroit's new quality automaking, writing, "GM, Ford and Chrysler are attacking with a vengeance, this time not with incentives, but with superior products" that are "beautifully-styled, superbly-crafted, presenting world-class ride" (Lutz 2011).

These advances were leaving the Japanese automakers, used to dominating the quality ratings, to face "tough road, hard work" ahead. Not so fast: three days after Lutz published his piece, J.D. Power and Associates released their initial quality ranking of 32 automobile brands. The list was topped by Lexus, Honda, and Acura, with Mazda in fifth place and Toyota in seventh place. Among American brands only Cadillac (ninth) and GMC (tenth) made it into the top ten. All other US makes ranked below the industry average of 107 problems per 100 vehicles, with Buick number 20, Ford, the strongest company of the Detroit Three, falling to 23rd place (with 116 problems for every 100 vehicles), and Dodge coming in last (J.D. Power and Associates 2011). And by July 2011, GM appeared to be having a truck supply overhang (the inventory of Silverados was worth more than six months of June sales) reminiscent of 2008 (Trudell and Armstrong 2011). The Detroit Three will be also limited (even when ignoring the exaggerated threat of new Chinese automakers) by Toyota's and Honda's determination to maintain their market share and by continuous aggressive expansion and upscaling by Hyundai and Kia Motors.

And any comeback will be even more limited for those manufacturing activities whose capacities have been reduced to an even greater extent than the automakers'. Pisano and Shih (2009) list the high-tech manufacturing capacities that have already been lost: fabless microchips; compact fluorescent lighting, electronic displays, lithium-ion batteries, advanced rechargeable batteries, crystalline and polycrystalline silicon solar cells, inverters, personal computers (desktop, notebook, and netbook), low-end servers, hard disk drives, consumer networking gear, advanced composite materials, advanced ceramics, and integrated circuit packaging. These products include both smaller, highly specialized industries as well as once globally dominant key sectors.

The best example in the first category is China's 95% or greater share of the world's supply of rare earth permanent magnets, with more than 100 companies producing the strongest neodymium-iron-boron devices (present in every hard drive), while the United States does not have a single maker (McCormack 2009). Printed circuit board and commercial photo masking are other highly specialized industries that now barely survive in the United States. Nothing illustrates the second kind of manufacturing demise, whose extent will limit any substantial future comeback, better than the plunge in the US production of machine tools. This critical manufacturing category was the country's great stronghold during the 1940s and 1950s, and by 1966 it was still producing 30% of the global output. by 2000 the share had fallen below 10% as imports rose from only about 5% during the late 1960s to about 70% of all machinery in the year 2000 (AMT 2004). By 2008 the output of $3.8 billion was less than 5% of the global total, putting the United States behind Taiwan, and equal to only about a quarter of the annual output of the two machine tool leaders, Germany and Japan (McCormack 2009).

Strong foreign competition has already limited the global reach of the United States' once unequaled aerospace industry, the manufacturing sector with apparently the strongest comparative advantage. I have already noted Boeing's losses to Airbus and the company's problems with the 787. Boeing's order books for 787 may be full, but it keeps announcing further slippages in the anticipated delivery of hundreds of planes (delays leading to some order cancellations). In 2011 the company lost further ground because of record orders for the new Airbus 320neo, with more than 1,200 orders placed in that year. This plane is directly competing with Boeing's best-selling model, the 737, whose low elevation makes it difficult to fit the more efficient engines that will be installed on a new version of the Airbus 320. Moreover, Airbus plans to reach parity with Boeing in China by 2013. Although a latecomer to that market, it already had a 45% share of the market by the end of 2010 and is adding a new assembly line.

And both Boeing and Airbus are under pressure from two smaller established aircraft makers that have already sold thousands of big small jets, the Canadian company Bombardier and Brazil's Embraer, and are now offering small big jetliners (the Bombardier C series, for 110–130 people, and the Embraer 195, for 106–188 passenger, are intended to compete against the Boeing 737), as well as from newcomers that have already entered or have plans to compete in the jetliner market with new commercial designs: Russia (Sukhoi Superjet, UAC MS-21), China (ARJ21 and C919), and Japan (Mitsubishi MRJ, Kawasaki YPX). In November 2010, China's Commercial Aircraft Corporation got its first 100 orders for the C919 (with 166 seats, in direct competition with the Boeing 737 and the Airbus A320), breaking the Boeing-Airbus duopoly. Arvai, Hamilton, and Schonland (2009) predict that the coming aerospace squeeze could cut in half the share of 100- to 200-seat single-aisle jetliners claimed by Airbus and Boeing.

Aircraft manufacturing is also a perfect example of another important factor that will limit future employment in US-based manufacturing, although it may increase the output and profit of companies headquartered in the United States. The new realities of globalized production mean that the large multinational companies that now form the core of the global business structure have no fundamental interest in structuring their affairs in a way that benefits a particular nation. As Nolan (2012) shows, the foreign assets of the world's top 100 multinationals are nearly 60% of their totals assets, with similar shares for foreign employment and sales. Not surprisingly, the relationship between those companies and their home countries has been steadily weakening, as their identity and interests are progressively less tied to those of the country where they were founded, and hence they have a diminishing incentive to work with the national governments to promote any specific industrial policy.

Subcontracting and outsourcing have made the concept of the country of origin of many manufactured goods a rather meaningless notion. Given this reality, any expectation that large multinational companies, and particularly those earning most of their profits abroad, should feel any obligation to maximize their American employment opportunities is as quaint as the idea of twenty-first-century industrial autarky. This has become a factor affecting not only production but also product design, and not just routine tasks outsourced to low-cost suppliers in low-income countries but also knowledge-intensive activities previously secured from specialized suppliers in high-wage nations.

MacPherson and Vanchan (2010) surveyed the 100 top US producers of durable goods and found that between 1995 and 2005, their share of externalized design activity had doubled for product design (to 26%), increased 3.5-fold for design research (to about 40%), and grown by 68% for all design activities. The process will only get more common, and while it may actually boost innovation originating under the corporate labels of Apple, Boeing, Caterpillar, Dell, or IBM, it surely does not create jobs in the United States. And the assembly of goods from parts designed and made in other countries is not limited to relatively inexpensive consumer electronics items such as the iPhone, whose cost and profit structure were explained in the previous chapter.

Boeing still assembles its jetliners in the United States (in Everett and Renton, Washington, and in North Charleston, South Carolina), and its corporate headquarters are now in Chicago. But most of its sales have been abroad, and that is where most of the components for its new planes originate. In June 2011 James F. Albaugh, executive vice president of Boeing, told the *China Daily* that "there is not a plane we built that doesn't have parts from China in it" (Li 2011)—and he might have repeated that claim in half a dozen other countries. Boeing airplanes are thus now no triumphs of American aircraft manufacturing as the company subcontracts major shares of fabrication to Japan (especially to Mitsubishi Heavy Industries), South Korea, Italy, France, and China.

With the Boeing 787, the company outsourced 70% of the design and development of work for the plane's key innovative feature, its all-composite wing, to a Japanese consortium (Harrigan 2006). In 1971 the Boeing 747 was an American plane; in 2011 the Boeing 787, finally in service after a three-year delay, is a plane whose parts are designed and made in many countries and whose final assembly takes place in the United States. In the short run this outsourcing brought immense problems with quality control and coordination; in the longer run it enables would-be competitors as the companies share and surrender their special know-how and engineer their own decline.

But no trend lasts forever, and counterintuitively, the world recession instigated a slow but unmistakable reappraisal of outsourcing. I have already quoted an astonishing admission by James McNerney, Boeing's CEO, about the lemming-like rush of US-based multinationals to extend their supply chains into Asia; here is a lesson learned. McNerney sees more manufacturing coming back to the United States, and GE's CEO Jeff Immelt, admitting an evolution of thinking on the value of outsourcing, sees "the opportunity to bring jobs—certain jobs, not every job—back" (Malone 2012). He believes that this will be true even in such areas as software, where outsourcing to India ruled for more than a decade.

Finally, US manufacturing would be helped by a global rebalancing as the countries that now run huge trade surpluses would consume more domestically and pull in more imports, creating new opportunities for exports. Many American economists and politicians have called for this grand global rebalancing, but an export expansion based on such a shift will not take place anytime soon. The most obvious reason is the sheer scale of the necessary adjustments. During the past decade the United States has not had a continuous trade surplus with even a single one of the world's 12 largest economies, a group that includes India, Brazil, and Russia, and with most of them it runs chronically deep deficits. The experience of trading with Japan shows how immutable these deficits seem to be.

In 1985, at the peak of concerns about Japan's economic expansion, the US trade deficit was $55 billion. After all supposedly corrective measures went into effect, the deficit was still $41 billion in 1990—and $60 billion in 2010; adjusting the latter total for inflation yields about $41 billion in 1990 monies. So the success has been nothing but a stabilization of a massive annual deficit. A closer look shows how entrenched these deficits have become. In 2000 and 2010 they were, respectively, $43 billion and $42 billion for transportation equipment and $15 billion and $14 billion for nonelectric machinery. The United States has large trade surpluses only in food and feed (wheat, corn, soybeans, meat; about $4 billion in 2000 and $6.5 billion in 2010), but those surpluses hardly make a dent in the overall deficit. During the quarter century between 1985 and 2010 the nominal trade deficit figure never slipped below $40 billion a year. It peaked at $90 billion in 2006 and averaged about $62 billion during the interval noted, and the aggregate added up to transferring about $1.6 trillion from the United States to Japan (USBC 2011b).

If this counts as a success, let us think of the prospects of modifying—given the Japanese precedent, the notion of reversing is impossible to entertain for a long time to come—the trade deficit with China, at $275 billion more than four times as large as that with Japan, and maintained by a country that is not only immune to any US appeals to deal with the imbalance but publicly scorns them. How intractable the situation is can be illustrated in many ways. One of the most convincing is the observation that even after US exports to China nearly sextupled between 2000 and 2010, the overall trade deficit still nearly tripled. And, recalling the cost structure of iPhone, even a rapid appreciation of the yuan would make little difference in the case of e-products assembled at such a low cost in China from foreign components (Xing 2011).

Other factors will limit the pace of global rebalancing. For many industries, an appreciation of Chinese currency and rising Chinese wages would have only one effect: the relocation of the affected manufacturing to other countries. After all, this is exactly what happened with the rise of China when the assembly work done elsewhere in Asia (mainly in Japan, Hong Kong, and Taiwan) moved, starting slowly during the late 1980s and accelerating after China's accession to the WTO, first to Guangdong and then to China's other coastal provinces. And while some sectors could repatriate the factories and jobs with relative ease, others would have to spend years and much capital building or rebuilding the inadequate production capacities and infrastructures.

Perhaps the most obvious example is the steel industry. Before the world recession of 2008–2009 the United States imported more than a quarter of its steel (compared to less than a fifth in 1970), and it simply could not raise its capacity by 20–30 Mt per year in a matter of years. Similar infrastructural obstacles would limit any rapid expansion of most manufacturing sectors that have been heavily reduced by imports. That is why I at least partially agree with Dadush (2011), who argues that the calls for global rebalancing are misguided as they divert attention from the real need, reforms at home. Or, in a counterintuitive rephrasing of the challenge, the United States has to start the rebalancing at home, as one of the principal causes of this disruptive phenomenon is the country's excessive consumption.

**Figure 6.1**
Is it a symbol of the past or a harbinger of new conquests? The original Boeing 747 flew commercially for the first time in 1969, and became the iconic machine of modern jet-powered long-distance flight. The new, redesigned Boeing 747–8 Intercontinental, shown here during its first flight, entered service in 2012, but it has to compete with the Airbus 380 and Airbus 340. Color image available at http://upload.wikimedia.org/wikipedia/commons/3/33/Boeing_747-8_first_flight_Everett,_WA.jpg.

# 6

# Chances of Success

*During the coming years America's reflexive optimism will be much tested. The odds of a strong social and economic rebound and of a broad-based manufacturing renaissance are no higher than even.*

The harsh reality, as far as I can see, is that the next 25 years (2013–2038) are highly unlikely to see more dramatic changes than science and technology produced in the last 25 (1987–2012).

—Niall Ferguson, "Don't Believe the Techno-Utopian Hype," *Newsweek,* July 30, 2012

We are poised to enter a new era that will come from the convergence of three technological transformations that have already happened: Big Data, the Wireless Wired World, and Computational Manufacturing. . . . Computational manufacturing is poised to become a trillion dollar industry, unleashing as big a change in how we make things as did mass production in an earlier era, and as did the agricultural revolution in how we grew things.

—Mark P. Mills, "The Next Great Growth Cycle," *The American,* August 25, 2012

Reflexive, perhaps even complacent, optimism is an essential part of the American outlook. Born of the hope of millions of immigrants, the country's westward expansion and the decades of its rapid technical rise during the latter half of the nineteenth century carried the message of inevitable progress into the twentieth century (Clarke 1985). Men as different as Andrew Carnegie and F. Scott Fitzgerald anticipated splendid futures: Carnegie saw "all sunshine," Fitzgerald's Gatsby believed in "the orgiastic future that year by year recedes before us . . . but that's no matter—tomorrow we will run faster, stretch out our arms further. . . . And one fine morning. . . ." The Great Depression dented these anticipations, but the Allied victory in World War II and the postwar economic expansion renewed the nation's faith in American exceptionalism. The doubts and downturns caused by the Vietnam War and the rise of Japanese, and later Chinese, economic power were soon erased by the "victory" in the Cold War and the Gulf War of 1991, and by the economic resurgence of the 1990s.

Even the attack on 9/11, the world recession of 2008–2009, and economic prostration and deepening social troubles could not destroy that persistent belief in America's exceptionalism. America's power to effect any positive change abroad seems to be almost entirely gone, but Joseph Nye, a senior Harvard man, counsels not to worry: "United States is likely to remain supreme for some time" (Nye 2011). But Nye must know that this kind of supremacy has made little difference in Afghanistan, Iran or North Korea, and even in Iraq, after so many lives lost and damaged and so many resources wasted during nearly a decade of war and occupation, the US now has virtually no influence.

The US government deficit is growing by more than a trillion dollars a year, but Paul Krugman—a Nobelian, no less!—is pleased that "the federal government is having no trouble raising money, and the price of that money—the interest rate on federal borrowing—is very low by historical standards. So there's no need to scramble to slash spending now now now" (2011a). How many more trillions of accumulated deficit will it take for Krugman's "now" to run out? What share of the federal budget spent on interest payments would make him reconsider?

As for the rise of America's key competitor, Summers (2011) thinks that it is easy "to overestimate our problems" while exaggerating what is happening in China as a result of the "seductive appeal to technology and public infrastructure" (the Shanghai maglev, rapid trains, new airports) and underestimating China's transformational challenges in political, environmental, financial, and social realms. Drezner (2011) assures us that "even on the financial side, the US still reigns." And Gross (2012) dismisses any talk of America's decline by claiming that the United States is stronger and faster than anyone else and that the jobs machine is clearly working again.

To Drezner I would say: what a glorious reign, with chronic budget and trade deficits, and with aggregate debt and other uncovered financial obligations that surpassed $120 trillion (National Debt Clock 2012). And with respect to being stronger than anyone else, Gross might also think of that half of the US citizenry that is now receiving some kind of government assistance, and of the misfiring jobs machine that in 2011 absorbed 1.48 million new workers when two million jobs would have been the minimum needed just to keep up with the country's population growth. Between 2001 and 2011 the United States created only 5.4 million net new jobs instead of the 20 million needed to keep its growing population working. And even though the latest international student assessment (PISA 2010) reveals another abysmal ranking of American students, Ben Wildavsky (2011) maintains that American kids are not falling behind. Is ranking 32nd on a math achievement scale another sign of supremacy?

Such claims should not be surprising, as they are part of a much larger exercise in collective denial. It is perhaps the surest sign of a country mired in deeply worrisome problems when its opinion-making elites claim that everything is more or less in order. The United States now has many serious challenges that are downplayed, even denied, by large segments of the country's ever-expanding commentariat, which still sees the United States as the undisputed number one, as an exceptional nation that has no equal and that will maintain this position into the foreseeable future. In light of this common perception, it should have been expected that the slightest economic gains in 2010 and 2011 would have been interpreted by some observers as harbingers of manufacturing's resurgence.

"Manufacturing booms as Deere exemplifies productivity surge," write Chen and Miller (2011), and "Manufacturing makes a comeback as shining star of the US economy," because in 2010 the sector's output grew by 7%, more than twice as fast as the economy as a whole, and during the first quarter of 2011 that difference grew even wider as "more manufacturing jobs were created in the first four months of this year than in any year since 1984" (Perry 2011). All true, but it is all no better than the proverbial grasping at straws. The sector's growth in 2010 was accompanied by a gain of only 117,000 jobs, and although more jobs (181,000) were added in 2011, the total net addition in those two years erased only about 5% of the total post-2000 manufacturing job loss—and the "shining star" was employing fewer people than at any time since the beginning of World War II.

The unemployment challenge has been particularly great. To some, the recent increase in unemployment has been a simple cyclical matter resulting from inadequate demand (Krugman 2011a); others have argued that structural shifts have played a role. Chen and colleagues (2011) took a closer look and found the latter to be true: during the world recession of 2008–2009 structural shocks (measured by an index of the cross section of variance of stock prices) accounted for about half the increase in the long-term duration of unemployment in that period. And the toll has been much greater than during previous recessions, when the average duration of unemployment was between 15 and 20 weeks, for this time it surpassed 35 weeks. In absolute terms, job losses were about 2.6 million 30 months after the peak job month during the 2001 recession; during the world recession the loss after 30 months was about 7.5 million below the peak, making the change in the US unemployment rate about twice that for the UK and Sweden and four times that for Australia and France, while Germany actually gained jobs (OECD 2010).

Most worrisome has been the increase in the number of jobless who cannot find work for 27 weeks or longer. During the previous post–World War II downturns, that share peaked at 15%–20%, and in the early 1980s it reached 25%, but during the recent world recession it surpassed 40% (IMF 2010). At least some observers have realized that all of this is not only exceptional but fundamentally transformational. Peck (2010, 42) offers perhaps the best summary:

> The Great Recession may be over, but this era of high joblessness is just beginning. Before it ends, it will likely change the life course and character of a generation of young adults. It will leave an indelible imprint on many blue-collar men. It could cripple marriage as an institution in many communities. It may already be plunging many inner cities into a despair not seen for decades. Ultimately, it is likely to warp our politics, our culture, and the character of our society for years to come.

And yet some observers are suggesting an imminent large-scale return of manufacturing capacities, from China to the United States. The Boston Consulting Group (2011) forecasts that the United States should see a manufacturing renaissance during the next five years as wage rises in China shrink the already narrowing wage gap and as location incentives and flexible work rules make many states increasingly competitive. They expect that such relocations will affect particularly the products whose manufacturing requires less labor, such as household appliances and construction equipment.

This conclusion has been confirmed by the U-turn taken by GE, America's leading manufacturer of electrical goods. Jeffrey Immelt, the company's CEO, affirmed not only that outsourcing is an outdated strategy for GE Appliances but, more generally, he concluded that outsourcing "based only on labor costs is yesterday's model" (Immelt 2012, 46). Consequently, GE began to repatriate some of its production lines (low-energy water heaters, stainless-steel dishwashers) from China to its Appliance Park in Louisville, Kentucky, where it opened a new assembly line in February 2012. Similarly, Apple announced in December 2012 that it will bring the production of its Macintosh computers (using American subcontractors) back to the United States.

These developments led some commentators to write about the in-sourcing boom, about "the startling, sustainable, just-getting started return of industry to the United States" (Fishman 2012, 45), about the global trade winds that might be finally blowing again toward America (Fallows 2012), and, most expansively, about the prospects of a US manufacturing renaissance (Pisano 2012). I agree with Pisano and Shih (2012) that such a renaissance is needed but what has been, so far, taking place does not deserve the description of rebirth.

Numbers behind GE's Appliance Park explain why: the facility's peak employment in 1973 was 23,000 people; by 2011 the total slid below 2,000, and by the end of 2012 it rose to 3,600 (Fishman 2012). What we have seen is a partial repatriation that may eventually double or triple the lowest employment numbers reached in the US manufacturing plants, or even in entire sectors, between 2008 and 2011—but that will still leave the totals as much as 80% below their highs of the 1970s and 1980s. Four factors will moderate, or outright limit, the future employment gains in the US manufacturing: improving competitiveness of foreign producers, continuing attractiveness of foreign markets, challenges accompanying plant repatriation, and, above all, inexorably advancing robotization of virtually all manufacturing tasks.

China and other formerly low-cost manufacturing countries will not simply stand by as the return of production to the United States keeps on unfolding and will respond by adjustments of their own. Obviously, many American companies will wish to keep on producing in countries that have become their principal markets for consumer and industrial goods, while other corporations will respond by shifting their production to new low-cost locations (the rise of Vietnamese manufacturing has already been remarkable). And many companies trying to repatriate their production from Asia will not find it easy to secure all the needed subcontractors in the United States and to fill all jobs requiring particular qualifications.

But even if most companies were to repatriate their outsourced production they would reinstate only a fraction of the jobs that American workers held before the plants were closed and the work moved to Asia. That is because the most important long-term threat to jobs in manufacturing is a steadily advancing robotization. Businesses relocating from China to the United States or abandoning plans to move to China have found that the best way to keep their costs low is to minimize labor costs by redesigning their products so that the assembly can be done by increasingly cheaper robots. Austen (2010) cites an example of a coffin factory in Tennessee that survived the influx of cheap Chinese imports by buying a robot that replaced four people and another one that did away with 16 workers. And GE Aviation's new manufacturing facility in Ellisville, Mississippi, built to produce advanced composite components for jet engines, will create just 250 jobs (Immelt 2012).

But robotization is a process that will transform virtually every category of modern manufacturing because it is poised to enter a qualitatively new stage. So far, a great deal of robotization has been driven primarily not by the quest for lower labor costs but by the unequaled accuracy, repeatability, speed, and quality with which industrial robots can operate, as well as by the opportunity to improve worker safety, avoid human exposure to potentially toxic substances, and enhance the flexibility of production (which can be achieved with a new set of software commands). During the late 1960s and 1970s, programmable robots began to take over welding, spray painting, and the manipulation of hazardous materials, with Japan in the lead. As prices declined and the average time between failures more than doubled, the robot count jumped by two orders of magnitude between 1980 and 2000. In 2012 the global total of industrial robots was in excess of one million machines, each expected to work for about 15 years.

And not only is the new generation of robots capable of executing a much wider variety of specific operations previously reserved for skilled employees but increasing computing power allows much greater flexibility, coordination with other machines, and multitasking. Multipurpose robots can locate, select, and grasp assorted parts, subject them to specific operations, or assemble them with high precision, while autonomous robotic couriers can convey raw materials, parts, and finished products. Moreover, the increasing integration of machines and processes activated by more complex software makes the term robotization obsolete. What is going on is intelligent automation that subsumes design, prototyping, and production.

It is this new, digitalized automated way of making things (whose initial use was in rapid prototyping) that is emerging as a production process of global importance. The *Economist* called its rise the third industrial revolution, following the mechanization of labor and the emergence of mass production (Markillie 2012), and Mills (2012) listed computational manufacturing (defined by high talent rather than by cheap labor) as one of three pillars of the next great growth cycle, the other two being big data (as computer processing power and data storage have become, for all practical purposes, free) and the delivery of information (the wireless wired world).

Computer-driven three-dimensional (3-D) printing is a form of additive manufacturing, producing objects from the sequential deposition of mini-layers of various materials (plastics, metals, alloys, ceramic powders, paper) and their solidification by heat, liquid binders, lamination, or laser sintering (Gibson, Rosen, and Stucker 2009). This is the opposite of the traditional subtractive production, in which objects are produced by the removal of materials by mechanized or manual machining (cutting, drilling, boring, chiseling). 3D printers have been getting larger and less expensive, and their use has advanced from rapid prototyping, the making of engineering and architectonic models, and the crafting of unique designer objects. The ultimate vision is to use this innovation to create a world where industrial products destined to become parts of more complex machines are designed by automated software and then go straight into 3D printers or, in the ultimate case, where 3D printers combine any number of needed raw materials to print complete machines.

For consumer products the only difference might be that production runs might be preceded by prototyping to gauge to the appeal, functionality, and acceptance of new items. The employment of 3D printing technology in manufacturing (a completely misleading term for that kind of production) would then consist only of programmers, as appropriately programmed additive printers could not only turn out serial products but could also make them themselves. A more likely reality for the next several years is a much more selective use of additive production, but the impact on manufacturing employment, both quantitative and qualitative, is bound to grow: although there would be less and less concern about the cost of massed labor, and although manufacturing could be done essentially in any place with a reliable supply of electricity and raw materials, there would be also fewer and fewer people employed in this new way of making things. And where will they go as intelligent automation takes over many service sectors, from retail to document processing, from stock trading to minimally invasive surgery, from patient care to book translation?

Again, for many economists, this state of affairs would be as it should be: they have consistently argued that it does not matter if established, large multinational companies are not the great generators of new jobs or if old industries and service do not return to the United States or are displaced by automation because new startups, those perennial favorites of entrepreneurial America, will compensate. A study by the Kauffman Foundation revealed that for all but seven years between 1977 and 2005, US startups, firms less than a year old, added an average of three million jobs a year, while older companies lost a million jobs a year (Kane 2010).

But as Grove (2010) so vigorously points out, belief in the superior job-creating capacity of startups is very mistaken because the ideas developed by such firms need considerable scaling up to be transformed into commercial successful products whose manufacturing will generate many new jobs. Hence it is not some inherent incapacity of large US firms to create jobs but the fact that an overwhelming majority of those companies have essentially given up on scaling up in the United States that is the issue. Grove illustrates the consequence of this reality with some devastating quantitative comparisons. In 2010 the employment in the entire US computer industry was less than before the first simple personal computer, the Altair 2800, was assembled in 1975, while Asian computer makers employ 1.5 million workers and Foxconn (Hon Hai), the principal maker of Apple products, has about 250,000 employees in China, ten times as many as Apple does in the United States. If the scaling-up of all new manufacturing sectors during the past three decades had taken place largely in the United States, the country would have now millions of new jobs.

None of America's recent electronic innovations, from the iPhone to the Kindle, has been scaled up to mass production in the United States, and "losing the ability to scale will ultimately damage our capacity to innovate" (Grove 2010). The consequences of this reality are perfectly illustrated by Linden, Dedrick, and Kraemer (2009). They traced all iPod-related jobs by country and category and found that only 30 of the more than 41,000 jobs were in US-based production. The largest category of domestic jobs (about18% of the total) was in retail, with about 15% in engineering and other professional positions, while production abroad accounted for about 47% of all iPod-related jobs and foreign retail and engineering for the remaining 20%. However, total compensation was more than twice as large in the United States as it was abroad, an expected consequence of two very different job categories (low-wage assembly in China, with annual earnings of about $1,500, and high-reward design in the United States, averaging about $85,000, while US retail pays only about $25,000 a year).

This reality is precisely why Grove's question about the future state of the nation goes to the very core of why manufacturing matters:

> You could say, as many do, that shipping jobs overseas is no big deal because the high-value work—and much of profits—remain in the US But what kind of a society are we going to have if it consists of highly paid people doing high-value-added work—and masses of unemployed? (Grove 2010)

I have been asking this very question, wording it in almost the same way, for more than a decade. Unfortunately, answers to it can be found in what is already there, in some truly worrisome numbers that cannot be dismissed as statistical artifacts or irrelevant measures.

Losses of well-paid manufacturing jobs have been a major reason for a pronounced polarization of job opportunities in the US labor market. As documented by Autor (2010), the demand for middle-skill jobs has been declining, and men have been disproportionately affected by this shift, resulting in a secular decline in male labor force participation, from about 76% in 1970 to 72% by the year 2000 and less than 64% in 2010 (BLS 2012). Moreover, as men have been forced out of middle-skill blue-collar jobs, they have generally moved down the occupational ladder, to lower-paid jobs demanding fewer skills. This is not a uniquely American phenomenon, but between 1996 and 2007 (the last period analyzed by Autor) the shift in that undesirable direction was stunning, as employment growth was heavily concentrated in the three lowest deciles of mean income, with job losses in deciles four through nine.

This reality is undoubtedly a major reason behind what is to me the most disconcerting trend, income inequality resembling more the distribution of wealth in China than in Canada or France. This income inequality has resulted in such troubling outcomes as nearly every fifth child in the United States living in poverty, and an astonishing total of some 45 million people (nearly the equivalent of the entire population of Spain) receiving food stamps in 2011 (USBC 2011a). But perhaps the United States is just in one of those temporary downturns, to be followed by a brighter tomorrow, much as (to recall just the last experience of such a see-saw) the economically vibrant 1990s followed the subdued 1980s. Or, as Fallows (2010, 55) reminded those forecasting the country's retreat, "America has been on the brink of ruination, or so we have heard, from the launch of *Sputnik*."

But that is a weak argument because this time things really have changed in too many fundamental ways. In 1957 the United States was the world's largest creditor nation, with large budget and trade surpluses. It was the world's largest producer of crude oil, had a very low unemployment rate, and was enjoying unequaled successes in rapidly deploying new industrial products ranging from large jetliners to tiny transistors, whose mass manufacturing it pioneered and perfected at home. And it really had no serious competitors, with the impoverished China on the verge of the world's largest, Mao-made famine, with Europe and Japan just a few years out from regaining their prewar production, and with the USSR, the exaggerated *Sputnik* scare notwithstanding, already on its trajectory of economic decline. Everything is different now. The United States, the largest ever debtor nation, keeps piling up enormous budget and trade deficits, has a real unemployment rate close to 20%, has not had a trade surplus in high-tech goods for more than a decade, and will not be able to keep postponing the government budget cuts for another decade. As Ruttan (2006) showed, America's general-purpose innovation has been so closely tied to military research that he titled his book examining these realities *Is War Necessary for Economic Growth?* What will happen to this link as "deeply destructive cuts" (the White House's phrasing in September 2012) hit the Pentagon's budget?

And, of course, there is a new China, the world's factory, with trillions of dollars in reserves and the largest holder of US government debt. Its economy is shifting to lower growth rates, and its multitude of social, political, and environmental challenges does not make it, as so many so uncritically claim, an invincible superpower, but there is no doubt that its post-1980 rise had a sapping effect on America. Add to this the visibly aged and inferior infrastructure, large-scale urban decay, and inferior public transportation, and foreign visitors to urban America often have the feeling of being in a struggling low-income country than in "the sole remaining superpower."

Is it because America does not aspire anymore? As Jack Welch, former CEO of GE, put it, you cannot run a grocery store without a basic strategy—but the United States has no fundamental strategy to be the "most innovative, the most productive, the most competitive country on Earth. . . . The Brazilians think they are exceptional and the Chinese think they are exceptional but we're not in America. I think we could be. That's what used to set us apart."

Similarly, Clyde Prestowitz (2010a) concluded that the United States has abandoned the economic principles that guided it to greatness: its support of domestic manufacturing, its investment in innovation, and its pursuit of only those trade deals that brought mutual benefits.

Immanuel Wallerstein (2011) is far more pessimistic as he believes that the global economy will not, "now or ever," recover from the downturn that began in 2008 because we are now experiencing "the next-to-last bubble" of the boom-bust sequence that began in the early 1970s and that will culminate in a final bubble of state indebtedness and national bankruptcies. Less dramatically, it is now necessary to ask an uncomfortable question. Has the United States exhausted those sources of innovation that it was able to mobilize in the past in order to generate many new manufacturing jobs? At the time of its IPO in May 2012, Facebook was valued at $104 billion, nearly twice as much as Boeing, with its total capitalization of $53 billion.

But Facebook is essentially just a communication and entertainment platform, an addictive and rapid means of verbal and pictorial messaging, gossiping and display, whose design and management employed about 3,200 people at the time of its IPO, whose operation depends overwhelmingly on devices made in Asia, and whose earnings (before taxes) in 2012 were just $2 billion. Boeing, on the other hand, is indisputably one of the creators of the modern age, a company whose order books have a backlog of planes worth $380 billion and that employs more than 170,000 people. Why should any economy applaud a decline or outright demise of its Boeings and cheer the emergence of its Facebooks?

But that is precisely what many economists are telling us to do. An editorialist in the *Economist* (April 21, 2012) wrote disparagingly about governments clinging "to a romantic belief that manufacturing is superior to services, let alone finance." I am not endowing manufacturing with any superior attributes, I am simply recognizing the obvious: we could obviously do quite well as an affluent civilization without a myriad of modern services, but our physical and mental well-being, from being able to access food and shelter to receiving health care and having reliable transportation, rests on an assured supply of a myriad of manufactured products. First things first: "superior" is a wrong term to use, but manufacturing (now including its many "service" components) is fundamentally more important than arranging dubious mortgages, investing in even more dubious hedge funds, and boasting about the exploits of a new dog on a Facebook page.

Within a decade we will know whether the Facebook route to economic might works—or whether the United States is sinking ever deeper into prolonged economic stagnation. While it can be argued that the past decade does not make a long-term trend, the indications have been worrisome. Here are average decadal growth rates of the US GDP: for the 1950s, 3.5%; the 1960s, 4.2%; the 1970s, 3.2%; the 1980s, 3.2%; the 1990s, 3.4%—and for the 2000s just 1.7%. This halving of GDP growth explains the loss of several million jobs and accounts for most of the disconcerting ending of a decadal series of net job creation: 6.9 million during the 1950s, 12.9 million during the 1960s, 20.6 million during the 1970s, 19.5 million during the 1980s, and 18.4 million during the 1990s (McKinsey Global Institute 2011)—but in the 10 years between the beginning of the year 2000 and the end of 2009 there was actually a net loss (gross job gains minus gross job losses) of about 3.8 million jobs in total private employment (BLS 2012). Are these figures harbingers of a great stagnation or just the aberrations of a dismal decade?

Might it be that Bismarck's famous 1898 *bon mot*—"God favors fools, drunkards, and the United States of America"—has not lost its validity? But only blind optimists could be confident that this favoritism persists: after more than a century there are abundant signs that the long run might be coming to its end. But I believe that in the affairs of large nations, no situation is ever completely hopeless—and as a lifelong critical observer of American society I am well aware how it has repeatedly demonstrated its impressive capacity for renewal. And yet I am not sure whether it can demonstrate it again as I have not seen, so far, enough commitment and resolve even to acknowledge fully the severity of the accumulated challenges. Even odds of success are thus the best bet I can offer—hoping that I will be wrong, fearing that I am expecting too much.

# Coda

## March 2013: Better News Still to Come

During the six months between the book's submission to MIT and proofreading the typeset pages, none of the key indicators of America's performance have shown any clear improvement: they have either remained unchanged or deteriorated even further. At 11.85 million, America's total manufacturing employment in January 2013 was no higher than during 2009 (the first full year of the economic downturn), and while the workforce in motor vehicles and parts sector was 16% above its 2009 level, broadly based deindustrialization of America has continued with new 2012 employment lows in communications equipment, semiconductors, computers and electronics products, furniture, textile mills, apparel, paper, printing, and chemicals. Reported unemployment fell below 8%, but real unemployment (counting discouraged workers who have not looked for a job for less than a year) was 14.4% at the end of 2012, and overall unemployment (including workers who have stopped looking) has reached just above 20%. The number of families on food stamps and those receiving some kind federal assistance has reached a new high: about half of the total population.

During 2012 the US federal debt rose by 17% from $14 to $16.4 trillion, and its share held by foreigners increased by about half a trillion dollars, with China holding a record amount—$1.2 trillion. The trade deficit remained near its historically high level with two marginal positives—a negligible decline (0.4%) in the overall deficit in trading goods and about an 8% lower deficit in advanced technology products (but still more than $90 billion a year in the red); however, there was another record trade deficit with China ($315 billion, nearly 7% higher than in 2011).

The country's most valuable company soared and then fell: in September 2012: Apple's stock reached $700, but by four months later, it had lost nearly 40% of its value. But that made little difference for American jobs, as Apple has not been manufacturing products in the United States. Boeing does, and it made a comeback by delivering 21 more planes than Airbus (601 vs. 580) and, much more impressively, by getting orders for 1203 new airplanes compared to 833 for Airbus. But most of those orders were for Boeing 787, whose flights and deliveries were suspended in January 13, 2013, after several on-board lithium-ion battery fires, the first time an airliner approved for commercial use was taken out of service for an indefinite period of time. Predictably, many knowledgeable observers blamed excessive outsourcing for the problem.

Hard to see anything promising in these developments . . .

# References


Abernathy, W., et al. 1982. *The Competitive Status of the US Auto Industry*. Washington, DC: National Academy Press.

Abramovitz, M. 1956. Resource and output trends in the United States since 1870. *American Economic Review* 46:5–23.

Acemoglu, D., et al. 2010. *The Environment and Directed Technical Change*. Milano: Fondazione ENI Enrico Mattei.

Adams, M. C. C. 1994. *The Best War Ever: America and World War II*. Baltimore, MD: Johns Hopkins University Press.

AFL-CIO. 2006. Petition [on China's repression of workers' rights]. Washington, DC: Office of the US Trade Representative.

Air Ministry. 1940. *A.P 1509B/J.2-W Merlin II and III Aero Engines*. London: Air Ministry.

Airbus. 2011. Airbus. http://www.airbus.com/.

Albert, M. 1993. *Capitalism Against Capitalism*. London: Whurr.

Albrecht, D., ed. 1995. *World War II and the American Dream: How Wartime Building Changed a Nation*. Cambridge, MA: MIT Press.

Alexander, J. D. 1994. Military conversion policies in the USA: 1940s and 1990s. *Journal of Peace Research* 31:19–33.

Allaud, L., and M. Martin. 1976. *Schlumberger: Histoire d'une technique*. Paris: Berger-Levrault.

Allen, R. C. 1979. International competition in iron and steel, 1850–1913. *Journal of Economic History* 39:911–937.

American Chemistry Council. 2008. Energy savings through American chemistry. http://www.steel.org/en/sitecore/content/Global/Document%20Types/News/2009/~/media/Files/AISI/General%20Docs/energy-climate-solutions-through-americanchemistry.ashx.

AMT (Association for Manufacturing Technology). 2004. *Why Do We Need Manufacturing Technology Made in America?* McLean, VA: Association for Manufacturing Technology.

Anderlini, J. 2010. Motorola claims espionage in Huawei lawsuit. *Financial Times,* July 22. http://www.ft.com/cms/s/0/616d2b34-953d-11df-b2e1-00144feab49a.html.

Anderson, K. 1981. *Wartime Women: Sex Roles, Family Relations, and the Status of Women during World War II.* Westport, CT: Greenwood Press.

AP. 1993. Wal-Mart will press ahead with Buy American, President tells stockholders. http://www.apnewsarchive.com/1993/Wal-Mart-Will-Press-Ahead-with-Buy-American-President-Tells-Stockholders/id-2e77340ee3ed11493fe9c3557893d00f.

Army Air Forces. 1945. *Army Air Forces Statistical Digest, World War II.* http://www.afhra.af.mil/shared/media/document/AFD-090608-039.pdf.

Arrow, K.J. 1962. Economic welfare and the allocation of resources for invention. Faculty paper, Department of Economics, Stanford, CA. http://papers.ssrn.com/sol3/papers.cfm?abstract_id=1497764.

Arvai, E. S., S. Hamilton, and A. Schonland. 2009. The coming aerospace squeeze. http://airinsight.com/store/the-coming-aerospace-squeeze/.

ASCE (American Society of Civil Engineers). 2011. Report card for America's infrastructure. http://www.infrastructurereportcard.org.

ASME (American Society of Mechanical Engineers). 1983. The American Society of Mechanical Engineers designates the Owens "AR" bottle machines as an international historic engineering landmark. http://www.utoledo.edu/library/canaday/exhibits/oi/OIExhibit/5612.pdf.

Atack, J., F. Bateman, and R. A. Margo. 2008. Steam power, establishment size, and labor productivity in nineteenth century American manufacturing. *Explorations in Economic History* 45:185–198.

Atkinson, R. D., et al. 2012. Worse than the Great Depression: What experts are missing about American manufacturing decline. Washington, DC: Information Technology and Innovation Foundation. http://www.itif.org/publications/worse-great-depression-what-experts-are-missing-about-american-manufacturing-decline.

Austen, B. 2010. The quick and the dead. *Atlantic*, December, 28–30.

Autor, D. 2010. The polarization of job opportunities in the US labor market. Center for American Progress, Washington, DC. http://economics.mit.edu/files/5554.

Ayres, R. U., L. W. Ayres, and B. Warr. 2003. Exergy, power and work in the US economy, 1900–1998. *Energy* 28:219–273.

Bacevich, A. J. 2011. The tyranny of Defense Inc. *Atlantic*, January–February, 74–79.

Bailey, B. F. 1911. *The Induction Motor*. New York: McGraw-Hill.

Ballard, J. S. 1983. *The Shock of Peace: Military and Economic Demobilization after World War II.* Washington, DC: University Press of America.

Banister, J., and G. Cook. 2011. China's employment and compensation costs in manufacturing through 2008. *Monthly Labor Review,* March, 39–52.

Bannister, R. L., and G. J. Silvestri. 1989. The evolution of central station steam turbines. *Mechanical Engineering (New York)* 111 (2): 70–78.

Barber, S., and M. Benson, eds. 2010. *Growth*. Kempen, Germany: te Neues.

Bardeen, J., and W. H. Brattain. 1950. Three-electron circuit element utilizing semiconductive materials. US Patent 2,524,035, October 3. US Patent and Trademark Office, Washington, DC. http://www.uspto.gov.

Bauer, Eugene E. 2000. *Boeing: The First Century*. Enumclaw, WA: TABA Publishers.

Beauchamp, Kenneth G. 1997. *Exhibiting Electricity*. London: Institution of Electrical Engineers.

Bell, D. A. 1973. *The Coming of Post-Industrial Society: A Venture in Social Forecasting*. New York: Basic Books.

Bell, I. Lothian. 1884. *Principles of the Manufacture of Iron and Steel*. London: George Routledge & Sons.

Bell System Memorial. 2011. Who really invented the transistor? http://www.porticus.org/bell/belllabs_transistor1.html.

Berliner, E. 1888. The gramophone. Paper read before the Franklin Institute, Philadelphia, May 16. Reprinted by the Berliner Gramophone Company, Montreal, 1909.

Bernard, A. B., and J. B. Jensen. 2004. Exporting and productivity in the USA. *Oxford Review of Economic Policy* 20:343–357.

Bernhardt, A., et al. 2008. *The Gloves-off Economy: Workplace Standards at the Bottom of America's Labor Market*. Champaign, IL: Labor and Employment Relations Association.

Berry, S., J. Levinsohn, and A. Pakes. 1999. Voluntary export restraints on automobiles: Valuating a trade policy. *American Economic Review* 89:400–430.

Bhagwati, J. 2010a. "Made in America" is not the way out. *FT.com,* August 9. http://www.ft.com/intl/cms/s/0/54a03eb6-a3eb-11df-9e3a-00144feabdc0.html.

Bhagwati, J. 2010b. The manufacturing fallacy. Project Syndicate, August 27. http://www.project-syndicate.org/commentary/bhagwati3/English.

Bhagwati, J., and A. S. Blinder. 2009. *Offshoring of American Jobs: What Response from US Economic Policy?* Cambridge, MA: MIT Press.

Binswanger, M. 2009. Is there a growth imperative in capitalist economies? A circular flow perspective. *Journal of Post Keynesian Economics* 31:707–727.

Bivens, J. 2011. *Failure by Design: The Story behind America's Broken Economy*. Ithaca, NY: Cornell University Press.

Blinder, A. S. 2009. Offshoring: Big deal, or business as usual? In *Offshoring of American Jobs*, ed. B. M. Friedman, 49. Cambridge, MA: MIT Press.

BLS (Bureau of Labor Statistics). 2012. Databases, Tables & Calculators by Subject. http://www.bls.gov/data.

Blumenthal, D. 2011. Why isn't China democratizing? Because it's not really capitalist. *The American,* April 26. http://www.american.com/archive/2011/april/why-isn2019t-china-democratizing-because-it2019s-not-really-capitalist.

Boeing. 2011. 737 Family. http://www.boeing.com/commercial/737family.

Bond, A. Russell. 1914. Going through the shops: I. *Scientific American* 110:8–10.

Boston Consulting Group. 2011. *Made in the USA, Again: Manufacturing Is Expected to Return to America as China's Rising Labor Costs Erase Most Savings from Offshoring*. Boston: Boston Consulting Group.

Brantly, J. E. 1971. *History of Oil Well Drilling*. Houston, TX: Gulf Publishing.

Bresnahan, T. F., and M. Trajtenberg. 1995. General purpose technologies "engines of growth"? *Journal of Econometrics* 65:83–108.

Brinkley, D. 2003. *Wheels for the World: Henry Ford, His Company, and a Century of Progress*. New York: Viking.

Broadberry, S. N. 1994. Comparative productivity in British and American manufacturing during the nineteenth century. *Explorations in Economic History* 31:521–548.

Broadberry, S. N. 1998. How did the United States and Germany overtake Britain? A sectoral analysis of comparative productivity levels, 1870–1990. *Journal of Economic History* 58:375–407.

Broda, C., and J. Romalis. 2008. Inequality and prices: Does China benefit the poor in America? http://www.etsg.org/ETSG2008/Papers/Romalis.pdf.

Buckley, C. 2011. China internal security spending jumps past army budget. Reuters, March 5. http://uk.reuters.com/article/2011/03/05/uk-china-unrest-idUKTRE7240B720110305.

Buffington, J. 2007. *An Easy Out: Corporate America's Addiction to Outsourcing*. Westport, CT: Praeger.

Bunker, J. G. 1972. *Liberty Ships*. New York: Arno Press.

Burks, A. R. 2002. *Who Invented the Computer? The Legal Battle That Changed Computing History*. New York: Prometheus Books.

Burks, A. W., and A. R. Burks. 1981. The ENIAC: The first general-purpose electronic computer. *Annals of the History of Computing* 3:310–389.

Burks, A. R., and A. W. Burks. 1988. *The First Electronic Computer: The Atanasoff Story*. Ann Arbor: University of Michigan Press.

Burwell, C. C. 1990. High-temperature electroprocessing: Steel and glass. In *Electricity in the American Economy*, ed. S. H. Schurr, W. D. Devine, and S. Sonenblum, 109–129. New York: Greenwood Press.

Busch, A. 2004. European integration, varieties of capitalism and the future of "Rhenish capitalism." Paper presented at "*Politik und Ökonomie*" conference, Cologne, December 3–4.

Bush, V., and H. Hazen. 1931. The differential analyzer: A new machine for solving differential equations. *Journal of the Franklin Institute* 212:447–488.

Cain, L. P., and D. G. Paterson. 1981. Factor biases and technological change in manufacturing: The American system, 1850–1919. *Journal of Economic History* 41:341–360.

Capozzola, S. 2012. Can Apple start making their products in the US again? The answer is YES. Campaign for America's Future, May 31. http://www.ourfuture

.org/blog-entry/2012052231/can-apple-start-making-their-product-us-again-answer-yes.

Carey, N., and J. B. Kelleher. 2011. Does corporate America kowtow to China? Reuters, April 27. http://www.reuters.com/article/2011/04/27/us-special-report-china-idUSTRE73Q10X20110427.

Catton, B. 1948. *Warlords of Washington*. New York: Harcourt.

CBO (Congressional Budget Office). 1980. *Current Problems of the US Automobile Industry and Policies to Address Them*. Washington, DC: Congressional Budget Office.

Cembalest, M. 2011. The capitol grill. *Eye on the Market*, July 29.

Ceruzzi, P. E. 2003. *A History of Modern Computing*. Cambridge, MA: MIT Press.

Chandler, A. D. 1977. *The Visible Hand: The Managerial Revolution in American Business*. Cambridge, MA: Belknap Press of Harvard University Press.

Charette, R. N. 2009. This car runs on code. *IEEE Spectrum*, February, 2009. http://spectrum.ieee.org/green-tech/advanced-cars/this-car-runs-on-code/0.

Chen, J., et al. 2011. *New Evidence on Cyclical and Structural Sources of Unemployment*. Washington, DC: IMF.

Chen, V. L., and R. Miller. 2011. Manufacturing booms as Deere exemplifies productivity surge. http://www.bloomberg.com/news/2011-05-08/manufacturing booms-as-deere-exemplifies-surge-in-productivity-across-u-s.html.

Cheney, Margaret. 1981. *Tesla: Man out of Time*. New York: Dorsett Press.

Chittum, R. 2010. (Ex)titans of industry against free trade fundamentalism. *Columbia Journalism Review*, July 9. http://www.cjr.org/the_audit/andy_grove_free_trade_jobs.php.

Christoff, C. 2012. Half of Detroit's streetlights may go out as city shrinks. *Bloomberg News*, May 24. http://www.bloomberg.com/news/print/2012-05-24/half-of-detroit-s-streetlights-may-go-out-as-city-shrinks.html.

Chuck, E. 2010. Geraldine Doyle, inspiration for "Rosie the Riveter," dies at 86. http://usnews.nbcnews.com/_news/2010/12/30/5738254-geraldine-doyle-inspiration-for-rosie-the-riveter-dies-at-86?lite.

Clarke, I. F. 1985. American anticipations. *Futures* 17:390–402.

Clarke, L., and C. Winch, eds. 2007. *Vocational Education: International Approaches, Developments and Systems*. London: Routledge.

Cleveland, C. J., and M. Ruth. 1999. Indicators of dematerialization and the materials intensity of use. *Journal of Industrial Ecology* 2:15–50.

Cline, W., and J. Williamson. 2010. *Estimating Consistent Fundamental Equilibrium Exchange Rates*. Washington, DC: Peterson Institute for International Economics.

Coad, J. 2005. *The Portsmouth Block Mills: Bentham, Brunel and the Start of the Royal Navy's Industrial Revolution*. London: English Heritage.

Cobet, Aaron E., and Gregory A. Wilson. 2002. Comparing 50 years of labor productivity in US and foreign manufacturing. *Monthly Labor Review*, June, 51–65.

Coe, B. 1988. *Kodak Cameras: The First Hundred Years*. London: Hove Books.

Cohen, B. 1999. *Howard Aiken: Portrait of a Computer Pioneer*. Cambridge, MA: MIT Press.

Cohen, S. S., and J. Zysman. 1987. *Manufacturing Matters: The Myth of the Post-Industrial Economy*. New York: HarperCollins.

Cole, J. R. 2009. *The Great American University: Its Rise to Preeminence, Its Indispensable National Role, and Why It Must Be Protected*. New York: Public Affairs.

Compton, A. H. 1956. *Atomic Quest*. New York: Oxford University Press.

Connery, R. H. 1951. *The Navy and the Industrial Mobilization in World War II*. Princeton, NJ: Princeton University Press.

Cortada, James W. 1993. *Before the Computer: IBM, NCR, Burroughs and Remington Rand and the Industry They Created*. Princeton, NJ: Princeton University Press.

Cowell, G. 1976. *D. H. Comet: The World's First Jet Airliner*. Hounslow, UK: Airline Publications and Sales.

Cowie, J., and J. Heathcott, eds. 2003. *Beyond the Ruins: The Meaning of Deindustrialization*. Ithaca, NY: Cornell University Press.

Crandall, R. W. 1987. The effects of US trade protection for autos and steel. *Brookings Papers on Economic Activity* 1:271–288.

Cuenot, F. 2009. $CO_2$ emissions from new cars and vehicle weight in Europe: How the EU regulation could have been avoided and how to reach it? *Energy Policy* 37:3832–3842.

Cyranoski, D., et al. 2011. The PhD factory. *Nature* 472:276–279.

Czech, B. 2000. *Shoveling Fuel for a Runaway Train: Errant Economists, Shameful Spenders, and a Plan to Stop Them All*. Berkeley: University of California Press.

Dadush, U. 2011. Global rebalancing: The dangerous obsession. *Current History*, January, 14–19.

Dale, W., D. W. Jorgenson, M. S. Ho, and K. J. Stiroh. 2002. *Projecting Productivity Growth: Lessons from the US Growth Resurgence*. Washington, DC: Resources for the Future. http://rff.org/RFF/Documents/RFF-DP-02-42.pdf.

David, P. A. 1990. The dynamo and the computer: An historical perspective on the modern productivity paradox. *American Economic Review* 80:355–361.

David, P. A. 1991. The hero and the herd in technological history: Reflections on Thomas Edison and the Battle of the Systems. In *Favorites of Fortune: Technology, Growth and Economic Development since the Industrial Revolution*, ed. P. Higonett, D. S. Landes, and H. Rosovsky, 72–119. Cambridge, MA: Harvard University Press.

De Loo, I., and L. Soete. 1999. *The Impact of Technology on Economic Growth: Some New Ideas and Empirical Considerations*. Maastricht: Maastricht Economic Research Institute on Innovation and Technology.

Deming, W. 2000. *Out of the Crisis*. Cambridge, MA: MIT Press.

Denison, E. F. 1985. *Trends in American Economic Growth, 1929–1982*. Washington, DC: Brookings Institution Press.

Detroit Residential Parcel Survey. 2011. Detroit Residential Parcel Survey. http://www.detroitparcelsurvey.org.

Devine, W. D., Jr. 1983. From shafts to wires: Historical perspective on electrification. *Journal of Economic History* 43:347–372.

Devol, G. C. 1961. Programmed Article Transfer. US Patent 2,988,237, June 13, 1961. US Patent and Trademark Office, Washington, DC. http://www.uspto.gov.

DeVol, R., and P. Wong. 2010. *Jobs for America: Investments and Policies for Economic Growth and Competitiveness*. Santa Monica, CA: Milken Institute.

Dewey & LeBoeuf. 2009. *Maintaining America's Competitive Edge: Government Policies Affecting Semiconductor Industry R&D and Manufacturing Activity*. Washington, DC: Semiconductor Institute of America.

Dickinson, H. W. 1939. *A Short History of the Steam Engine*. Cambridge: Cambridge University Press.

DiFrancesco, C. A., et al. eds. 2010. Iron and steel statistics. US Geological Survey, Washington, DC. http://minerals.usgs.gov/ds/2005/140/ironsteel.pdf.

Drayse, M. H. 2008. Globalization and regional change in the US furniture industry. *Growth and Change* 39:252–282.

Drezner, D. W. 2011. . . . and China isn't beating the US. *Foreign Policy*, January–February, 67. http://www.foreignpolicy.com/articles/2011/01/02/unconventional_wisdom.

Drucker, P. J. 2001. The next society. *Economist*, November 1. http://www.economist.com/node/770861.

DuBoff, R. B. 1979. *Electric Power in American Manufacturing, 1889–1958*. New York: Arno Press.

Duesterberg, T. J., and E. H. Preeg, eds. 2003. *US Manufacturing: The Engine for Growth in a Global Economy*. Westport, CT: Praeger.

Duesterberg, T. J. 2009. MAPI's view on manufacturing. http://www.qualitydigest.com/inside/quality-insider-article/mapis-view-us-manufacturing.html.

Dunsheath, P. 1962. *A History of Electrical Industry*. London: Faber and Faber.

Dyer, Frank L., and Thomas C. Martin. 1929. *Edison: His Life and Inventions*. New York: Harper & Brothers.

*Economist*. 2012. Manufacturing: The third industrial revolution. *Economist*, April 21. http://www.economist.com/node/21553017.

Eisenhower, D. D. 1961. Military-industrial complex speech. Avalon Project, Yale University Law School, New Haven, CT. http://avalon.law.yale.edu/20th_century/eisenhower001.asp.

Ellis, H. 1977. *The Lore of the Train*. New York: Crescent Books.

Ellsworth, L. F. 1969. *The American Leather Industry*. Chicago: Rand McNally.

Elphick, P. 2001. *Liberty: The Ships That Won the War*. Annapolis, MD: Naval Institute Press.

Engelberger, J. F. 1980. *Robotics in Practice: Management and Applications of Industrial Robots*. New York: AMACOM.

Ethell, J. L. 1981. *Mustang: A Documentary History of the P-51*. London: Jane's Publishing.

EU. 2005. Material deprivation in the EU. http://epp.eurostat.ec.europa.eu/portal/page/portal/product_details/publication?p_product_code=KS-NK-05-021.

Evenson, A. E. 2000. *The Telephone Patent Conspiracy of 1876: The Elisha Gray-Alexander Bell Controversy*. Jefferson, NC: McFarland.

Ewing, James A. 1911. Steam engine. In *Encyclopaedia Britannica*. 11th ed., vol. 25, 818–850. Cambridge: Cambridge University Press.

Fackler, M. 2010. Japan goes from dynamic to disheartened. *New York Times*, October 16.

Fallows, J. 2010. How America can rise again. *Atlantic*, January–February, 38–55. http://www.theatlantic.com/magazine/archive/2010/01/how-america-can-rise-again/7839.

Fallows, J. 2012. Mr. China comes to America. *The Atlantic*, December, 54–66.

Feenstra, R. C. 1984. Voluntary export restraint in US autos, 1980–81: Quality, employment, and welfare effects. In *The Structure and Evolution of Recent US Trade Policy*, ed. R. E. Baldwin and A. O. Krueger, 35–66. Chicago: University of Chicago Press.

Ferguson, N. 2012. Don't believe the techno-utopian hype. *Newsweek*, July 20. http://www.thedailybeast.com/newsweek/2012/07/29/niall-ferguson-don-t-believe-the-techno-utopian-hype.html.

Ferguson, R. G. 2005. One thousand planes a day: Ford, Grumman, General Motors and the arsenal of democracy. *History and Technology* 21:149–175.

Field, A. J. 2003. The most technologically progressive decade of the century. *American Economic Review* 93:1399–1414.

Field, A. J. 2006. Technological change and US productivity growth in the interwar years. *Journal of Economic History* 66:203–236.

Field, A. J. 2008. The impact of the Second World War on US productivity growth. *Economic History Review* 61:672–694.

Field, A. J. 2009. US economic growth in the Gilded Age. *Journal of Macroeconomics* 31:173–190.

Fishman, C. 2012. The insourcing boom. *The Atlantic*, December, 45–52.

Fletcher, I. 2011. *Free Trade Doesn't Work*. Sheffield, MA: Coalition for a Prosperous America.

Flink, J. J. 1985. Innovation in automotive technology. *American Scientist* 73:151–161.

Flink, J. J. 1988. *The Automobile Age*. Cambridge, MA: MIT Press.

Flipo, F., and F. Schneider, eds. 2008. *Proceedings of the First International Conference on Economic De-Growth for Ecological Sustainability and Social Equity,* Paris, April 18–19. http://events.it-sudparis.eu/degrowthconference/appel/Degrowth%20Conference%20-%20Proceedings.pdf.

Floud, R. C. 1974. The adolescence of American engineering competition, 1860–1900. *Economic History Review* 27:57–71.

FMC (Ford Motor Company). 1908. Ford Motor Cars, Detroit, MI. http://www.mtfca.com.

Fogel, R. 2010. 123,000,000,000,000. *Foreign Policy,* January–February, 70–75.

Ford, H. 1922. *My Life and Work*. New York: Doubleday.

Ford. 2011. *Fusion* quality can't be beat. Advertisement in the US media in 2011.

Freed, J., et al. 2010. *Creating a Clean Energy Century*. http://content.thirdway.org/publications/351/Third_Way_Report_-_Creating_a_Clean_Energy_Century.pdf.

Friedel, Robert, and Paul Israel. 1986. *Edison's Electric Light*. New Brunswick, NJ: Rutgers University Press.

Fruehan, R., ed. 1998. *The Making, Shaping and Treating of Steel Steelmaking and Refining Volume*. Pittsburgh, PA: The AISE Steel Foundation.

Fujimoto, T. 1999/. *The Evolution of a Manufacturing System at Toyota*. New York: Oxford University Press.

Gallup. 2011. Gallup finds US unemployment hitting10.3% in February. Gallup, March 3. http://www.gallup.com/poll/146453/gallup-finds-unemployment-hitting-february.aspx.

Garcke, Emil. 1911. Telephone. In *Encyclopaedia Britannica*. 11th ed. vol. 26, 547–557. Cambridge: Cambridge University Press.

Geiser, K. 2001. *Materials Matter: Toward a Sustainable Materials Policy*. Cambridge, MA: MIT Press.

Georgescu-Roegen, N. 1971. *The Entropy Law and the Economic Process*. Cambridge, MA: Harvard University Press.

Gibson, I., D. W. Rosen, and B. Stucker. 2009. *Additive Manufacturing Technologies: Rapid Prototyping to Direct Digital Manufacturing*. New York: Springer.

Global Automakers. 2012. *Global Automakers*. http://www.globalautomakers.org/

Gluck, S. B. 1987. *Rosie the Riveter Revisited: Women, the War, and Social Change*. Boston: Twayne Publishers.

GM. 2011. GM powers the Burlington Zephyr. http://history.gmheritagecenter.com/wiki/index.php/GM_Powers_the_Burlington_Zephyr.

Gold, B., et al. 1984. *Technological Progress and Industrial Leadership: The Growth of the US Steel Industry, 1900–1970*. Lexington, MA: Lexington Books.

Goldfarb, B. 2005. Diffusion of general-purpose technologies: Understanding patterns in the electrification of US manufacturing 1880–1930. *Industrial and Corporate Change* 14:745–773.

Goldin, C., and R. A. Margo. 1992. The Great Compression: The wage structure in the United States at mid-century. *Quarterly Journal of Economics* 101:1–34.

Golley, J., and F. Whittle. 1987. *Whittle, the True Story*. Washington, DC: Smithsonian Institution Press.

Grebler, L., D. M. Blank, and L. Winnick. 1956. *Capital Formation in Residential Real Estate: Trends and Prospects*. Princeton, NJ: Princeton University Press.

Greene, J. P. 2010. *Administrative Bloat at American Universities: The Real Reason for High Costs in Higher Education*. Phoenix, AZ: Goldwater Institute.

Gross, D. 2012. *Better, Stronger, Faster: The Myth of American Decline . . . and the Rise of a New Economy*. New York: Free Press.

Grossman, G. M., and E. Helpman. 1991. *Innovation and Growth in the Global Economy*. Cambridge, MA: MIT Press.

Grove, A. 2010. How America can create jobs. *Bloomberg BusinessWeek,* July 1. http://www.businessweek.com/magazine/content/10_28/b4186048358596.htm.

Groves, L. 1962. *Now It Can Be Told: The Story of the Manhattan Project*. New York: Harper.

Hacker, A., and C. Dreifus. 2010. *Higher Education? How Colleges Are Wasting Our Money and Failing Our Kids—and What We Can Do About It*. New York: Times Books.

Haley, U. 2007. Shedding light on energy subsidies in China: An analysis of China's steel industry from 2000–2007. Alliance for American Manufacturing, Washington, DC. http://www.americanmanufacturing.org/files/energy-subsidies-in-china-jan-8-08.pdf.

Haley, U. 2010. No paper tiger: Subsidies to China's paper industry from 2002–2009. Alliance for American Manufacturing, Washington, DC. http://www.americanmanufacturing.org/files/briefingpaper264_final.pdf.

Hall, E. C. 1996. *Journey to the Moon: The History of the Apollo Guidance Computer*. Reston, VA: American Institute of Aeronautics and Astronautics.

Hamilton, A. 1791. Report on manufactures. http://constitution.org/ah/rpt_manufactures.pdf.

Hanushek, E. A., P. E. Peterson, and L. Woessman 2010. U. S. math performance in global perspective: How well does each state do at producing high-achieving students? Faculty paper, Harvard University, Cambridge, MA. http://www.hks.harvard.edu/pepg/PDF/Papers/PEPG10-19_HanushekPetersonWoessmann.pdf.

Harrison, M., ed. 1998. *The Economics of World War II: Six Great Powers in International Comparison*. Cambridge: Cambridge University Press.

Hayes, R. H., and W. J. Abernathy. 1985. Managing our way to economic decline. *Harvard Business Review* 85:138–149.

Herman, A. 2012. *Freedom's Forge: How American Business Produced Victory in World War II*. New York: Random House.

Hermes, Matthew E. 1996. *Enough for One Lifetime: Wallace Carothers, Inventor of Nylon*. Washington, DC: American Chemical Society and the Chemical Heritage Foundation.

Herrigel, G. 2010. *Manufacturing Possibilities: Creative Action and Industrial Recomposition in the United States, Germany, and Japan*. New York: Oxford University Press.

High, S., and D. W. Lewis. 2007. *Corporate Wasteland: The Landscape and Memory of Deindustrialization*. Ithaca, NY: Cornell University Press.

Hira, R., and A. Hira. 2005. *Outsourcing America*. New York: American Management Association.

Hirst, E., et al. 1983. Recent changes in US energy consumption: What happened and why. *Annual Review of Energy* 8:193–245.

Hoff, M. E., S. Mazor, and F. Fagin. 1974. Memory system for a multi- chip digital computer. US Patent 3,821,715, June 28, 1974. Washington, DC: US Patent and Trademark Office. http://www.uspto.gov.

Hogan, W. T. 1971. *Economic History of the Iron and Steel Industry in the United States*. Vol. 1, pts. I and II. Lexington, MA: Lexington Books.

Holley, I. B. 1964. *Buying Aircraft: Matériel Procurement for the Army Air Forces*. Washington, DC: Department of the Army.

Holley, I. B. 1987. Detroit dream of mass-produced fighter aircraft: The XP-75 fiasco. *Technology and Culture* 28:578–593.

Hooks, G. 1991. *Forging the Military-Industrial Complex: World War II's Battle of the Potomac*. Urbana, IL: University of Illinois Press.

Hounshell, D. A. 1984. *From the American System to Mass Production, 1800–1932: The Development of Manufacturing Technology in the United States*. Baltimore, MD: Johns Hopkins University Press.

Houseman, S. 2007. Outsourcing, offshoring and productivity measurement in United States manufacturing. *International Labour Review* 146:61–80.

Houston, R. E. 1927. Model T Ford production. Model T Ford Club of America, Centerville, IN. http://www.mtfca.com/encyclo/fdprod.htm.

Hughes, T. P. 1983. *Networks of Power*. Baltimore, MD: Johns Hopkins University Press.

Hunter, Louis C., and Lynwood Bryant. 1991. *A History of Industrial Power in the United States, 1780–1930. Vol. 3. The Transmission of Power*. Cambridge, MA: MIT Press.

Illich, I. 1973. *Tools for Conviviality*. London: Calder and Boyars.

IMF (International Monetary Fund). 2010. United States: Selected issues paper. International Monetary Fund, Washington, DC. http://www.imf.org/external/pubs/ft/scr/2010/cr10248.pdf.

Immelt, J. R. 2012. How we did it . . . The CEO of General Electric on sparking an American manufacturing renewal. *Harvard Business Review*, March, 43–46.

Ingham, J. N. 1978. *The Iron Barons: A Social Analysis of an American Urban Elite, 1874–1965*. Westport, CT: Greenwood Press.

Intel. 2011. The Intel 4004. http://www.intel4004.com.

Irwin, D. 2011. *Peddling Protectionism: Smoot-Hawley and the Great Depression*. Princeton, NJ: Princeton University Press.

Irwin, D. A., and P. J. Klenow. 1996. Sematech: Purpose and performance. *Proceedings of the National Academy of Sciences of the United States of America* 93:12739–12742.

ITA. 2011a. *Flight Plan 2011: Analysis of the US Aerospace Industry*. Washington, DC: International Trade Administration.

ITA. 2011b. US aerospace industry statistics. http://www.trade.gov/mas/manufacturing/oaai/tg_oaai_003646.asp.

Ives, F. E. 1928. *The Autobiography of an Amateur Inventor*. Philadelphia: Privately printed.

Jackson, T. 2009. *Prosperity without Growth: Economics for a Finite Planet*. London: Earthscan.

James, J. A. 1983. Structural change in American manufacturing, 1850–1890. *Journal of Economic History* 43:433–459.

Janeway, E. 1951. *The Struggle for Survival: A Chronicle of Economic Mobilization in World War II*. New Haven, CT: Yale University Press.

J. D. Power and Associates. 2011. Tracking. http://www.jdpower.com/business-services/services/tracking.htm.

Jeffries, J. W. 1996. *Wartime America: The World War II Home Front*. Chicago: Ivan R. Dee.

Jensen, O. O. 1975. *The American Heritage History of Railroads in America*. New York: American Heritage Books.

Jerome, H. 1934. *Mechanization in Industry*. New York: National Bureau of Economic Research.

Josephson, M. 1959. *Edison: A Biography*. New York: John Wiley.

Kane, T. 2010. The importance of startups in job creation and job destruction. Kauffman Foundation, Kansas City, MO. http://www.kauffman.org/research-and-policy/the-importance-of-startups-in-job-creation-and-job-desctruction.aspx.

Kanigel, Robert. 1997. *The One Best Way: Frederick Winslow Taylor and the Enigma of Efficiency*. New York: Viking.

Kapur, A., N. Macleod, and N. Singh. 2005. Plutonomy: Buying luxury, explaining global imbalances. Citigroup, New York. http://cryptome.org/0005/rich-pander.pdf.

Katz, B., and E. Istrate. 2011. *Boosting Exports, Delivering Jobs and Economic Growth*. New York: Brookings-Rockefeller Project on State and Metropolitan Innovation.

Keidel, A. 2011. China's exchange rate controversy: A balanced analysis. *Eurasian Geography and Economics* 52:347–374.

Kendrick, J. 1961. *Productivity Trends in the United States*. Washington, DC: National Bureau of Economic Research.

Kilby, J. S. 1964. Miniaturized electronic circuits. US Patent 3,138,743, June 23, 1964. US Patent and Trademark Office, Washington, DC. http://www.uspto.gov.

Kilby, J. S., J. D. Merryman, and J. H. Van Tassel. 1974. Miniature electronic calculator. US Patent 3,819,921, June 25, 1974. US Patent and Trademark Office, Washington, DC. http://www.uspto.gov.

Kimball, W. F. 1969. *The Most Unsordid Act: Lend-lease, 1939–1941*. Baltimore, MD: Johns Hopkins University Press.

King, C. D. 1948. *Seventy-five Years of Progress in Iron and Steel*. New York: American Institute of Mining and Metallurgical Engineers.

Klein, J. 2011. Scenes from the class struggle. *Atlantic*, June, 66–77.

Knox, J. J. 1900. *A History of Banking in the United States*. New York: B. Rhodes & Company.

Krugman, P. 2011a. Dumbing deficits down. http://www.nytimes.com/2011/03/11/opinion/11krugman.html?_r=0

Krugman, P. 2011b. No JOLTS to complacency. *New York Times*, March 16, 2011. http://krugman.blogs.nytimes.com/2011/03/16/no-jolts-to-complacency.

Lane, F. C. 2001. *Ships for Victory: A History of Shipbuilding under the US Maritime Commission in World War II*. Baltimore, MD: Johns Hopkins University Press.

Leary, J. P. 2011. Detroitism. *Guernica*. http://www.guernicamag.com/features/leary_1_15_11.

Lécuyer, C., and D. C. Brock. 2010. *Makers of the Microchip: A Documentary History of Fairchild Semiconductor*. Cambridge, MA: MIT Press.

Leland, A., and M. Oboroceanu. 2010. *American War and Military Operations Casualties: Lists and Statistics*. Washington, DC: Congressional Research Service.

LeMay, C., and B. Yenne. 1988. *Super Fortress*. London: Berkley Books.

Lescaroux, F. 2008. Decomposition of US manufacturing energy intensity and elasticities of components with respect to energy prices. *Energy Economics* 30:1068–1080.

Levinson, M. 2012. U.S. manufacturing in international perspective. Congressional Research Service, Washington, DC. http://www.fas.org/sgp/crs/misc/R42135.pdf.

Lewchuk, W. 1989. Fordism and the moving assembly line: The British and American experience, 1895–1930. In *On the Line: Essays in the History of Auto Work*, ed. Nelson Lichtenstein and Stephen Meyer, 17–41. Urbana:: University of Illinois Press.

Lewis, H. G. 1986. *Union Relative Wage Effects: A Survey*. Chicago: University of Chicago Press.

Li, X. 2011. Boeing's reach is woven into China's aviation industry. *China Daily*, January 14. http://www.chinadaily.com.cn/bizchina/2011-01/14/content_11854659.htm.

Lilienfeld, E. J. 1930. Method and apparatus for controlling electric currents. US Patent 1,745,175, January 28, 1930. Washington, DC: US Patent and Trademark Office.

Linden, G., J. Dedrick, and K. L. Kraemer. 2009. Innovation and job creation in a global economy: The case of Apple's iPod. http://pcic.merage.uci.edu/papers/2009/InnovationAndJobCreation.pdf

Lipscomb, T. 2011. *Re-Made in the USA*. New York: John Wiley.

Litterer, J. A. 1961. Systematic management: The search for order and integration. *History Review* 35:461–476.

Liveris, A. 2011. *Make It in America*. New York: John Wiley.

Lutz, B. 2011. Yes, there is a difference between American and Japanese cars. Reuters, June 20. http://blogs.reuters.com/japan/2011/06/20/yes-there-is-a-difference-between-american-and-japanese-cars.

MacArthur, D. 1964. *Reminiscences*. New York: McGraw-Hill.

MacLaren, Malcolm. 1943. *The Rise of the Electrical Industry during the Nineteenth Century*. Princeton, NJ: Princeton University Press.

MacPherson, A., and V. Vanchan. 2010. The outsourcing of industrial design services by large US manufacturing companies. *International Regional Science Review* 33:3–30.

Maddison, A. 2007. *Contours of the World Economy, 1–2030 AD*. Oxford: Oxford University Press.

Malone, S. 2012. After "lemming" exodus, manufacturers look to US Reuters, February 13. http://www.reuters.com/article/2012/02/14/us-usa-manufacturing-onshoring-idUSTRE81C1B720120214.

The Manhattan Project Heritage Preservation Association. 2012. *Manhattan Project History*. Manhattan Project Historical Preservation Association, Montour Falls, NY. http://www.mphpa.org/classic/index.htm.

Mann, J. 2007. James Mann before the US-China Economic and Security Commission hearing on "US-China Relationship: Economics and Security in Perspective." http://www.uscc.gov/hearings/2007hearings/written_testimonies/07_02_01_02wrts/07_02_1_2_mann_james_statement.pdf.

Markillie, P. 2012. A third industrial revolution. *Economist,* April 21.

Martin, M. F. 2009. What's the difference?—Comparing US and Chinese trade data. Congressional Research Service, Washington, DC. http://fpc.state.gov/documents/organization/122443.pdf.

Martinez, L. 2011. Foreign CEOs: Hard to find skilled US workers. http://abcnews.go.com/blogs/politics/2011/10/foreign-ceos-hard-to-find-skilled-us-workers.

Maxton, G. P., and J. Wormald. 2004. *Time for Model Change: Re-engineering the Global Automotive Industry*. Cambridge: Cambridge University Press.

Mazor, S. 1995. The history of microcomputer—Invention and evolution. *Proceedings of the IEEE* 83:1600–1608.

McAllister, J. 1989. Colonial America, 1607–1776. *Economic History Review* 52:245–259.

McCallum, H. D., and T. Frances. 1965. *The Wire That Fenced the West.* Norman: University of Oklahoma Press.

McCormack, R. 2006. Council on Competitiveness says US has little to fear, but fear itself: By most measures, US is way ahead of global competitors. *Manufacturing & Technology News* 13 (21): 1–7.

McCormack, R. A. 2009. US machines tool industry is on the brink: How does an industry survive without any orders? *Manufacturing & Technology News* 16 (5): 1–4.

McCormack, R. A. 2010. You don't know where your drugs come from and neither does the FDA: US imports 90 percent of its antibiotics (and vitamin A) from China. *Manufacturing & Technology News* 18 (17): 1–4.

McKinsey Global Institute. 2011. *An Economy That Works: Job Creation and America's Future.* San Francisco: McKinsey Global Institute. http://www.mckinsey.com/Insights/MGI/Research/Labor_Markets/An_economy_that_works_for_US_job_creation.

McMillion, C. W. 2009. *China's Soaring Commercial and Financial Power: How It Is Affecting the US and the World.* Washington, DC: US-China Economic and Security Review Commission. http://www.uscc.gov/researchpapers/2009/MBG%20Info%20Svs%20US-China%20Trade%20Report%20--%20FINAL%20June%202009.pdf.

Media.Ford.Com. 2010. Ford Fusion and Fusion Hybrid continue momentum in 2010. http://media.ford.com/article_display.cfm?article_id=32165.

Mellberg, William F. 2003. Transportation revolution. *Mechanical Engineering Supplement: 100 Years of Flight,* 22–25.

Menzel, P. 1994. *Material World: A Global Family Portrait.* Berkeley:: University of California Press.

Meyer, D. E. 2011. GMC trucks helped win World War II. http://history.gmheritagecenter.com/wiki/index.php/GMC_Trucks_Helped_Win_World_War_II.

MI (Manufacturing Institute). 2009. *The Facts about Modern Manufacturing.* http://www.nist.gov/mep/upload/FINAL_NAM_REPORT_PAGES.pdf.

Mills, M. P. 2012. The next great growth cycle. *American,* August 25. http://www.american.com/archive/2012/august/the-next-great-growth-cycle.

Milward, A. S. 1979. *War, Economy, and Society, 1939–1945.* Berkeley: University of California Press.

Minchin, T. J. 2009. "It knocked this city to its knees": The closure of Pillowtex Mills in Kannapolis, North Carolina, and the decline of the US textile industry. *Labor History* 50:287–311.

Misa, T. J. 1995. *A Nation of Steel.* Baltimore, MD: Johns Hopkins University Press.

MOFCOM (Ministry of Commerce of the People's Republic of China). 2012. Regular press conference of the Ministry of Commerce, January 18. http://english.mofcom.gov.cn/aarticle/newsrelease/press/201202/20120207966907.html.

Mokyr, J. 2002. *The Gifts of Athena: Historical Origins of the Knowledge Economy*. Princeton, NJ: Princeton University Press.

Montgomery Ward & Company. 2008 (1895). *Catalogue and Buyers' Guide 1895*. New York: Skyhorse Publishing.

Moore, G. 1965. Cramming more components onto integrated circuits. *Electronics* 38 (8): 114–117.

Moore, G. 1975. Progress in digital integrated electronics. *IEEE. IEDM Tech Digest* 1975:11–13.

Morgan, T. 2010. End-game: The denouement of exponentials. Tullett Prebon, London. http://www.tullettprebon.com/Documents/strategyinsights/tp0610d_tpsi_006.pdf.

Morgan & Company. 2011. US auto sales analysis by Morgan & Company. http://www.morgancom.com/salesanalysis.htm.

Morin, R., and P. Taylor. 2009. *Luxury or Necessity? The Public Makes a U-Turn*. Washington, DC: Pew Research Center. http://www.pewsocialtrends.org/2009/04/23/luxury-or-necessity-the-public-makes-a-u-turn.

Moritz, M. 1984. *The Little Kingdom: The Private Story of Apple Computer*. New York: William Morrow.

Morrison, W. M. 2011. *China-US Trade Issues*. Washington, DC: Congressional Research Service.

Mott, F. L. 1957. *A History of American Magazines, 1885–1905*. Cambridge, MA: Harvard University Press.

MVMA (Motor Vehicle Manufacturers Association). 1980. *Facts and Figures*. Detroit, MI: Motor Vehicle Manufacturers Association.

MVMA. 1985. *Facts and Figures*. Detroit, MI: Motor Vehicle Manufacturers Association.

Nader, R. 1965. *Unsafe at Any Speed: The Designed-in Dangers of the American Automobile*. New York: Grossman Publishers.

Nagengast, B. 2000. It's a cool story. *Mechanical Engineering* 122 (5):56–63.

NAHB (National Association of Home Builders). 2010. Smaller homes to remain popular even after recession's end. http://www.housingzone.com/design/nahb-smaller-homes-remain-popular-even-after-recessions-end.

NAICS (North American Industry Classification System). 2008. NAICS code description. http://www.naics.com/free-code-search/naicsdescription.php?code=31.

NAM (National Association of Manufacturers). 2011a. Manufacturing strategy for jobs and a competitive America. http://www.nam.org/~/media/99977BFAD78B4DA1B812C4DD3F3CC94F.ashx.

NAM. 2011b. The United States exports half as much of its manufacturing production as other countries do. http://www.nam.org/~/media/FDD7F13666F84C3BA7C814982A8E8469/US_Exports_Half_as_Much_of_its_Manufacturing_Production_as_Other_Countries_Do.pdf.

Nash, G. D. 1985. *The American West Transformed: The Impact of the Second World War*. Lincoln: University of Nebraska Press.

National Debt Clock. 2012. National debt clock. http://www.usdebtclock.org.

National Export Initiative. 2010. *Report to the President on the National Export Initiative: The Export Promotion Cabinet's Plan for Doubling US Exports in Five Years*. Washington, DC: National Export Initiative.

Naval Historical Center. 2011. Quonset hut. http://www.history.navy.mil/faqs/faq75-1.htm.

NCTO (National Council of Textile Organizations). 2011. Trade and jobs. http://www.ncto.org.

NEED (National Energy Education Development) Project. 2011. Energy consumption. http://www.need.org/needpdf/infobook_activities/IntInfo/ConsI.pdf.

Nelson, D. M. 1946. *Arsenal of Democracy: The Story of American Wartime Production*. New York: Harcourt Brace.

Nixon, R. 1959. The kitchen debate (Nixon and Khrushchev, July 1959). http://www.youtube.com/watch?v=D7HqOrAakco.

Noble, David F. 1984. *Forces of Production: A Social History of Industrial Automation*. New York: Knopf.

Nolan, P. 2012. *Is China Buying the World?* Cambridge: Polity Press.

Noyce, Robert N. 1961. Semiconductor device-and-lead structure. US Patent 2,981,877, April 25. US Patent and Trademark Office, Washington, DC. http://www.uspto.gov.

NSF (National Science Foundation). 2010. *Science and Engineering Indicators: 2010*. National Science Foundation, Washington, DC. http://www.nsf.gov/statistics/seind10.

Nutter, G. W., and H. A. Einhorn. 1969. *Enterprise Monopoly in the United States: 1899–1958*. New York: Columbia University Press.

Nye, J. 2011. Joe Nye answers your questions on the future of American power. CNN, *Global Public Square*. http://globalpublicsquare.blogs.cnn.com/2011/03/15/joseph-nye-answers-your-questions-on-the-future-of-american-power.

OECD (Organisation for Economic Co-operation and Development). 2009. PISA 2009 key findings. http://www.oecd.org/pisa/pisaproducts/pisa2009/pisa2009keyfindings.htm.

OECD. 2010. *Taxation of Corporate and Capital Income*. Paris: Organisation for Economic Co-operation and Development.

OECD. 2011. *Labour Statistics*. Paris: Organisation for Economic Co-operation and Development.

OECD. 2012. Central government debt. http://stats.oecd.org/index.aspx?queryid=8089.

Offer, A. 2006. *The Challenge of Affluence: Self-Control and Well-Being in the United States and Britain since 1950*. Oxford: Oxford University Press.

Ohnsman, A., M. Kitamura, and J. Green. 2011. Toyota's "big damage" brings Sony-style decline. Bloomberg.com, January 11. http://www.bloomberg.com/news/2011-01-11/toyota-hegemony-fades-as-damage-brings-sony-style-decline.html.

Okumura, H. 1994. Recent trends and future prospects of continuous casting technology. *Nippon Steel Technical Report* 61:9–14.

O'Leary, M. 2010. *P-51 Mustang: The Story of Manufacturing North American's Legendary World War II Fighter in Original Photos*. North Branch, MN: Specialty Press.

OTEXA (Office of Textiles and Apparel). 2012. Trade data: US textiles and apparel imports by category. http://otexa.ita.doc.gov/Msrcat.htm.

Otis Elevator Company. 1953. *The First One Hundred Years*. New York: Otis Elevator Co.

Parsons, Robert H. 1936. *The Development of Parsons Steam Turbine*. London: Constable & Co.

Paus, E., ed. 2007. *Global Capitalism Unbound: Winners and Losers from Offshore Outsourcing*. London: Palgrave Macmillan.

Payne, H. 2011. SUVs saved Chrysler. *The Detroit News*, May 24. http://blogs.detroitnews.com/politics/2011/05/24/payne-suvs-saved-chrysler-the-michigan-vies-05-24-11.

PBGC (Pension Benefit Guaranty Corporation). 2011. Pension Benefit Guaranty Corporation. http://www.pbgc.gov.

Peck, D. 2010. How a new jobless era will transform America. *Atlantic*, March, 42–56.

Peck, D. 2011. Can the middle class be saved? *Atlantic*, September, 60–78.

Perry, M. J. 2011. Manufacturing makes a comeback as shining star of the US economy. *AEI Ideas*, May 10. http://www.aei-ideas.org/2011/05/manufacturing-makes-a-comeback-as-shining-star-of-the-u-s-economy.

Perry, M. J. 2012. Manufacturing's declining share of GDP is a global phenomenon, and it's something to celebrate. National Chamber Foundation, March 22. http://ncf.uschamber.com/blog/2012/03/manufacturing%E2%80%99sdeclining-share-gdp.

Picketty, T., and E. Saez. 2003. Income inequality in the United States, 1913–1998. *Quarterly Journal of Economics* 118:1–39.

PISA (Program for International Student Assessment). 2010. *PISA 2009 Results*. http://www.oecd.org/pisa/pisa2009keyfindings.htm.

Pisano, G. P. 2012. Will Apple spark a US manufacturing renaissance? *Harvard Business Review*. http://blogs.hbr.org/cs/2012/12/will_apple_spark_a_us_manufact.html.

Pisano, G. P., and W. C. Shih. 2009. Restoring American competitiveness. *Harvard Business Review* 87 (7/8): 114–125.

Pisano, G. P., and W. C. Shih. 2012. *Producing Prosperity: Why America Needs a Manufacturing Renaissance*. Cambridge, MA: Harvard Business Review Press.

Platzer, M. D. 2009. *US Aerospace Manufacturing: Industry Overview and Prospects*. Washington, DC: Congressional Research Service. http://www.fas.org/sgp/crs/misc/R40967.pdf.

Pohl, E., and R. Müller, eds. 1984. *150 Jahre Elektromotor, 1834–1984*. Würzburg: Vogel-Verlag.

Pope, C. 2012. America's dirty war against manufacturing. *Bloomberg View*, January 17. http://www.bloomberg.com/news/2012-01-18/america-s-dirty-war-against-manufacturing-part-1-carl-pope.html.

Porter, M. E. 2007. Understanding competitiveness and its causes. In *Competitiveness Index: Where America Stands*, 9. New York: Council on Competitiveness.

Prestowitz, C. 2010a. *The Betrayal of American Prosperity*. New York: Free Press.

Prestowitz, C. 2010b. Lie of the tiger. *Foreign Policy*, November, 36. http://www.foreignpolicy.com/articles/2010/10/11/lie_of_the_tiger.

Prestowitz, C. 2010c. Should we be concerned with American manufacturing? http://www.futureofuschinatrade.com/article/should-we-be-concerned-american-manufacturing.

Princen, T. 2005. *The Logic of Sufficiency*. Cambridge, MA: MIT Press.

Princen, T., M. Maniates, and K. Conca, eds. 2002. *Confronting Consumption*. Cambridge, MA: MIT Press.

Ramrattan, L., and M. Szenberg. 2007. *Distressed Industries in the Era of Globalization*. Aldershot, UK: Ashgate..

Rassweiler, A. 2009. iPhone 3GS carries $178.96 BOM and manufacturing cost, iSuppli teardown reveals. http://www.isuppli.com/Teardowns/News/Pages/iPhone-3G-S-Carries-178-96-BOM-and-Manufacturing-Cost-iSuppli-Teardown-Reveals.aspx.

Ratzlaff, J. T., and L. I. Anderson. 1979. *Dr. Nikola Tesla Bibliography*. San Carlos, CA: Ragusan Press.

Reed, C. 2011. From Treasury vault to the Manhattan Project. *American Scientist* 99:40–47.

Reich, E. S. 2011. US legislation aims to simplify rules for inventors. *Nature* 471:149.

Reich, R. 2011. The truth about the American economy. http://robertreich.org/post/5993482080.

ReviewCars.com. 2011. 2010 Ford Fusion; 2010 Toyota Camry. http://www.reviewcars.com.

Reynolds, A. 2007. *Has US Income Inequality Really Increased?* Washington, DC: Cato Institute.

Rhodes, R. 1986. *The Making of the Atomic Bomb*. New York: Simon and Schuster.

Ripley, A. 2010. Your child left behind. *Atlantic*, December, 94–98.

Rohde, D. 2012. How Zippos, dredges and vitamin can save the American middle class. Reuters, May 25. http://blogs.reuters.com/david-rohde/2012/05/25/how-zippos-dredges-and-vitamins-can-save-the-american-middle-class.

Rojas, R., and U. Hashagen, eds. 2000. *The First Computers: History and Architectures*. Cambridge, MA: MIT Press.

Rolt, L.T.C. 1963. *Thomas Newcomen: The Prehistory of the Steam Engine*. Dawlish, UK: David and Charles.

Romer, P. 1990. Endogenous Technological Change. *Journal of Political Economy* 98:S71–S102.

Rostow, W. W. 1960. *The Stages of Economic Growth: A Non-Communist Manifesto*. Cambridge: Cambridge University Press.

Rostow, W. W. 1990. *Theories of Economic Growth from David Hume to the Present*. New York: Oxford University Press.

Rowthorn, R., and R. Ramaswamy. 1997. *Deindustrialization: Causes and Implications*. Washington, DC: International Monetary Fund.

Russ, J. S. 2009. *Global Motivations: Honda, Toyota, and the Drive Toward American Manufacturing*. Lanham, MD: University Press of America.

Ruttan, V. W. 2006. *Is War Necessary for Economic Growth? Military Procurement and Technology Development*. New York: Oxford University Press.

Saez, E. 2010. Striking it richer: The evolution of top incomes in the United States (updated with 2008 estimates). Faculty paper, University of California, Berkeley. http://elsa.berkeley.edu/~saez/saez-UStopincomes-2008.pdf.

Sakiya, T. 1982. *Honda Motor: The Men, the Management, the Machines*. New York: Kodansha International.

Sale, A. E. 2000. The Colossus of Bletchley Park: The German cipher system. In *The First Computers: History and Architectures*, ed. Raúl Rojas and Ulf Hashagen, 351–364. Cambridge, MA: MIT Press.

Schipper, J. E. 1919. The Liberty engine. *Flight* 11 (1): 6–10.

Schipper, L., R. B. Howarth, and H. Geller. 1990. United States energy use from 1973 to1987: The impacts of improved efficiency. *Annual Review of Energy* 15:455–504.

Schmitt, J. 2009. *Inequality as Policy: The United States since 1979*. Washington, DC: Center for Economic and Policy Research.

Schuman, M. 2011. How Germany became the China of Europe. *Time*, March 7. http://www.time.com/time/magazine/article/0,9171,2055176,00.html.

Schurr, S. H. 1984. Energy use, technological change, and productive efficiency: An economic-historical interpretation. *Annual Review of Energy* 9:409–425.

Schurr, S. H., and B. C. Netschert. 1960. *Energy in the American Economy 1850–1975*. Baltimore, MD: Johns Hopkins University Press.

Schurr, S. H., C.C. Burwell, W.D. Devine, and S. Sonenblum, eds. 1990. *Electricity in the American Economy: Agent of Technological Progress*. New York: Greenwood Press.

Scott, Peter B. 1984. *The Robotics Revolution*. Oxford: Basil Blackwell.

Scott, R. E. 2007. The Wal-Mart effect: Its Chinese imports have displaced nearly 200,000 US jobs. Economic Policy Institute, Washington, DC. http://www.epi.org/publication/ib235.

Scott, R. E. 2010. Unfair China trade costs local jobs. Economic Policy Institute, Washington, DC. http://epi.3cdn.net/91b2eeeffce66c1a10_v5m6beqhi.pdf.

Sears, Roebuck & Company. 2007 (1897). *1897 Consumers Guide*. New York: Skyhorse Publishing.

Seifer, M. J. 1996. *Wizard: The Life and Times of Nikola Tesla—Biography of a Genius*. New York: Birch Lane.

SEMATECH. 2010. *2009: A Year in Review*. Austin, TX: SEMATECH. http://www.sematech.org/corporate/annual/annual09.pdf.

SEMATECH. 2011. SEMATECH timeline. http://www.sematech.org/corporate/timeline.htm.

Serafino, N., C. Tarnoff, and D. K. Nanto. 2006. *US Occupation Assistance: Iraq, Germany and Japan Compared*. Washington, DC: Congressional Research Service.

Sherrill Manufacturing. 2010. http://www.sherrillmfg.com/index.asp.

Shigemitsu, M. 1958. *Japan and Her Destiny: My Struggle for Peace*. New York: Dutton.

Shockley, W. 1951. Circuit element utilizing semiconductive material. US Patent 2,569,347, September 25, 1951. US Patent and Trademark Office, Washington, DC. http://www.uspto.gov.

Shockley, William. 1964. Transistor technology evokes new physics. In *Nobel Lectures: Physics 1942–1962*, 344–374. Amsterdam: Elsevier.

SIA (Semiconductor Industry Association). 2010. *Doubling Semiconductor Exports over the Next Five Years: An Economic Analysis by the Semiconductor Industry Association*. San Jose, CA: Semiconductor Industry Association. http://www.sia-online.org/clientuploads/directory/DocumentSIA/Export/Doubling_Exports_Paper_0610.pdf.

SIA. 2011. STATS: Global billings report history (3-month moving average), 1976–January 2011. http://www.sia-online.org/industry_statistics/historical_billing_reports.

Simon, H. 2009. *Hidden Champions of the 21st Century: Success Strategies of Unknown World Market Leaders*. London: Springer.

Singla, V. 2011. US competitiveness becoming a tale of two economies. CNBC, June 21. http://www.cnbc.com/id/43424130/U_S_Competitiveness_Becoming_A_Tale_of_Two_Economies.

Sivak, M., and O. Tsimhoni. 2009. Fuel efficiency of vehicles on US roads: 1936–2006. *Energy Policy* 37:3168–3170.

Slade, G. 2006. *Made to Break: Technology and Obsolescence in America*. Cambridge, MA: Harvard University Press.

Smil, V. 2001. *Feeding the World: A Challenge for the Twenty-First Century*. Cambridge, MA: MIT Press.

Smil, V. 2005. *Creating the Twentieth Century: Technical Innovations of 1867–1914 and Their Lasting Impact*. New York: Oxford University Press.

Smil, V. 2006. *Transforming the 20th Century: Technical Innovations and Their Consequences*. New York: Oxford University Press.

Smil, V. 2008. *Energy in Nature and Society: General Energetics of Complex Systems*. Cambridge, MA: MIT Press.

Smil, V. 2010. *Prime Movers of Globalization: The History and Impact of Diesel Engines and Gas Turbines*. Cambridge, MA: MIT Press.

Smil, V. 2011. Harvesting the biosphere: The human impact. *Population and Development Review* 37:613–636.

Smith, Adam. 1776. *The Wealth of Nations*. London: W. Strahan and T. Cadell. http://www.gutenberg.org/files/3300/3300-h/3300-h.htm.

Smith, D. K., and R. C. Alexander. 1988. *Fumbling the Future: How Xerox Invented, Then Ignored, the First Personal Computer*. New York: William Morrow.

Solow, R. M. 1987. Growth theory and after. http://www.nobelprize.org/nobel_prizes/economics/laureates/1987/solow-lecture.html.

Sommer, M. 2009. *Why Has Japan Been Hit So Hard by the Global Recession?* Washington, DC: International Monetary Fund. http://www.imf.org/external/pubs/ft/spn/2009/spn0905.pdf.

Sousa, B. A. 1982. Regulating Japanese automobile imports: Some implications of the voluntary quota system. *Boston College International and Comparative Law Review* 5:431–460.

Stahel, W. R. 1997. The service economy: "Wealth without resource consumption"? *Philosophical Transactions of the Royal Society of London, Series A, Mathematical and Physical Sciences* 355:1309–1319.

Stanley, W. 1912. Alternating-current development in America. *Journal of the Franklin Institute* 173:561–580.

Steindel, C. 2004. The relationship between manufacturing production and goods output. *Current Issues in Economics and Finance* 10:1–7.

Stieglitz, J. E. 2011. Of the 1%, by the 1%, for the 1%. *Vanity Fair*, May. http://www.vanityfair.com/society/features/2011/05/top-one-percent-201105.

Summers, L. 2011. Larry Summers exit interview. *International Economy*, Winter, 8–11, 67.

Tanner, A. Heinrich. 1998. *Continuous Casting: A Revolution in Steel*. Fort Lauderdale: Write Stuff Enterprises.

Tarbell, I. M. 1904. *The History of the Standard Oil Company*. Gloucester, MA: Peter Smith.

Tassava, C. 2008. The American Economy during World War II. *EH.Net Encyclopedia*, ed. R. Whaples. February 10. http://eh.net/encyclopedia/article/tassava.WWII.

Tassey, G. 2010. Rationales and mechanisms for revitalizing US manufacturing R&D strategies. *Journal of Technology Transfer* 35:283–333.

Taylor, F. W. 1911. *The Principles of Scientific Management*. New York: Harper and Brothers.

Taylor, P., C. Funk, and A. Clark. 2006. *Luxury or Necessity? Things We Can't Live Without: The List Has Grown in the Past Decade*. Washington, DC: Pew Research Center. http://www.pewsocialtrends.org/2009/04/23/luxury-or-necessity-the-public-makes-a-u-turn.

Temin, P. 1964. *Iron and Steel in Nineteenth Century America*. Cambridge, MA: MIT Press.

Texas Instruments. 2011. TI introduces first commercial silicon transistor. http://www.ti.com/corp/docs/company/history/timeline/semicon/1950/docs/54commercial.htm.

Thoreson, R., R. E. Rowberg, and J. F. Ryan. 1985. Industrial fuel use: Structure and trends. *Annual Review of Energy* 10:165–199.

Thruelsen, Richard. 1976. *The Grumman Story*. New York: Praeger.

Tomlinson, Ray. 2002. The invention of e-mail just seemed like a neat idea. SAP.info. http://www.sap.info.

Toyota. 2011. Toyota history. http://www.toyoland.com/history.html.

Trudell, C., and J. Armstrong. 2011. Widening GM truck supply reminiscent of 2008 "bad habits." Bloomberg.com, July 5. http://www.bloomberg.com/news/2011-07-05/gm-s-widening-truck-inventories-risk-return-to-bad-habits-of-2008-cars.html.

Tschetter, J. 2010. Exports support American jobs. International Trade Research Report no. 1. http://trade.gov/publications/pdfs/exports-support-american-jobs.pdf.

Turak, T. 1986. *William Le Baron Jenney: A Pioneer of Modern Architecture*. Ann Arbor, MI: UMI Research Press.

Twain, M. 1889. *A Connecticut Yankee in King Arthur's Court*. New York: Charles L. Webster Co.

Twain, M., and C. D. Warner. 1873. *The Gilded Age: A Tale of Today*. New York: American Publishing Co.

Typewriter Topics. 1924. *The Typewriter: History & Encyclopedia*. New York: Typewriter Topics.

UN (United Nations). 2012. National Accounts Main Aggregates Base. http://unstats.un.org/unsd/snaama/dnllist.asp.

Unander, F. 2007. Decomposition of manufacturing energy-use in IEA countries: How do recent developments compare with historical trends? *Applied Energy* 84:771–780.

Unander, F., et al. 1999. Manufacturing energy use in OECD countries: Decomposition of long-term trends. *Energy Policy* 27:769–778.

UNCTAD (United Nations Conference on Trade and Development). 2012. UNCTAD statistics. http://unctad.org/en/Pages/Statistics.aspx.

UNDP (United Nations Development Programme). 2011. International Human Development Indicators. http://hdrstats.undp.org/en/indicators/67106.html.

USBC (US Bureau of the Census). 1975. Historical statistics of the United States: Colonial times to 1970. http://www2.census.gov/prod2/statcomp/documents/CT1970p1-01.pdf.

USBC. 2009. Median and average square feet of floor area in new single-family houses completed by location: Built for sale. http://www.census.gov/const/C25Ann/sfforsalemedavgsqft.pdf.

USBC. 2010. Sector 31—Manufacturing. https://epic.od.nih.gov/naics/31Manu.htm.

USBC. 2011a. Food Stamp/Supplemental Nutrition Assistance Program (SNAP) Receipt in the past 12 Months for Households by State: 2008 and 2009. http://www.fns.usda.gov/snap.

USBC. 2011b. Foreign trade. http://www.census.gov/indicator/www/ustrade.html.

USBC. 2011c. Poverty status in the past 12 months. http://factfinder2.census.gov/bkmk/table/1.0/en/ACS/11_1YR/S1701/1600000US4835000.

USBC. 2012. The 2011 statistical abstract. http://www.census.gov/compendia/statab.

US Department of Veterans Affairs. 2011. GI Bill history. http://www.gibill.va.gov/benefits/history_timeline/index.html.

US Department of the Treasury. 2012. US /gross external debt. http://www.treasury.gov/resource-center/data-chart-center/tic/Pages/external-debt.aspx.

US EIA (US Energy Information Agency). 2012. Electricity. http://www.eia.gov/cneaf/electricity/page/eia826.html.

US EPA (US Environmental Protection Agency). 2012. *Light-Duty Automotive Technology, Carbon Dioxide Emissions, and Fuel Economy Trends: 1975 through 2011*. http://www.epa.gov/otaq/cert/mpg/fetrends/2012/420s12001.pdf.

USITC (US International Trade Commission). 2010. USITC makes determination in five-year (sunset) review concerning wooden bedroom furniture from China. Press release, November 30. http://www.usitc.gov/press_room/news_release/2010/er1130hh1.htm.

US Maritime Commission. 2011. *Liberty Ships Built by the United States Maritime Commission in World War II*. http://www.usmm.org/libertyships.html.

Vander Meulen, J. 1995. *Building the B-29*. Washington, DC: Smithsonian Books.

Van Ark, B., and M. Timmer. 2001. PPPs and international productivity comparisons: Bottlenecks and new directions. http://www.oecd.org/std/pricesandpurchasingpowerparitiesppp/2424747.pdf.

van Opstal, D. 2008. *Thrive: The Skills Imperative*. New York: Council on Competitiveness http://www.compete.org/publications/detail/472/thrive.

van Opstal, D. 2010. Commentary on Gregory Tassey's "Rationales and mechanisms for revitalizing US manufacturing R&D strategies." *Journal of Technology Transfer* 35:355–359.

VDMA (Verband Deutscher Maschinen- und Anlagenbau). 2011. *Maschinenbau in Zahl und Bild*. Frankfurt: VDMA. http://www.sdg.vdma.org/wps/wcm/connect/

c6ce3800467e8f3284d0965629cf6c64/MbauinZuB2011.pdf?MOD=AJPERES &CACHEID=c6ce3800467e8f3284d0965629cf6c64.

Victor, P. 2008. *Managing Without Growth: Slower by Design, Not Disaster.* Cheltenham, UK: Edward Elgar.

von der Leyden, U. 2011. Keeping Germany at work. In *OECD Yearbook 2011*, 41. Paris: Organisation for Economic Co-operation and Development.

von Neumann, J. 1945. First draft of a report on the EDVAC. Moore School of Electrical Engineering, University of Pennsylvania, Philadelphia. http://virtual travelog.net.s115267.gridserver.com/wp/wp-content/media/2003-08-TheFirst Draft.pdf.

Wade, Louise Carroll. 1987. *Chicago's Pride: The Stockyards, Packingtown, and Environs in the Nineteenth Century*. Urbana: University of Illinois Press.

Waldrop, M. M. 2001. *The Dream Machine: J.C.R. Licklider and the Revolution That Made Computing Personal*. New York: Viking Press.

Walker, D. M., et al. 2011. Sovereign Fiscal Responsibility Index 2011. Comeback America Initiative, Stanford, CA. http://siepr.stanford.edu/system/files/shared/ documents/policybrief_04_2011.pdf.

Walker, R., et al. 2002. *The Commission on the Future of the US Aerospace Industry*. http://trade.gov/static/aero_rpt_aero_commission.pdf.

Wallerstein, I. 2011. The global economy won't recover, now or ever. *Foreign Policy,* March, 76. http://coyoteprime-runningcauseicantfly.blogspot.com/2011/03/ immanuel-wallerstein-global-economy.html.

Walmart. 2012. *Walmart 2011 Annual Report*. http://www.walmartstores.com/ sites/annualreport/2011/financials/Walmart_2011_Annual_Report.pdf.

Wal-Mart Watch. 2007. Buy American becomes buy Chinese: Wal-Mart dumps the Walton legacy. http://makingchangeatwalmart.org/press/buy-american-becomes -buy-chinese-wal-mart-dumps-the-walton-legacy.

Walton, S. 1985. *Sam Walton, Made in America: My Story*. New York: Doubleday.

Ward's Communications. 2010. *Ward's Motor Vehicle Facts & Figures 2010*. Southfield, MI: Ward's Communications.

Warren, K. 1973. *The American Steel Industry 1850–1970*. Oxford: Clarendon Press.

Wärtsilä. 2012. Products. http://www.wartsila.com/en/engines.

Watson, P. 2010. *The German Genius*. New York: Simon & Schuster.

Weik, M. H. 1961. The ENIAC story. Aberdeen, MD: Ordnance Ballistic Research Laboratories. http://ftp.arl.army.mil/~mike/comphist/eniac-story.html.

Weiss, T. 1993. Long-term changes in US agricultural output per worker, 1800-1900. *Economic History Review* 46:324–341.

Welch, J. 2011. US lacks vision, strategy to be exceptional. CNBC, June 13. http:// www.cnbc.com/id/43379665/US_Lacks_Vision_Strategy_to_Be_Exceptional_ Welch.

White, E. B. 1936. Farewell, my lovely! *New Yorker*, May, 15. http://www.newyorker .com/archive/1936/05/16/1936_05_16_020_TNY_CARDS_000161110.

White House. 2010. Executive Order—National Export Initiative. http://www.whitehouse.gov/the-press-office/executive-order-national-export-initiative.

White House. 2012. The Budget. http://www.whitehouse.gov/omb/budget.

Wildavsky, B. 2011. Relax, America. *Foreign Affairs,* March–April, 49–52.

Wilkinson, R., and K. Pickett. 2009. *The Spirit Level: Why More Equal Societies Almost Always Do Better*. London: Allan Lane.

Willis, D. 2007. Boeing B-29 and B-50 Superfortress. *International Air Power Review* 22:136–169.

Wilson, J. M., and A. McKinlay. 2010. Rethinking the assembly line: Organisation, performance and productivity in Ford Motor Company, c. 1908–27. *Business History* 52:760–778.

Wilson, P. 2011. Maintaining US leadership in semiconductors. Paper presented at the AAAS annual meeting, Washington, DC, February 18. http://www.aaas.org/spp/rd/presentations/20110218PatrickWilson.pdf.

Woltjer, P. 2010. New estimates of comparative German-American manufacturing productivity, 1935–6. Paper prepared for the Fifth Global Euronet Summer School, Madrid 2010. http://www.rug.nl/staff/p.j.woltjer/WoltjerGlobalEuronet.pdf.

Womack, J. P., D. T. Jones, and D. Roos. 1990. *The Machine That Changed the World: The Story of Lean Production*. New York: Harper Perennial.

Wood, S. 1993. The Japanization of Fordism. *Economic and Industrial Democracy* 14:535–555.

Woolf, A. G. 1984. Electricity, productivity, and labor saving: American manufacturing, 1900–1929. *Explorations in Economic History* 21:176–191.

World Bank. 2011. Exports of goods and services (% of GDP). http://data.worldbank.org/indicator/NE.EXP.GNFS.ZS.

Worrell, E., and C. Galitsky. 2008. *Energy Efficiency Improvement and Cost Saving Opportunities for Cement Making*. Berkeley, CA: Ernest Orlando Lawrence Berkeley National Laboratory. http://www.energystar.gov/ia/business/industry/LBNL-54036.pdf.

Wright, G. 1990. The origins of American industrial success, 1879–1940. *American Economic Review* 80:651–666.

WSA (World Steel Association). 2011. World steel top producers 2012. http://www.worldsteel.org/statistics/top-producers.html.

WTO (World Trade Organization). 2011. International trade and tariff data. http://www.wto.org/english/res_e/statis_e/statis_e.htm.

WTO. 2012. International trade and tariff data. http://www.wto.org/english/res_e/statis_e/statis_e.htm.

Xerox PARC. 2011. Xerox PARC history. http://www.parc.com/about.

Xing, Y. 2011. How the iPhone widens the US trade deficit with China. http://www3.grips.ac.jp/~pinc/data/10-21.pdf.

Xing, Y., and N. Detert. 2010. How the iPhone widens the United States trade deficit with the People's Republic of China. Tokyo: National Graduate Institute for Policy Studies. http://www3.grips.ac.jp/~pinc/data/10-21.pdf.

Yenne, B. 2006. *The American Aircraft Factory in WW II*. Minneapolis, MN: Zenith Press.

YouTube. 2009. The Kitchen Debate (Nixon and Khrushchev, 1959). http://www.youtube.com/watch?v=D7HqOrAakco.

Yuan, T., K. Fukao, and H. X. Wu. 2010. Comparative output and labor productivity in manufacturing between China, Japan, Korea and the United States for ca. 1935: A production-side PPP approach. *Explorations in Economic History* 47:325–346.

Zellers, John Adam. 1948. *The Typewriter: A Short History, On Its 75th Anniversary, 1873–1948*. New York: Newcomen Society of England, American Branch.

# Name Index

# Subject Index